Measuring Progress in Adapting to a Changing Climate

INSIGHTS FROM OECD COUNTRIES

OECD
BETTER POLICIES FOR BETTER LIVES

Please cite this publication as:
OECD (2024), *Measuring Progress in Adapting to a Changing Climate: Insights from OECD countries*, OECD Publishing, Paris, https://doi.org/10.1787/8cfe45af-en.

ISBN 978-92-64-44905-3 (print)
ISBN 978-92-64-64034-4 (PDF)
ISBN 978-92-64-56223-3 (HTML)
ISBN 978-92-64-43127-0 (epub)

Photo credits: Cover © faithie/shutterstock.com.

Corrigenda to OECD publications may be found on line at: www.oecd.org/about/publishing/corrigenda.htm.

Foreword

Despite the continued rise in temperatures, record-breaking heatwaves, and the devastating droughts, fires and floods around the world, adaptation to climate change is not happening at the speed and scale needed to protect humans, nature and livelihoods. The 2022 IPCC 6th Assessment and the 2023 UN Environment Programme Adaptation Gap reports warned that the adaptation finance gap is widening and that the pace of planning and implementation of adaptation efforts must accelerate in light of future expected climate impacts.

There are, however, encouraging signs that momentum is building. The 2023 United Arab Emirates Framework for Global Climate Resilience reflects the international community's intention to strengthen adaptation action, in line with what the Paris Agreement set out to do. The Framework's establishment of global objectives and targets to guide adaptation efforts in all countries promises to be a step-change. At the national level, too, countries need to better understand whether they are advancing at the pace needed to build climate resilience and make informed decisions on how to bridge adaptation gaps effectively. Being able to demonstrate tangible adaptation progress will increase transparency and accountability and may also help to give adaptation the political momentum it has long needed.

This report contributes to ongoing discussions on measuring adaptation progress at the national level, by taking stock of how OECD member countries, and several partner countries, are advancing with measurement and monitoring. While it highlights that much work still remains to be done to demonstrate progress comprehensively, the good news is that all OECD countries have adopted national adaptation policies and most have set up mechanisms to measure their implementation progress at sectoral and subnational levels. However, a varied set of indicators is needed to grasp the diverse sources and drivers of climate risks and impacts, as well as to reflect progress appropriately. The data requirements are significant, and include complex scientific information on hazards, as well as a diversity of demographic, economic and ecosystem data, to name just a few. Harmonising and aggregating information from different data owners and levels is particularly challenging, as is demonstrating clear links between actions and climate change resilience building.

This OECD report provides a stocktake of country efforts and reflects OECD members' strong interest in developing and using indicators to measure their climate adaptation progress. The OECD is taking forward the results of this work to develop thematic adaptation indicators, in support of international discussions on the Global Goal on Adaptation. Through this work, the OECD will continue to assist governments in designing measurement frameworks to strengthen the implementation of their adaptation plans. I hope the findings in this report will serve as a reference for policy makers in meeting this challenge.

Jo Tyndall

Director, Environment Directorate, OECD

Acknowledgements

This report was developed by the OECD Environment Directorate, directed by Jo Tyndall, under the guidance of Walid Oueslati, Head of the Climate, Water and Biodiversity Division. This report was co-ordinated by Mikaela Rambali, under the guidance of Catherine Gamper. Chapter 1 was authored by Mikaela Rambali and Maike Kirsch, with substantive contributions from Catherine Gamper and Simon Touboul. Chapter 2 was authored by Mikaela Rambali and Maike Kirsch. Chapter 3 was authored by Gladys Santis, Maritza Jadrijevic, and Micaela Jara from the Ministry of the Environment of Chile and Camilo Prats, consultant for the Capacity Building Initiative for Transparency Project of Chile. A preliminary version of Chapter 4 was authored by Young-Il Song, Je-Woo Hong, Huicheul Jung, Songmi Park (Korea Environment Institute). The full version of chapter 5 was authored by Katarína Nánásiová, Ján Dráb, Martin Gális, Hana Arnold, Veronika Tóth and Karin Hrnčiarová (Institute for Environmental Policy (IEP) of Ministry of Environment of the Slovak Republic). Research input was provided by Nathan Rueche and Johanne Trotin.

In addition to the case study authors, we would like to acknowledge the contributions of the following colleagues who provided invaluable support and insights: Megan Bickle, Andrew Carr, Ashley Diggins and James Ward (UK Department for Environment, Food and Rural Affairs), Brendan Freeman, Miriam Kennedy and Cara Labuschagne (UK Climate Change Committee). The OECD Secretariat is also grateful for receiving substantive inputs from a number of institutions across devolved administrations and local authorities for the case study on the United Kingdom.

This report is an output of the OECD Environmental Policy Committee (EPOC) and its Working Party on Climate Change (WPCC). The Secretariat would like to thank the EPOC and WPCC delegates for their feedback on the earlier drafts of this report. The extensive responses to the OECD survey from delegates from the OECD member and partner countries are also gratefully acknowledged.

Camilo Jimenez and Elodie Prata Leal (OECD Environment Directorate) provided administrative support. The report also benefited from support with communication and outreach aspects from Sama Al Taher-Cucci and Beth Del Bourgo (OECD Environment Directorate). The report also received editorial support from Fiona Hinchcliffe (independent editor).

Table of contents

FIGURES

TABLES

Abbreviations and acronyms

Acronym	Full name
25-YEP	25-Year Environment Plan
AC	Adaptation Committee
ARClim	Climate Risk Atlas
ARP	Adaptation Reporting Power
BMK	Bundesministerium für Klimaschutz, Umwelt, Energie, Mobilität, Innovation und Technologie [Ministry for Climate Protection, Environment, Energy, Mobility, Innovation and Technology Austria]
CARO	Climate Action regional Office
CCC	Climate Change Committee
CCRA	Climate Change Risk Assessment
Climate NI	Climate Northern Ireland
CNC	Carbon Neutrality Committee
CRA	Climate Risk Assessment
CRIA	Climate Risk Independent Assessment
DAERA	Department of Agriculture, Environment and Rural Affairs (Northern Ireland government)
Defra	Department for Environment, Food and Rural Affairs
DESNZ	Department for Energy Security and Net Zero
DIP	Detailed Implementation Plan
EA	Environment Agency
EC	European Commission
EEA	European Environment Agency
ETICC	Technical Inter-Ministerial Committee on Climate Change
EU	European Union
GGA	Global Goal on Adaptation
INECC	Instituto Nacional de Ecología y Cambio Climático [National Institute of Ecology and Climate Change Mexico]
IPCC	Intergovernmental Panel on Climate Change
KACCC	Korea Adaptation Center for Climate Change
KCCAR	Korea Climate Change Assessment Report
KMA	Korea Meteorological Administration
LAAP	Local Adaptation Advisory Panel
M&E	Monitoring & Evaluation
M&R	Monitoring & Reporting
MEL	Monitoring, Evaluation & Learning
MoE	Ministry of Environment
NAF	National Adaptation Framework (Ireland)
NAO	National Audit Office
NAP	National Adaptation Programme or Plan
NAS	National Adaptation Strategy
NDC	Nationally Determined Contribution
NGO	Non-Governmental Organisation
NICCAP	Northern Ireland Climate Change Adaptation Programme
NOS	National Office for Statistics

NSW	New South Wales (Australia)
PfACCW	Prosperity for All: A Climate Conscious Wales
PRA	Prudential Regulatory Authority
SAP	Sectoral Adaptation Plan
SCCAP	Scotland Climate Change Adaptation Programme
SDG	Sustainable Development Goals
TCFD	Task Force on Climate-related Financial Disclosures
UBA	Umweltbundesamt [Environment Agency Germany]
UK	United Kingdom
UKCIP	United Kingdom Climate Impacts Programme
UNECE	United Nations Economic Commission for Europe
UNEP	United Nations Environmental Programme
UNFCCC	United Nations Framework Convention on Climate Change

Executive Summary

Global greenhouse gas emissions are still on the rise and the impacts of climate change, manifested for example with extensive drought episodes or sea level rise, will increasingly be experienced across countries. To address these impacts, many countries are making climate change adaptation a national priority, adopting comprehensive national policies which lay out adaptation priorities and objectives for cross-government actions.

With growing country efforts to adapt to climate change, it is important to demonstrate progress and results in the implementation of adaptation policies. Progress measurement is critical to inform and improve the planning and prioritisation of adaptation actions, to engage resources effectively and to collectively monitor the strengthening of climate resilience nationally and internationally.

Measuring adaptation progress is complex and cannot be captured in a single metric. The OECD's work on adaptation measurement seeks to support countries in capturing the complexity of adaptation and to help demonstrate the impact of adaptation actions over time. The OECD's approach to adaptation measurement goes beyond the project or programme level, instead evaluating nationwide, cross-cutting adaptation efforts. This approach involves four main steps: 1) assessing climate risks as measurement baselines; 2) translating adaptation needs into measurable objectives and targets; 3) tracking implementation progress towards achieving these adaptation targets; and 4) measuring the effectiveness of adaptation policies in reducing climate impacts over time.

This report presents findings of an OECD-wide stocktake of countries' efforts in measuring adaptation, which are informed by a cross-country survey of OECD and partner countries, four country case studies (Chile, Korea, Slovak Republic and the United Kingdom) and insights gathered during OECD expert workshops.

Key Findings

Baseline climate hazard and exposure information is becoming widely available. Robust, granular and regularly updated climate hazard, exposure and vulnerability information allow to determine adaptation needs and to formulate and adjust adaptation objectives and targets. While hazard assessments are increasingly available – in 60% of surveyed countries – only 40% assess the exposure of people, socio-economic assets, and ecosystems to climate impacts. Of the 22 survey responding countries that conduct regular climate risk assessments, 16 also include vulnerability assessments. However, their coverage, method and depth vary widely.

Countries are increasingly defining adaptation objectives and measuring progress towards them over time. Building on climate risk information, adaptation objectives break down a high-level adaptation vision into sub-national and sectoral adaptation objectives for which targets can be set for specific timeframes. The great majority (97%) of respondent countries report that their climate risk data inform the development of their national adaptation policies. Sixty percent of surveyed countries use this information to define adaptation objectives at the sub-national level, and 73% do so by sector. Implementation progress is also widely reported, with 70% of all surveyed countries tracking resources (inputs) allocated to adaptation as well as outputs produced, such as the structural and non-structural measures implemented.

Assessing adaptation effectiveness remains the greatest measurement challenge. Measuring whether adaptation policies reduce climate impacts over time is reported as a challenge by 80% of responding countries. One reason is that information on observed climate impacts is only partially reported. For example, while insured losses may be readily available, ecosystem damage by extreme events may not be. Secondly, establishing causal links between adaptation actions and the resulting change in climate impacts is complicated. Most causal inference studies involve in-depth research, which makes them difficult to conduct more systematically. Many countries rely on qualitative assessments, such as expert interviews, to capture successes and failures of adaptation actions, and to attribute progress to policy action over time.

The data requirements for adaptation measurement are significant. In addition to hazard modelling and climate change projections, population, household and administrative data are needed. Additional information, e.g. on climate impacts and implementation progress, needs to be collected to gather a complete picture of adaptation progress. Countries are working to bring longitudinal and spatial data together and to harmonise information from across levels of government and sectors. Stronger communication between data owners and policy makers will help to fully leverage the range of existing information and data.

Indicators play a prominent role in adaptation measurement, as reflected by the number of countries (83% of surveyed countries) using or intending to use indicators to measure adaptation progress. Indicators help to simplify, synthesise and standardise information, and thereby facilitate communication and comparability. While some countries compile indicators from existing data, others produce a wish list of indicators, which in turn drives data collection.

Strong institutional frameworks can foster adaptation measurement and the use of its results, provided there is capacity to do so. Many OECD countries are anchoring adaptation measurement in their national adaptation planning process, with results informing subsequent phases of national adaptation plans. Work is needed to increase the engagement and contribution to adaptation measurement by all relevant stakeholders. Given the wide-ranging nature of adaptation, environment ministries cannot do this alone. Legal instruments, such as incorporating adaptation measurement in climate laws, can strengthen ownership and improve data and reporting across all agencies involved. This will also strengthen the use of measurement results.

Key recommendations

- Bridge data and information gaps, including by increasing the granularity of information, to understand how adaptation policies might affect the exposure and vulnerability of populations, economies and the environment over time. Much of the data needed to measure adaptation progress already exists within sectors (e.g. water management, agriculture…). Consultative processes can help elicit relevant data that can be tied to measuring adaptation progress.
- Formulate clear objectives targeted at reducing climate impacts over time and expand the development and use of indicators to assess progress.
- Allocate appropriate and sufficient technical and financial resources to measure progress on adaptation and develop a conducive institutional framework.
- Use results of adaptation measurement to inform policy decisions. An important objective of adaptation measurement is to inform policy and resource allocation decisions. In doing so, the results of adaptation measurement can reinforce accountability and transparency, and increase the efficiency of resources deployed for adaptation.

1 Measuring progress in implementing national adaptation policies

This chapter presents the main findings from this report. It first discusses the rationale for adaptation measurement, including a framing discussion on what needs to be measured and how. This is complemented by findings from a stocktake of OECD countries' current practices and achievements in measuring progress in implementing national adaptation policies. The chapter is informed by a cross-country survey carried out in OECD member and partner countries, as well as expert workshops, and in-depth country case studies in Chile, Korea, the Slovak Republic, and the United Kingdom.

1.1. Introduction

1.1.1. Rationale for measuring adaptation progress

Global greenhouse gas emissions are still on the rise and the impacts of global warming are increasingly being felt across countries. Ocean acidification, sea level rise, heatwaves, droughts, wildfires, storms, extreme precipitation periods and floods are all taking a rising social, economic and environmental toll on countries. To address these impacts, many countries have made climate change adaptation a national priority. Adaptation policies and actions are rolled out as part of a process of adjustment to actual or expected climate change and its effects. They seek to moderate or avoid harm as well as exploit beneficial opportunities in human systems (IPCC, 2022[1]).

Countries' adaptation policies and practices have advanced significantly in recent years. All OECD countries have adopted national adaptation strategies (NAS) or plans (NAPs), which lay out adaptation priorities and objectives for cross-government actions at national, sectoral and sub-national levels over a multi-annual period, such as three or five years. Many countries have NAS/NAPs that are already in their second or third iterations. In this process, adaptation objectives and actions are adjusted to constantly evolving knowledge of climate risks and impacts, and as experience is gained in implementing adaptation actions.

Measuring adaptation progress is key for informing and adjusting adaptation policies, priorities and practices. It involves assessing climate risk, tracking adaptation implementation, helping to understand what is effective for reducing climate impacts (and under what circumstances), and informing policy design. Countries have made significant strides in measuring adaptation. Half of OECD countries (19 countries) have developed at least one report that documents the implementation status of their national policies (OECD, 2022[2]). Globally nearly 40% of countries (63 countries) that have adopted a national adaptation policy have started to track its implementation (Leiter, 2021[3]).

Adaptation measurement is critical for understanding implementation progress and adjusting adaptation policies. It helps to understand changes in the level of losses and damages suffered from extreme climate events, and identify adaptation needs and policy gaps. It also informs and improves the planning of ongoing and future adaptation actions and enables decision makers to adjust policies and actions to evolving socio-economic and climate conditions (Lamhauge, Lanzi and Agrawala, 2012[4]; EEA, 2015[5]). Adaptation measurement is also key for evaluating accountability and enhancing transparency to ensure resources earmarked for adaptation contribute to agreed objectives (OECD, 2015[6]; IPCC, 2018[7]; EEA, 2015[5]) and in an efficient way (Adaptation Committee, 2021[8]; UNFCCC, 2022[9]) (Berrang-Ford et al., 2019[10]).

At the international level too, adaptation measurement is becoming increasingly important. On the one hand it is needed for documenting the progress made towards various international framework goals, such as the Paris Agreement – notably on the Global Goal on Adaptation (GGA), see Box 1.1 – and the Sustainable Development Goals (SDGs) (UNFCCC, 2012[11]; OECD, 2020[12]). Ideally, the information required for international reporting is included in countries' national adaptation measurement systems, instead of requiring additional efforts (Jeudy-Hugo, Errendal and Kotani, 2022[13]). On the other hand, international reporting mechanisms can support national adaptation measurement efforts by enabling peer-learning between countries on best practices for implementing adaptation actions.

Box 1.1. Measuring progress towards the Global Goal on Adaptation

The Paris Agreement established the Global Goal on Adaptation (GGA) in 2015 to enhance adaptive capacity, strengthening resilience and reducing vulnerability to climate change. This overarching goal has been discussed and refined over the years, notably through the two-year Glasgow-Sharm el-Sheikh work programme, which aims to accelerate action guided by a set of thematic targets. The targets highlight priorities for adaptation in the sectors of water, food and agriculture, health, ecosystems and biodiversity, poverty and livelihoods, infrastructure, and cultural heritage. The targets were adopted at COP28 in 2023 as part of the United Arab Emirates (UAE) Framework for Global Climate Resilience, which also sets out further work to develop indicators.

Although the Paris Agreement did not specify whether and how progress on the implementation and the effectiveness of adaptation actions needed to be assessed, countries that have submitted adaptation communications outline efforts to enhance the ability to track and understand adaptation effects. These include an increasing number of quantitative time-bound targets, more detailed indicator frameworks to monitor progress, and comprehensive information on synergies between adaptation and mitigation as well as sustainable development.

Sources: (UNFCCC, 2023[14]); (UNFCCC, 2022[9]); (Jeudy-Hugo, Errendal and Kotani, 2022[13]); (UNFCCC, 2021[15]) (UNEP, 2021[16]); (UNFCCC, 2023[17]);

Nevertheless, countries face difficulties in assessing whether and how their adaptation actions contribute to achieving their objectives and whether they are ultimately and effectively increasing their resilience to climate change. This is primarily due to the difficulty of identifying a causal relationship between adaptation action and a reduction in climate risks, and the achievement of the desired impacts on society, the environment and economy. The OECD survey conducted as part of this report (see Section 1.1.3), on measuring progress in implementing national adaptation policies, found that countries face several difficulties, with the two most challenging being the complexity of adaptation as a topic and measuring effectiveness (Figure 1.1).

Figure 1.1. Countries face a range of challenges in measuring progress

Country responses to "To what extent are the challenges in measuring progress listed below experienced by your country?

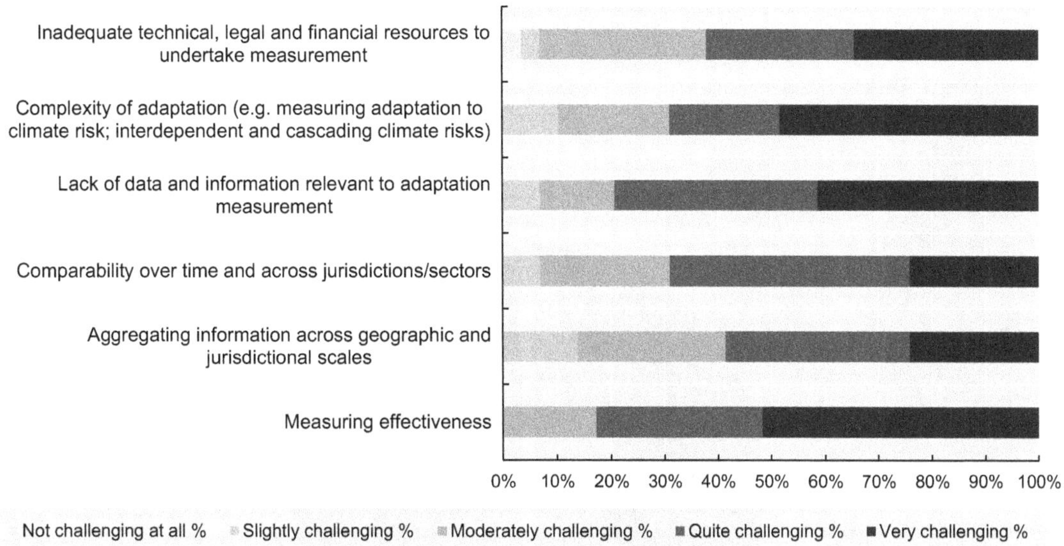

Note: Share of responding countries (29 responses) to question 22: "To what extent are the challenges in measuring progress listed below experienced by your country?". Responses of countries that selected "other": Costa Rica: "Use of climate information, use of climate services, use of historical information on losses and damages by territories"; Indonesia: "Adaptation literacy".
Source: (OECD, 2022[2]), *OECD Survey on Measuring Progress in Implementing National Adaptation Policies*. Details in Annex A.

1.1.2. Defining adaptation measurement

In the context of the OECD's work, adaptation measurement refers to all efforts that track progress in implementing adaptation policies and that seek to evaluate their effectiveness. Therefore, adaptation measurement is defined as the processes, methodologies and tools for measuring the degree of implementation of adaptation policies over time and space, with the aim of evaluating the effect of such efforts on reducing exposure and vulnerability, as well as reducing climate impacts.

Other terms and definitions are closely linked and can be used in different contexts. For example, monitoring and evaluation (M&E), monitoring and reporting (M&R), and monitoring, evaluation and learning (MEL) are all terms often used in the context of development co-operation interventions and applied predominantly to interventions at project (rather than programme) level (Noltze et al., 2021[18]). Earlier OECD work has explored the complementarity of assessing specific interventions at the project level with assessments of national strategies to strengthen adaptation (Lamhauge, Lanzi and Agrawala, 2012[4]). Adaptation measurement, as interpreted in the OECD's work, aims to help countries evaluate nationwide, cross-cutting efforts to adapt to climate change. It seeks to move beyond a project or programme-specific approach in order to comprehensively capture adaptation progress.

The process of adaptation measurement is informed by each step of the adaptation policy cycle (Figure 1.2). The first step involves establishing a baseline of current and projected climate risks (including climate hazard levels, as well as exposure and vulnerability), and ideally the likely impacts on society, economy and environment (e.g. climate change could lead to an average annual agricultural yield loss of 10-20% between 2020 and 2050 due to greater water scarcity). The second step includes defining adaptation objectives – grounded in identified climate risks and impacts – against which progress can be assessed (e.g. increase agricultural water use efficiency). This step involves setting objectives and possibly targets that are measurable and achievable within a specific timeframe (e.g. introduce water-saving measures by 2025). Subsequently, adaptation measurement seeks not just to monitor implementation progress, but also to evaluate whether implemented adaptation actions are effective and efficient in reducing climate risks and their impacts (e.g. would crop yield losses due to droughts decline if a drought of the same severity recurs at some point in the future).

Figure 1.2. Adaptation measurement is linked to all steps of the adaptation policy cycle

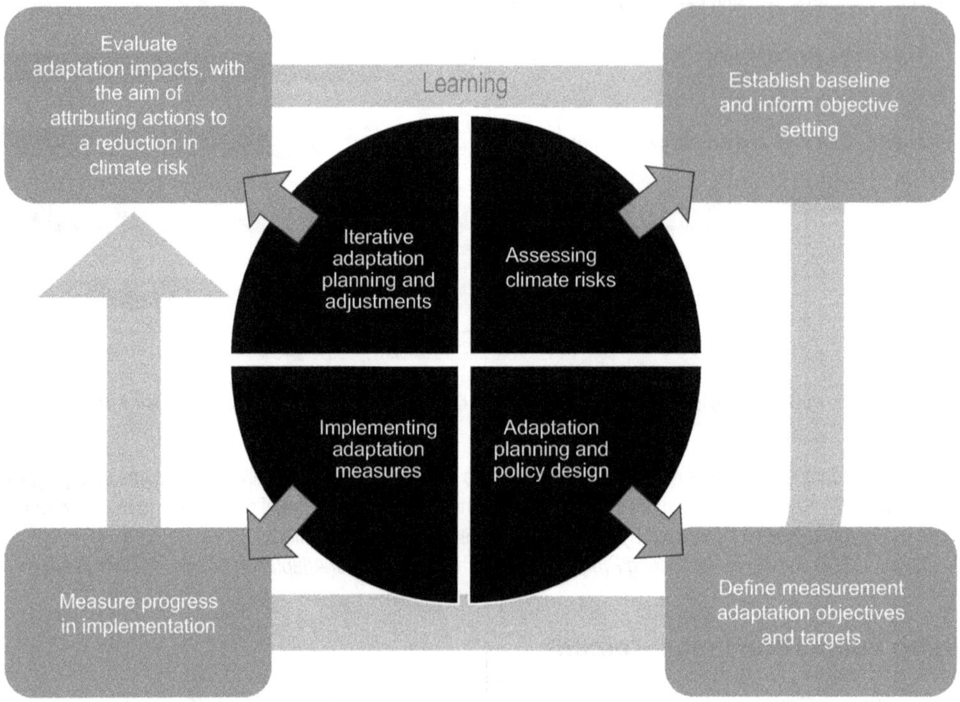

1.1.3. Report methodology

This chapter presents the findings of a stocktaking exercise that sought to shed light on countries' approaches, objectives and achievements in measuring progress in implementing their national adaptation policies. The findings build on a cross-country survey, four country case studies, and expert workshops organised by the OECD:

- The cross-country survey (see Annex A) was sent to 48 countries and targeted national government officials working on climate adaptation. The countries included 38 OECD member countries, 6 OECD accession countries (Argentina, Brazil, Bulgaria, Croatia, Peru, Romania), 4 OECD key partner countries (The People's Republic of China, India, Indonesia, South Africa) and the European Union (EU). Of these, 30 countries responded to the survey, which corresponds to a 62.5% response rate. The survey gathered information on countries' existing practices, achievements and persisting challenges faced in measuring adaptation progress at the national level.
- Four OECD country case studies were carried out: in the United Kingdom (Chapter 2), Chile (Chapter 3), Korea (Chapter 4) and the Slovak Republic (Chapter 5). The case studies sought to document and compare countries' adaptation measurement approaches, achievements and challenges. The case studies were guided by a structure and research questions so as to maximise comparability of the results (Annex B). The main national counterparts consulted in all countries were the ministries of environment.

- Two expert workshops were organised to inform the report's findings. The first expert workshop was co-convened by the OECD and the United Kingdom's Climate Change Committee. It aimed to bring together country and academic experts to share and discuss progress in developing measurement frameworks and instruments. The second expert meeting focused on developing meaningful adaptation policy indicators, and sought to establish an exchange between environmental information and adaptation experts from OECD countries to discuss how existing information can be used to build adaptation indicators. Additional country dialogues were organised at the COP26 and COP27.

This chapter looks at the main elements of adaptation measurement, building on the results of the survey, case studies and experts discussions. In addition to presenting the rationale for measuring progress on implementing adaptation policies, it describes how climate risk assessments serve as the measurement baseline when setting and measuring adaptation objectives and target. The chapter also dives into the importance of developing and presenting relevant data and information for adaptation measurement. Finally, the chapter looks at the institutional framework and how the results of adaptation measurement inform policy development.

1.2. Adaptation measurement: from establishing baselines to measuring results

1.2.1. Assessing climate change risks and impacts

The starting point for measuring adaptation progress is understanding current and future climate risk (Figure 1.2). This is done through climate risk assessments (CRA)[1] that bring together knowledge of climate change hazards, exposure (e.g. location of assets, infrastructure, value chains, ecosystems, communities), and vulnerabilities across multiple geographies and timescales (Figure 1.3):

- Information on climate hazard includes the likelihood and intensity of the occurrence of floods, wildfires and other climate events, and their expected change in intensity and frequency under given climate change scenarios.
- Exposure determines the degree to which a population, physical assets or ecosystems are exposed to climate hazards. It can be measured in terms of exposed population (e.g. number of people in a flood-prone area), assets (e.g. number of businesses, hospitals) or ecosystems (e.g. biodiversity, wetlands) in areas at risk, for example of flooding or coastal erosion.
- Measuring vulnerability provides complementary information on the propensity or predisposition of natural, built, and human systems to be adversely affected by a climate hazard (2019[19]; ISO, 2021[20]; IPCC, 2022[1]). While different people and assets might be exposed to the same level of climate hazard, their likelihood of suffering damage and loss differs. By combining social, environmental and economic factors that determine the level of vulnerability, policy makers can identify at-risk individuals, assets or ecosystems and prioritise adaptation efforts accordingly.

While adaptation cannot change the likelihood of a hazard occurring or its intensity, it can influence exposure and vulnerability, and thus determine the level of climate impacts. Understanding all components of climate risk, including hazards, is important to determine the areas that are hazard-prone and thus assess the exposure of people and assets in these areas.

Figure 1.3. Climate risk conceptual framework

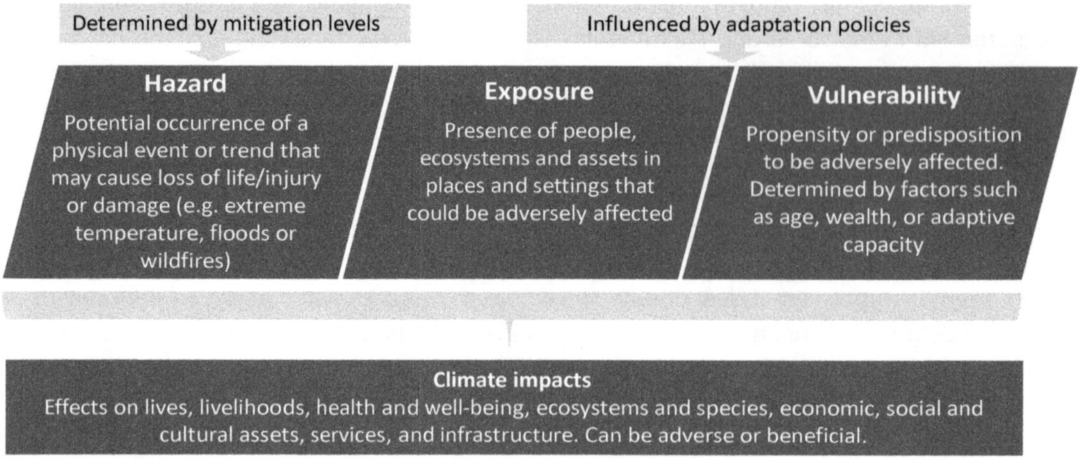

Source: Based on (IPCC, 2022[1])

CRAs allow countries to determine areas where adaptation efforts are most needed and serve as a baseline to measure whether adaptation actions are reducing the exposure and vulnerability of people, sectors or regions over time. Since climate risks are significantly shaped by climate mitigation efforts, as well as socio-economic development and adaptation responses, the CRA must be updated regularly to track changing hazard levels, exposure and vulnerability. Doing so provides relevant baselines for measuring adaptation progress over time. Regular assessments of climate risks also allow for a comparison of current and past risk levels to understand the factors responsible for changes in climate risk, and whether progress has been made in reducing exposure and vulnerability to prevailing hazard risk levels.

CRAs are increasingly becoming standard practice for countries. However, the extent to which countries measure different elements of climate risks and impacts varies depending on data availability and interpretation of the concepts of hazards, exposure and vulnerability (Singh et al., 2021[21]). The OECD survey (Annex A) finds that the large majority of responding countries have undertaken some form of CRA, with 23 countries (80% of respondents) reporting having developed a national or sectoral CRA (OECD, 2022[2]). Most countries update their CRAs regularly, often every five years. This is the case for several EU Member States, as this is the interval recommended by the EU (EEA, 2022[22]).

Measuring climate risk starts by identifying climate hazards threatening the country, while taking into account uncertainty surrounding future climate change. Of the survey respondents, 60% (18) report that they assess climate hazards (

Figure 1.4). Given the interdependence of climate hazards with future emissions pathways, different climate scenarios are usually considered when assessing expected hazard recurrence and severity. For example, for each risk identified in the United Kingdom's (UK) CRA was assessed in the in the context of a 2 and 4 degrees Celsius global warming scenario, disaggregated into regional scenarios (CCC, 2021[23]). The Slovak Republic, in comparison, uses the RCP4.5 scenario for all of its hazard projections for 2041-2070. This moderate scenario projects emissions to peak around 2040 and decline thereafter, and assumes a global temperature rise of between 2 and 3 degrees Celsius by 2100 (OECD, 2023[24]). Indicating the probability of each hazard to occur can help comprehend the degree of uncertainty attached to the results (EC & EEA, 2019[25]).

While OECD countries have made progress in identifying the hazards threatening their territory, fewer of them assess exposure to a changing climate. Out of the 23 countries reporting conducting CRAs, only 12 assess the exposure of people, socio-economic assets, ecosystems and environmental services (

Figure 1.4) (OECD, 2022[2]). For example, the UK CRA finds that around 10% of hospitals, 23% of listed buildings and 18% of scheduled monuments in England are at risk of significant flooding (CCC, 2021[23]). The Slovak Republic finds that more than 16% of the country's population resides in areas at high risk of extreme heat (OECD, 2023[24]).

Figure 1.4. Various elements are assessed in climate risk assessments

Country responses to "If a climate risk assessment has been developed, what does it assess?"

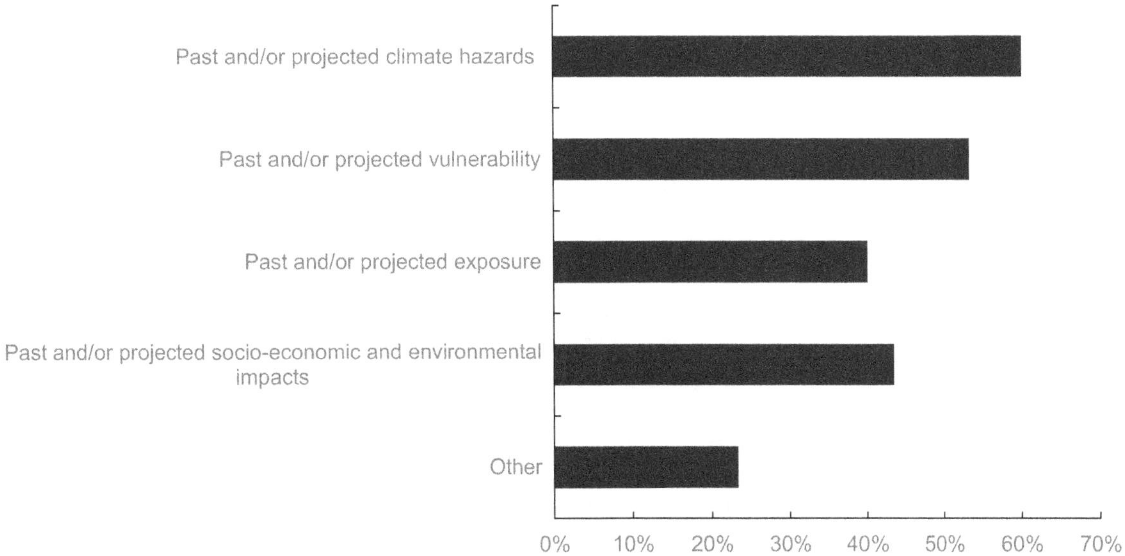

Note: Share of responding countries who state having developed a CRA (23 responses) to question 2: "If a climate risk assessment has been developed, what does it assess?"; All response options are referred to as "past and/or projected" in the survey. Responses under "other" include the following: France: cost of inaction; Germany: adaptive capacity, climate risk with and without adaptation; Hungary: vulnerability analyses of the Hungarian National Adaptation Geo-Information System; Lithuania: inter-connected risks; UK: actions being taken, adaptation shortfall and potential for actions, and prioritisation of risks using an urgency framework. Fewer countries state that they measure exposure (12) than vulnerability (16). This is likely due to differing characterisations of vulnerability. Some of the countries that report assessing vulnerability do not in fact assess the variables that reflect the vulnerability definitions set out above. Instead, they actually assess exposure variables. Overall, existing climate risk assessments have a better assessment of exposure than vulnerability because the concept of vulnerability is complex and data are scarce and difficult to measure.
Source: (OECD, 2022[2]), *OECD Survey on Measuring Progress in Implementing National Adaptation Policies*. Details in Annex A.

Similarly, the quality of information on vulnerability varies significantly across countries because of methodological and data limitations. Assessing vulnerability requires, for example, spatial micro data on households' socio-economic characteristics (such as age, income, gender, education and migration backgrounds), which need to be mapped with exposure information, and updated regularly. As a result, vulnerability information remains limited or coarse, with 16 out of 23 countries reporting conducting regular CRAs that include vulnerability assessments (OECD, 2022[2]). The Slovak Republic, for instance, has identified indicators as children aged below 4, elderly people aged over 70 years, municipalities with high shares of low-income groups and unemployment to characterise vulnerability. It maps these indicators spatially by district (Figure 1.5), which is good practice (OECD, 2023[24]). In some other countries, vulnerability is described qualitatively, for example for particular groups, assets or ecosystems vulnerable to specific hazards, and is not demonstrated using data.

Figure 1.5. The Slovak Republic has mapped factors that make people vulnerable to climate change

Vulnerable population aged ≥ 70 (%) (upper left); vulnerable population aged ≤ 3 (%) (upper right); unemployment rate (%) (lower left); municipal income per capita (EUR) (lower right)

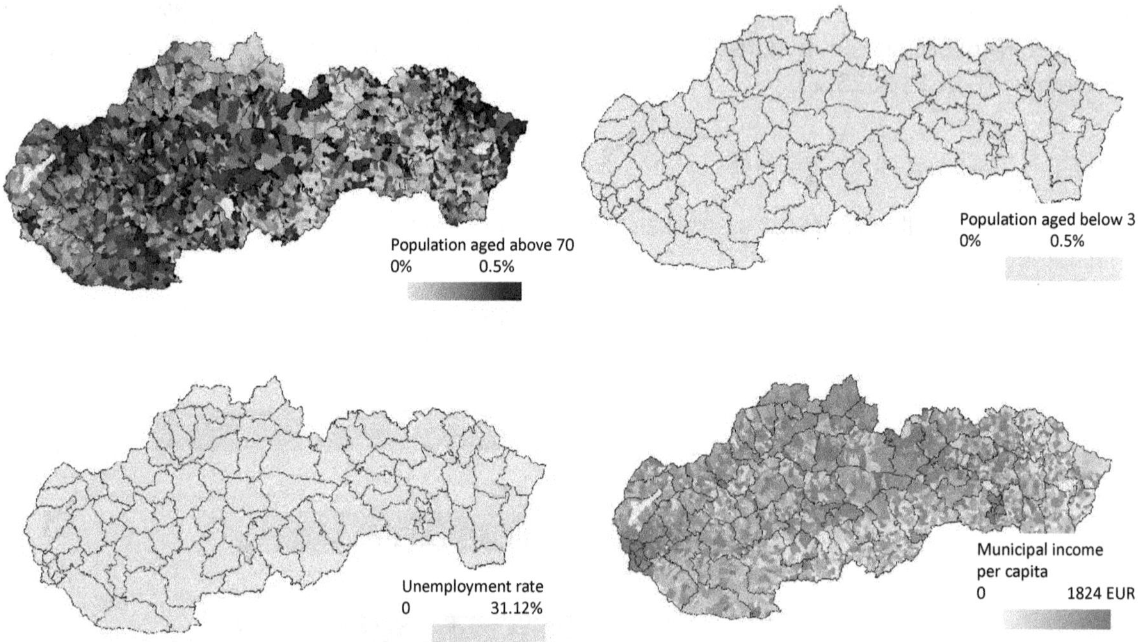

Source: (OECD, 2023[24]).

Finally, some OECD countries also make use of information on historical climate related impacts to identify areas and communities at risk from climate change. Of the responding countries, 13 (43%) document past socio-economic and environmental impacts as part of their CRA (

Figure 1.4). For example, the UK documents in its CRA a wide range of past and anticipated future impacts (though not always quantitatively projected) on people's health, livelihoods, ecosystems, and the economy. These impacts include health and productivity, deterioration in soil health and agricultural productivity, and impacts on water availability and energy supply (see Chapter 2). Germany has quantified losses and damages from past climate hazards between 2000 and 2021, and includes both direct losses, as well as those caused through indirect effects, such as reduced worker productivity due to heatwaves (OECD, 2022[2]; Prognos, 2022[26]; UBA, 2021[27]).

To conclude, the wider the coverage of detailed information on climate hazard, exposure and vulnerability, the easier it is to measure adaptation progress. Robust and regularly updated exposure and vulnerability information enables adaptation objectives and targets to be determined and adjusted, and greatly facilitates the measurement task. For example, if the baseline finds that 50% of the elderly population live in high flood risk zones, an adaptation objective could be to reduce this share by a target date.

1.2.2. Setting adaptation objectives and targets

The second step in adaptation measurement is to lay out clear, and ideally measurable, adaptation policy objectives (Figure 1.2). In setting objectives, countries define the level of ambition of their adaptation policies for addressing climate risks and reducing impacts, thereby determining the acceptable levels of risks. For instance, France's objective is to implement measures to adapt to warming of 4°C by 2100 (Ministry of Ecological Transition and Territorial Cohesion & Ministry of Energy Transition France, 2023[28]).

This section sheds light on current country practices in defining adaptation objectives, using baselines and defining targets. It also highlights the need for a collaborative process in defining objectives.

Using climate risk assessments to define adaptation objectives

As indicated above, climate risk assessments enable to create a baseline to inform adaptation objectives against which progress can be measured. The OECD survey finds that most responding countries use their CRA to inform their national adaptation policies (Figure 1.6) (OECD, 2022[2]). The UK, Costa Rica, New Zealand, Portugal and Czechia use information on exposure and vulnerability to determine their adaptation policy objectives (Defra, 2018[29]; Ministry for the Environment New Zealand, 2022[30]; Ministry of the Environment Czechia, 2021[31]; Environment Agency Portugal, 2019[32]; OECD, 2022[2]). The UK links objectives to the climate risks that the NAP responds to (CCC, 2021[33]). For instance, the UK's third NAP includes the objective to "minimise the impact on the transport network of climate change-driven increases in incidences of river, surface water and ground water flooding, so that assets remain operational throughout their design life, the risk of fatalities and major disruption are reduced as far as possible, and resilience plans enable people and freight to move safely in the event of a loss of service on any given route, while also ensuring staff safety" (Defra, 2023[34]). Another objective is to "protect critical infrastructure assets from flooding to 1-in-1 000-year flood event standards".

Figure 1.6. Most climate risk assessments inform national adaptation policies

Number of responding countries to "If a climate risk assessment has been developed, to what extent does it inform the development of adaptation policies in terms of priority and objectives setting?"

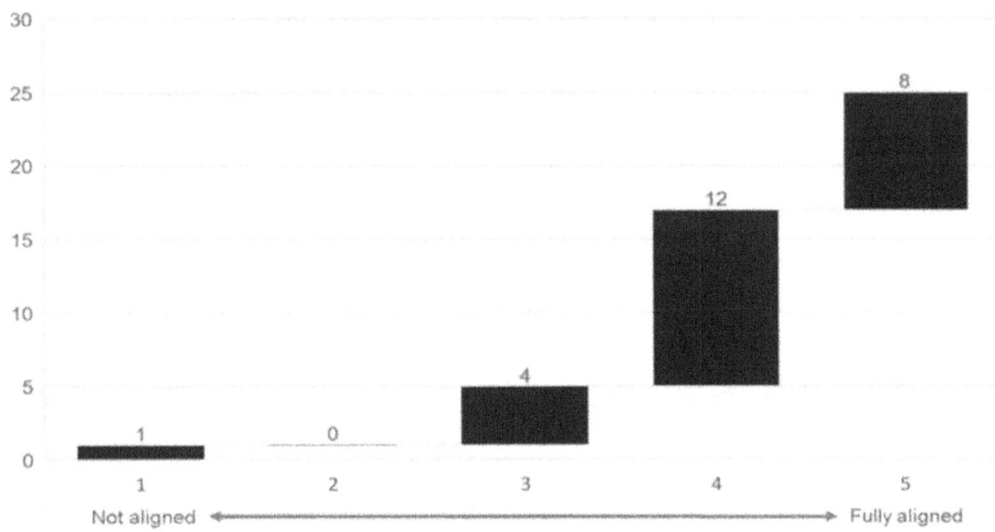

Note: 25 responses received to question 3: "If a climate risk assessment has been developed, to what extent does it inform the development of adaptation policies in terms of priority and objectives setting?". Number indicated above bars represents the number of responding countries, while horizontal axis shows a range from 1 (not at all) to 5 (fully aligned). Only respondents that answered "yes" to having developed a "National or sectoral climate risk assessment" in question 1 were able to answer to this question.
Source: (OECD, 2022[2]), *OECD Survey on Measuring Progress in Implementing National Adaptation Policies*. Details in Annex A.

Characterising robust adaptation objectives

Robust adaptation objectives encompass a range of characteristics, from the definition of a country-wide vision to the identification of sectoral and/or regional actions. A first step in setting adaption objectives is therefore to break down broad, higher-level adaptation visions into concrete objectives. A hierarchy of objectives can help translate an overarching vision into measurable objectives. Canada's NAP, for example, sets out the following vision: people "living in Canada, communities, and the natural environment are resilient in the face of a changing climate". It then sets further direction for adaptation for five interconnected systems of society, represented in Figure 1.7 (Government of Canada, 2023[35]).

All countries responding to the OECD survey have adaptation objectives that state the medium to long-term impact that they aim to achieve by implementing policies and actions; 27 responding countries (90%) report that they have defined a broad vision – or high-level objective – for adaptation (OECD, 2022[2]).

Figure 1.7. Adaptation objectives can be broken down from broader vision to concrete targets

Example from the health sector

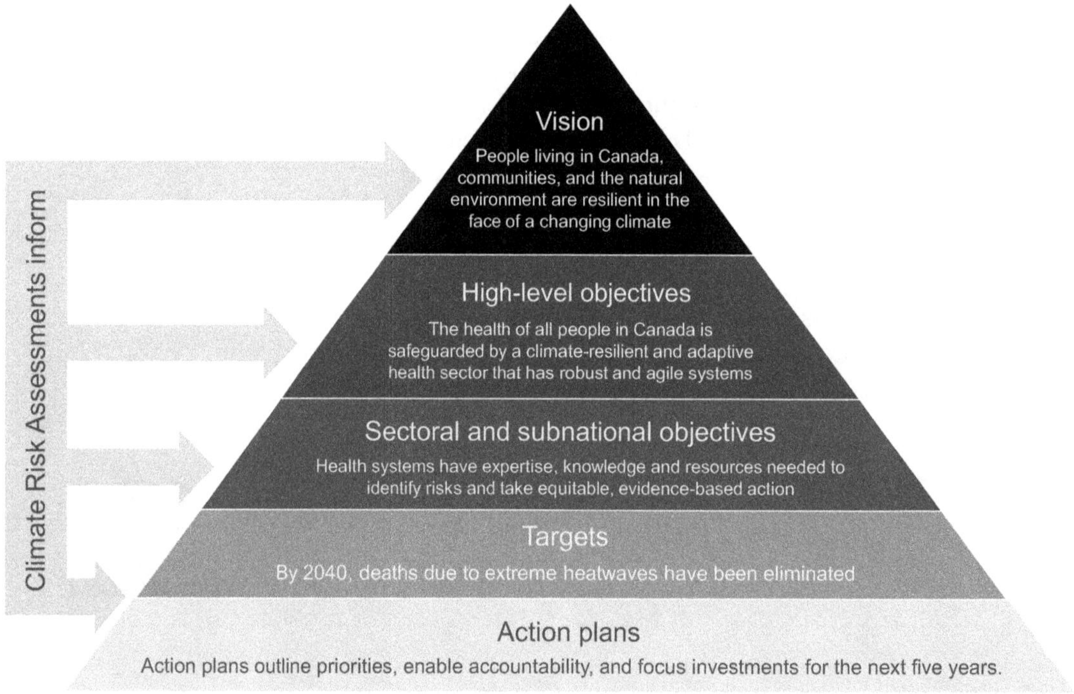

Note: The number of objectives, and respective targets and indicators may vary by objective or target. Examples are adapted from Canada's NAP.
Source: Authors, based on (Government of Canada, 2023[35]), Canada's National Adaptation Strategy: Building Resilient Communities and a Strong Economy.

Robust adaptation objectives reflect spatial differences within countries. As different regions within a country may vary in their exposure to specific climate risks, defining sub-national adaptation objectives helps reflect territorial disparities and enables policy makers to adjust adaptation action accordingly. Countries define their adaptation objectives at different levels of jurisdictions. All but one of the OECD countries responding to the survey define objectives at the national level, while 60% also set sub-national objectives (OECD, 2022[2]; OECD, 2023[36]).

Similarly, sectoral adaptation objectives help to allocate responsibility for actions to relevant line ministries and agencies, thereby strengthening accountability for adaptation actions across government. Most countries (70% of responding countries) classify their adaptation objectives by sector. Table 1.1 gives some examples of countries' sectoral objectives, which include better adapting agricultural production, improving irrigation water use, fostering the climate resilience of infrastructure, reducing climate-related diseases or diversifying energy resources. Austria has defined 14 sectoral objectives (for health, transport, spatial planning, etc.) and subdivided them into lower-level objectives, each associated with a number of actions to achieve them. Thus its overarching objective for the health sector is subdivided into nine specific objectives that focus on raising awareness, informing the public and improving the capabilities of co-ordinated emergency services to prevent or minimise health risks and lower fatal casualties in cases of extreme events or outbreaks of infectious diseases. These detailed objectives allow Austria to narrow down what it needs to assess when measuring adaptation progress (e.g. whether climate-related topics have been included in medical studies and in training of nursing staff, paramedics, and home helpers) (BMK, 2021[37]).

Table 1.1. OECD country examples of sectoral adaptation objectives

Policy area	Example of sectoral adaptation objective	Country
Agriculture	Ensuring sustainable, resource-conserving and climate-friendly agricultural production as well as maintaining and improving the ecological services of agriculture under changed climatic conditions; efficiency improvements in irrigation and water use through the introduction of modern technological developments	Austria
Infrastructure	Strengthening regulations and guidelines for public investment with criteria for adaptation to climate change to guarantee the design of resilient infrastructure and services, ensure their useful life and the continuity of services	Costa Rica
Health	Robust biosecurity to reduce the risk of new pests and diseases spreading	New Zealand
Energy	Diversification of energy sources, decentralisation of the energy system and reduction of energy consumption to reduce vulnerability to climate impacts	Austria
Disaster risk reduction	Strengthening disaster risk management against the impacts of climate change	Chile
Water management	Ensuring ecological stability and provision of ecosystem services for aquatic and water-related ecosystems, with an emphasis on strengthening the natural water regime of the landscape and to meet the needs of human society and sustainable water use	Czechia
Urban planning	Significantly strengthening the resilience of human settlements, including their public and green infrastructure, with an emphasis on the protection of human health	Czechia

Source: (BMK, 2021[37]); (Ministry of Environment Chile, 2017[38]); (Ministry of Environment and Energy Costa Rica, 2022[39]); (Ministry for the Environment New Zealand, 2022[30]); (Ministry of the Environment Czechia, 2021[31]).

Most countries then associate their objectives with actions to be implemented. All responding countries (except one) report having associated the adaptation actions set in their NAS or NAP to a specific objective (OECD, 2022[2]). New Zealand, for instance, has assigned a number of actions to each of the 14 objectives set out in its NAP, distinguishing them as critical actions (31 in total) and supporting actions (40 in total). As an example, New Zealand's NAP lists a number of actions to achieve the objective of reducing the vulnerability of infrastructure assets exposed to climate change. These include defining a resilience standard or code for infrastructure and integrating adaptation into Treasury decisions on infrastructure (Ministry for the Environment New Zealand, 2022[30]).

To be measurable, objectives should be associated with targets, together with a baseline and a timeframe towards which progresss will be measured. Adding targets to objectives helps formulate what actions would be expected in a given timeframe (see examples of targets in Table 1.2). A target is a nearer-term goal that should be specific enough, measurable (i.e. defines a quantitative threshold that leads towards the objective), achievable, realistic/relevant and time-bound (SMART). Targets, timeframes and baselines should be modified as new information becomes available, or as predictions of climate change evolve. An example of a target is for 100% of public institutions to integrate climate adaptation actions into their operational planning by a certain date. Canada, Costa Rica and the UK, for instance, have developed targets for some objectives on the natural environment and adaptation capacity (Table 1.2). Figure 1.8 shows that while the great majority of responding countries include a timeframe for some objectives, only 10 countries do this consistently for all objectives (OECD, 2022[2]). However, more than 40% of responding countries do not establish baseline values for their targets at all and those that do only define baselines for some targets (Figure 1.8). Korea and Mexico are among the few countries that link each of their adaptation progress indicators to both a baseline and a timeframe (see Chapter 4. Korea).

Figure 1.8. Most countries include a timeframe for some objectives, but only a few do so consistently for all objectives

Country responses to "Are the objectives and/or targets associated with a baseline? and "Are the objectives and/or targets time-bound?""

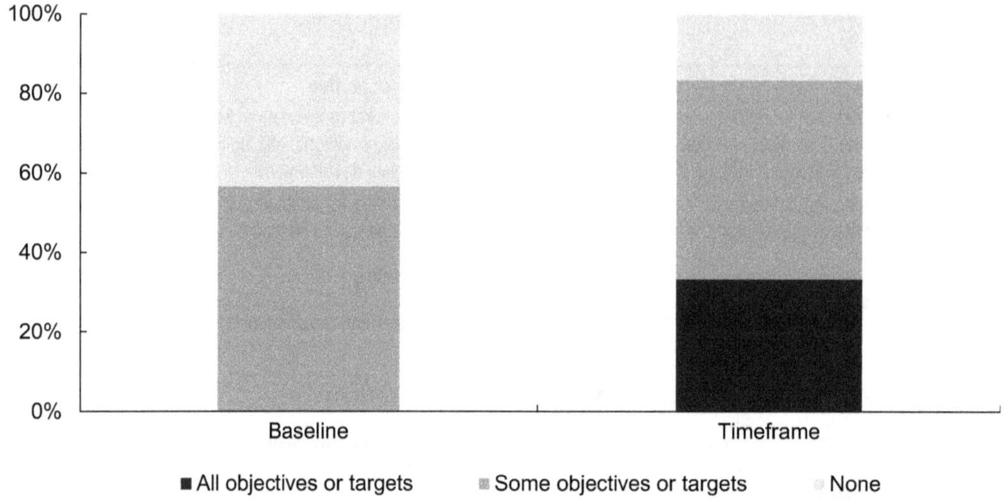

Note: As share of respondents based on 30 responses received to both question 7.b: "Are the objectives and/or targets time-bound?" and question 7.d: "Are the objectives and/or targets associated with a baseline?" out of a total of 30 respondents to the questionnaire.
Source: (OECD, 2022[2]), *OECD Survey on Measuring Progress in Implementing National Adaptation Policies*. Details in Annex A.

Table 1.2. Country examples of adaptation targets linked to an objective

Country	Objective	Associated target
Canada	Everyone in Canada has equitable access to the tools and support needed to prepare for, reduce, and respond to climate change impacts	By 2030, all northern and Indigenous communities have the resources to develop, or have access to, culturally appropriate tools and information to address climate risks
Costa Rica	Develop criteria and guidelines for adaptation in sectoral, regional, and territorial, marine, and coastal planning instruments at different scales	100% of public institutions integrate climate adaptation and risk management actions into their annual operational planning
	Incorporate adaptation criteria into municipal regulatory plans, urban corridors and canton-level planning instruments	100% of coastal and territorial planning instruments presented between 2022-26 incorporate criteria and actions for adaptation
	Promote adaptation-based ecosystems outside the natural heritage of the state, through biodiversity conservation, to allow for sustainable production, promotion of connectivity between natural ecosystems, and control of invasive species	At least 3 997 contracts are maintained under the Payment for Environmental Services Programme, of which 791 are formalised with women owners or co-owners of farms, and 53 are formalised in Indigenous Territories
UK	Protect and improve our protected sites and our other areas of important wildlife habitat	Restoring 75% of terrestrial and freshwater sites to favourable condition

Source: Authors' compilation integrating examples from (Ministry of Environment and Energy Costa Rica, 2022[39]); (Defra, 2018[29]).

Setting adaptation objectives through a collaborative process

In addition to CRAs, adaptation objectives are often also informed by consultations with relevant stakeholders. Generally, consulting a wide range of stakeholders in the objective-setting process helps reflect diverse knowledge on key climate risks as well as potentially differing views on what an objective should aim to achieve. Stakeholder engagement can also help to analyse acceptable levels of risk and what is achievable in terms of cost, timescales and political will (in the light of international, national and regional landscapes). Furthermore, it establishes accountability and legitimacy for the decision-making process, building confidence among stakeholders that the objectives are grounded in credible evidence. According to the OECD survey, objectives are often defined through both expert consultations and inter-ministerial consultations (both 93% of responding countries) (Figure 1.9). France, Japan and Luxembourg all launched public consultations to inform the development of objectives in their NAPs. Peru explicitly seeks to involve indigenous or native people, Afro-Peruvian people, women and youth in setting its adaptation objectives.

Some countries have also set up cross-agency committees to facilitate organised and inclusive co-ordination across the relevant stakeholders. Portugal has established the Co-ordination Group of the Portuguese NAS, including representatives from the Portuguese Environment Agency, nine different sectors, its autonomous regions and municipality associations (OECD, 2022[2]). As part of its NAP development process, Costa Rica set up a NAP Technical Committee composed of 150 actors from relevant sectors, regions and institutions who play a strategic role in environmental planning processes climate risk management; as well as representatives of academia and civil society.

Figure 1.9. Most countries consult widely when defining adaptation objectives

Country responses to "If applicable, what is the process followed for developing the objectives and targets?"

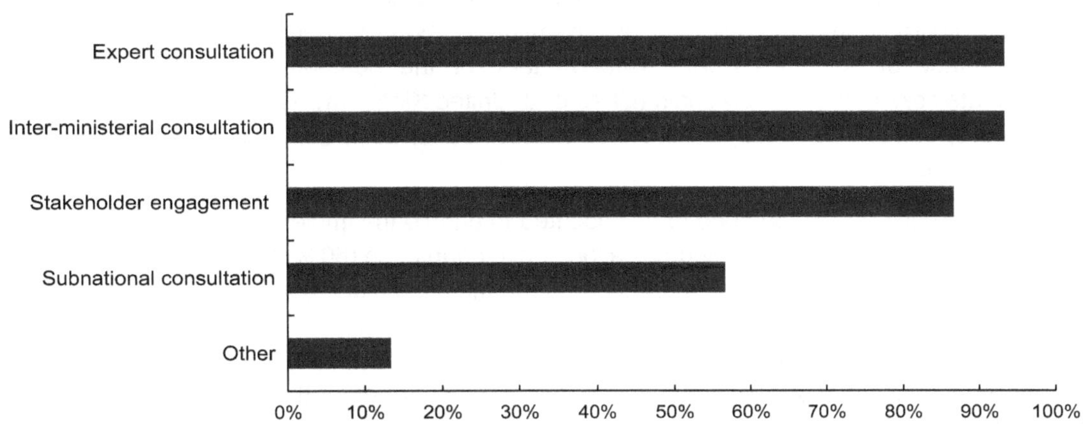

Note: 30 responses were received to question 6: "If applicable, what is the process followed for developing the objectives and targets?", out of 30 respondents to the questionnaire. Respondents could provide multiple answers. "Other" types of consultation (i.e. public consultation and sectoral consultation) were reported by 13% of country respondents and included public consultations and sectoral consultations with different ministries.
Source: (OECD, 2022[2]), *OECD Survey on Measuring Progress in Implementing National Adaptation Policies*. Details in Annex A.

Involving the ministries responsible for implementing the various adaptation interventions in defining objectives is not only useful to ensure that the objectives are appropriate, but can also help increase their buy-in for implementing adaptation actions (UNEP DTU Partnership, 2018[40]). Developing sectoral adaptation targets jointly can help achieve a shared understanding of the acceptable level of risk, ambition and accountability in each sector. Existing sectoral policies, issues, standards, guidance and research should be considered, as well as regional priorities and cross-sectoral issues. Germany is in the process of developing measurable objectives and corresponding indicators and has put each sectoral ministry in charge of defining sectoral objectives and targets, underpinned by a broad stakeholder consultation process (Federal Parliament Germany, 2023[41]).

1.2.3. Measuring adaptation policy progress and effectiveness

Once the risks and adaptation needs have been assessed, countries implement adaptation policies to achieve the defined objectives (Figure 1.2). Progress against these objectives needs to be assessed, including measuring the implementation of adaptation policies and actions, and evaluating the effectiveness and relevance of the actions taken, both quantitatively and qualitatively.

Measuring progress in policy implementation

Tracking the implementation status of the actions listed in national or sectoral plans helps gauge whether an action has been completed within a set timeframe and budget. Implementation monitoring is a well-established practice in adaptation. In the UK, the NAP Monitoring Tracker tool demonstrated the status (on-track, off-track, delivered) of each of the 253 actions set out in the second NAP (CCC, 2021[33]). Similarly, Ireland tracks implementation progress for 423 climate action measures, of which 60 focus on adaptation (Government of Ireland, 2022[42]). France also monitors the implementation progress of its 240 NAP actions, indicating implementation status as percentage progress towards completion. Regular reports also indicate whether the actions are completed, ongoing, delayed or abandoned (Ministry of Ecology, Sustainable Development and Energy France, 2015[43]).

Most OECD countries (70% of all responding countries) report tracking implementation outputs from their adaptation policies (OECD, 2022[2]). These include for example the implementation of physical adaptation measures, regulations, strategies or plans, institutional changes, or capacity and awareness strengthening measures (e.g. research activities or communication tools). The elements reported can also represent social, environmental or economic changes resulting from a policy, for instance, the extent of marine protected area, share of impermeable land in urban areas, flood warning registrations, reported and forecast percentage of households with water meters, or the percentage of FTSE100 companies evaluating climate risks to their supply chain (Chapter 2. United Kingdom). These elements are commonly measured as they can rely on readily available data collected for other activities related to infrastructure, agriculture or businesses.

As additional resources (or inputs) need to be allocated to enable the implementation of planned actions, a majority of countries also track the resources allocated to adaptation (60% of surveyed countries). Ideally the level of resources needed (expressed either in staff time, financial resources or equipment), and the source of resources (e.g. national, sectoral, or local funds), are spelled out in the initial adaptation planning process. However, planned level and source of resources are not commonly integrated into OECD countries' national or sectoral planning documents, and it is even rarer for the resources actually engaged to be reported (OECD, 2022[2]). An exception is Korea, which in its third NAP determines the level of budget needed for each adaptation action and documents the percentage budget execution rate, indicating how much of the planned budget has been spent at different implementation intervals (Chapter 4. Korea). Germany assesses the extent to which resources and competencies are sufficient for implementing the country's NAS in the absence of an overall record of direct and indirect national public expenditure on climate adaptation (UBA, 2019[44]).

In addition to measuring the ressources allocated to the implementation of adaptation actions and their direct results, many countries also look into factors that influence their enabling environment. This can refer to the institutional context for adaptation or co-ordination processes (Norway, Germany), or the level of mainstreaming of adaptation across other policy domains. To a lesser extent it can also include indirect drivers of vulnerability or adaptive capacity (social, economic and environmental). Finland, for example, assesses sectors' institutional capacities for responding to climate change risks, the role of stakeholder participation in promoting NAP implementation, and the level of collaboration between different actors and sectors. It also collects evidence of lessons learnt from implementation, notably on successes and challenges (Ministry of Agriculture and Forestry Finland, 2020[45]).

Quantifying the effectiveness of adaptation policies

In complement to implementation tracking, a key objective of adaptation measurement is to understand the effectiveness of adaptation actions and policies. Adaptation effectiveness is defined as the extent to which an action reduces vulnerability and exposure, increases resilience, and avoids maladaptation (IPCC, 2022[1]). This is the most complex measurement step as it seeks to establish a causal link between adaptation actions and the impact resulting from a reduction in exposure and vulnerability. In practice, measuring effectiveness requires attributing a change in climate impacts to a given adaptation action or policy. An increasing number of countries are seeking to assess the effectiveness of their national adaptation policies and even mandate such evaluations in their legal framework. Yet, 80% of responding countries reported finding it "quite" or "very" challenging to measure the effectiveness of their respective adaptation policies (OECD, 2022[2]), mainly due to the challenge of attribution.

While about one-third (30%) of responding countries state that they measure the impact of their policies, they predominantly measure changes in climate impacts, without assessing whether an implemented action or policy has contributed to these changes (i.e. attribution). Several countries, such as Colombia, Germany and the UK, have developed climate impact indicators – such as annual damage from coastal and river flooding, agricultural losses from drought, or the number of heat-related deaths per year – which they use as proxy to measure policy impact (Table 1.3).[2]

Table 1.3. Ease of measuring climate impacts

Event type	Easy-to-measure impacts	Difficult-to-measure impacts	Rarely-measured impacts
Heatwave	Excess mortality from heat, heat-related hospitalisations	infrastructure damage**	Productivity and other indirect economic losses***
Flooding	Insured asset damage, direct mortality*	Uninsured asset damage. Crop losses**	Mental health impacts, disease outbreaks***
Drought	Crop losses*	Food insecurity and malnutrition ***	Heat-related impacts during drought. Other indirect economic losses***
Wildfire	Insured asset damage, direct mortality**	Uninsured asset damage. Adverse health outcomes from related air pollution ***	Productivity and other indirect economic losses***

Note: *commonly reported, ** typically reported only by OECD countries, *** not routinely reported, and requiring bespoke analysis to yield an impact estimate.
Source: adapted from (OECD, 2021[46]), *Managing Climate Risks, Facing up to Losses and Damages*, https://doi.org/10.1787/55ea1cc9-en.

Countries face methodological and empirical challenges in attributing implemented actions to the measured impacts on climate risk reduction. A first difficulty in assessing effectiveness is measuring climate change impacts. Climate impacts measure the level of actual (not projected) losses and damages caused by climate variability and extremes. Climate impacts result from climate risk, compounded of hazard, exposure and vulnerability (IPCC, 2022[1]). Impacts can be represented, for example, by the number of people wounded, the number of buildings damaged or the level of business disruption. The assessment of climate impacts is limited by information availability. Some types of climate impacts get more frequently measured than others (Table 1.3). For example, insured losses are commonly reported by insurance companies and therefore readily available, at least in an aggregate form. Other types of losses, such as reduced worker productivity (assessed by Germany for some past heatwaves), require in-depth analysis and data and are therefore rarely regularly documented. In the UK, efforts are being undertaken by the UK Climate Change Committee to produce new indicators for climate impacts such as the prevalence of flooding impacts, deaths from overheating or monetary impacts of climate-related water shortages (Chapter 2. United Kingdom).

Attributing changes in climate impacts to a given action or policy is also challenging. Isolating the effect of adaptation requires the evaluation of a change in impact, controlling for the intensity, duration and location of the hazard. An observed reduction in losses and damages may be caused by actions taken outside of the planned and monitored public actions. For example, private actions driven by economic interests or policies that do not target adaptation can also reduce impact. A dam constructed by a private power operator to produce electricity (driven by a policy favouring the production of renewable energy) can affect flood risks downstream.

While quantitative impact assessments exist that highlight impacts on beneficiaries and understand attribution levels, to date these are mainly carried out for individual programmes or projects and are predominantly found in academic research. Causal inference methods range from randomised control trials to natural experiments that identify before and after affects in defined regions or population groups. One such study in Korea assessed the effect of heatwave alerts and health plans on reducing the mortality risk of heatwaves. For this study, a difference-in-difference method was used to measure the difference in outcomes for programme participants before and after the implementation of the programme, compared with non-participants in seven major cities between 2009 and 2014 (Heo et al., 2019[47]).

In complement, cost-effectiveness studies can help select adaptation measures that maximise a result based on comparable levels of resources employed. For instance, Dottori et al. (2023[48]) used flood risk modelling and cost-effectiveness analysis to assess four key adaptation strategies to reduce flood risk across Europe (building-based flood proofing, relocation measures, strengthening of dykes, and reducing flood peaks using detention areas). By estimating by how much each of these solutions can lower projected flood losses in Europe, they can assess their relative cost-effectiveness. Effectiveness can also be assessed ex-ante by predicting how effective specific adaptation measures will be in future scenarios. This can help policy makers select and implement adaptation actions. For example, in Toronto and Montreal (Canada), researchers calculated the expected impacts of a heat mitigation strategy involving increasing the albedo effect on roofs, walls and ground on the reduction in heat-related mortality (excess heat-related deaths). They did so by coupling a weather forecasting model with an urban canopy model. The impact on heat-related mortality was assessed by measuring the intermediate effect of increasing surface albedo on air and dew-point temperature and near-surface wind speed (Jandaghian and Akbari, 2020[49]).

Qualitative approaches to measuring the impact of adaptation policies

Due to the complexity and limitations of quantitative effectiveness assessments, many OECD countries rely on qualitative assessments of the impact of their policies. For example, some countries adopt a theory of change approach to understand the causal relationship between actions and results. This approach links inputs to outputs, outcomes and finally overall impacts (Table 1.4) and enables a qualitative discussion on which part of the results can be attributed to the policy action. In Germany's evaluation of its NAS, it assessed adaptation impacts by establishing plausible causal relations between inputs, implemented actions, outputs, outcomes and policy impact. In Mexico, an evaluation co-ordination group held workshops which identified 13 conditions and steps needed to achieve long-term climate policy objectives and attribute actions to outcomes. This evaluation compares, to the extent possible, the information used to assess objectives and associated indicators against the conditions identified in the theory of change (INECC, 2017[50]).

Table 1.4. Selected examples of theory-of-change step indicators across policy areas

	Input	Output	Outcomes	Climate impact
Natural environment	Resources spent to support habitat creation and restoration and for protected areas	Extent, quality and conditions of habitats in grant areas (relative to non-grant areas) or protected areas	Trends in restored habitats relative to changes in climatic variables; distribution and abundance of species in protected areas (relative to non-protected areas)	Species' extinction risk (e.g. red-list assessment), species abundance, ecosystem service provision
Infrastructure	Reported and forecast investment in flood defences	Number of flood warning registrations	Number of people and properties at risk of flooding (for return period of 1/30 per year)	Annual damages from coastal and river flooding
Agriculture	Agricultural R&D funding for adaptation measures (water storage and drainage infrastructure, water efficiency)	Total number of farms implementing water efficiency measures	Volume of abstraction for agriculture from catchments at risk of water scarcity	Annual agricultural losses from droughts
Health	Spending on passive cooling measures in buildings (residential and healthcare facilities)	Number of hospitals implementing heatwave plans	Number of patients treated for heatstroke and days spent in hospitals	Number of heat-related deaths per year

Source: Authors, based on (Pearce-Higgins et al., 2022[51]); (CCC, 2021[52]).

Another qualitative approach to gauging policy impact and attribution is to consult experts and relevant stakeholders. For example, Austria discusses the impact of policy implementation using expert interviews or surveys of stakeholders responsible for implementing specific actions. Some countries guide the consultation with evaluation criteria or questions that aim to qualitatively assess the effectiveness of implemented actions. Finland, for instance, asks effectiveness-related questions of sectoral and sub-national government officials as well as independent experts, such as "How and in what ways has the NAP promoted risk reduction and adaptive capacity?" (Ministry of Agriculture and Forestry Finland, 2020[45]). Germany also asks whether the measures are sufficient to manage the six key climate risks identified in the country's CRA[3] and to shed light on potential implementation gaps (UBA, 2019[44]). Interestingly some countries also seek second opinions to validate the findings (see Section 1.4).

Some countries also focus on assessing the quality of their adaptation plan. Germany, for instance, assesses whether the adaptation policies are suitable by documenting their development, the extent to which the content reflects the main challenges of adaptation and climate risks assessed, the quality of exchange and co-ordination between government levels and sectors (UBA, 2019[44]). The UK, in its 2021 adaptation progress report, looks into whether the plans in place prepare for a 2-degree Celsius rise in global temperature and consider the risks of a 4-degree Celsius scenario. The progress report assesses whether the objectives are specific, measurable, attainable, relevant and time-bound (SMART), whether they clearly state outcomes that are appropriate, consider short-term and long-term climate impacts, have an effective monitoring and evaluation framework and demonstrate clear links between the outcomes and corresponding actions (CCC, 2021[53]). The EU recently published guidance on developing and updating good quality adaptation strategies and plans, highlighting the importance of creating an institutional framework and ensuring stakeholder buy-in, conducting CRAs, identifying and prioritising adaptation options, as well as essential elements of an action plan (e.g. accounting for different emission scenarios, establishing instruments to mainstream adaptation, estimation of investment needs) and an M&E framework (EC, 2023[54]).

In parrallel, some countries (Czechia, Finland and Ireland) qualitatively review the challenges, barriers, maladaptation and potential limits identified in the implementation of measures (UNFCCC, 2022[9]). Generally, adaptation actions can result in a spectrum of outcomes, ranging from maladaptation to successful adaptation, reflecting a range from decreasing to increasing resilience. Maladaptation, of which there is increasing evidence across sectors and regions (e.g. increasing use of air conditioning), can lock people into situations of vulnerability and exposure that can exacerbate inequalities and might be difficult to change (Schipper, 2020[55]). Finland, for instance, evaluates barriers related to legislation, information and co-operation in the implementation of its adaptation measures (Ministry of Agriculture and Forestry Finland, 2020[45]). Ireland looks into the reasons for delays in the implementation of their NAP: these include administrative delays (e.g. approval processes), capacity and capability constraints (e.g. resourcing and competing priorities), public and stakeholder consultation efforts (e.g. the need to consult in the first instance and the required analysis of submissions), technical and physical limitations, and legislative delays (e.g. drafting, passing and enacting bills) (Climate Change Advisory Council Ireland, 2022[56]).

Finally, although rarer, some countries qualitatively assess whether adaptive capacity has increased overall (i.e. whether society, ecosystems and the economy are better prepared and able to cope with climate related hazards) as a result of their invested resources and implemented actions. For example, Finland identifies processes and practices relevant for increasing adaptive capacity, namely advances made in research, communication and education of climate risks and awareness, and incorporation of climate risks by businesses (Ministry of Agriculture and Forestry Finland, 2020[45]).

1.3. Data and information for adaptation measurement

Data identification, collection and preparation is fundamental for adaptation measurement. This section discusses current country practices in data management for adaptation measurement. It also covers the use of indicator-based frameworks and highlights the related resources and technical constraints that countries may face when establishing databases.

1.3.1. Collecting data and information for adaptation measurement

Data and information requirements for adaptation measurement

Countries rely on a mix of qualitative and quantitave data and information to measure progress on adaptation. While quantitative information can help track progress over time, enable comparison between jurisdictions, and is easy for policy makers to grasp, qualitative information can provide essential information on the "why" and "how" of adaptation successes and failures. Qualitative data can also provide complementary information: for instance, as part of a survey to collect societal perceptions of climate risks and their impacts, German citizens were asked whether they believed heatwaves would affect their work efficiency (UBA, 2019[57]). As both quantitative and qualitative data have different advantages and disadvantages, combining them can ensure that the overall narrative of adaptation progress and performance is robust, consistent and contextualised (EC, 2023[54]).

Countries already have useful and relevant data and information at their disposal. Most responding countries (80%) mainly rely on existing data and information to measure adaptation, often extracted from publicly available sources (Figure 1.10). Environment agencies, meteorological offices and other public bodies are key owners of information on climate hazards and exposure. Different government agencies hold sectorally relevant adaptation information, such as the health, agriculture or infrastructure ministries. Similarly, governments can collect relevant information from the private sector through publicly available corporate disclosures on climate-related information or specific reporting mandates.

Figure 1.10. Most country respondents use existing data to measure progress on adaptation

Country responses to "How is relevant data and information to measure progress on adaptation collected or generated?"

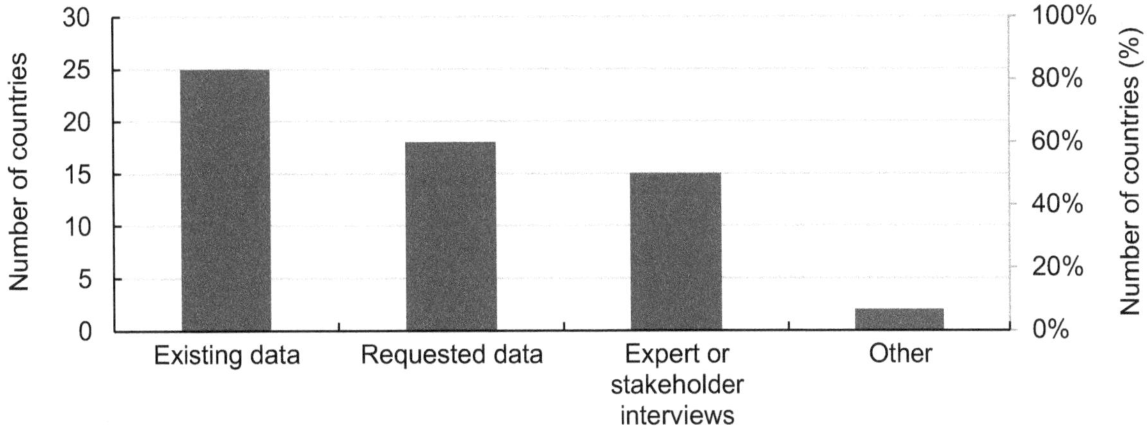

Note: 28 responses were received to question 11: "How is relevant data and information to measure progress on adaptation collected or generated?" out of a total of 30 respondents to the questionnaire. Two countries mentioned 'Other' – the UK's Climate Change Committee (CCC) uses commissioned research, and Indonesia, which noted: "methodologies and instruments for monitoring and evaluation, validation and verification". Multiple answer question.

Source: (OECD, 2022[2]), *OECD Survey on Measuring Progress in Implementing National Adaptation Policies*. Details in Annex A.

Countries need historical and projected data on temperature and precipitation, as well as relevant information on other hazards (e.g. soil moisture levels to assess drought risk). Most countries have temperature and precipitation data at their disposal, but may struggle to integrate climate change projections into hazard models and data. To assess exposure, countries need data on the size and location of populations and assets, or the area of ecosystems exposed to a specific climate hazard. While census data often provide sufficient figures on population levels and density, geospatial data on non-public assets can be difficult and resource-intensive to retrieve. Spatial disaggregation of hazard and exposure data more broadly remains an issue, as local data are often lacking, incomplete or inconsistent (Adger, Brown and Surminski, 2018[58]).

Measuring vulnerability to hazards requires refined socio-economic data. Chile, for instance, assesses poverty levels; density levels of children under five, elderly over 65, and female-headed households with dependent people (children, adolescents and older adults); as well as population densities in urban areas (Ministry of Environment Chile, 2020[59]). As vulnerability factors are highly varied and context-specific – ranging from the age of materials and use rates of services and infrastructure to climate risk awareness among citizens – collecting data to assess these factors at the national level can be extremely resource-intensive. As a result, the quality of information on vulnerability varies significantly across countries and some vulnerability information remains limited or coarse.

To assess progress on the implementation of adaptation actions, countries need to document information on the measures implemented, such as the number of strategies developed, investment measures carried out, regulations updated or introduced or communication campaigns carried out. Implementation progress reporting also requires data on environmental and socio-economic changes that may have been achieved as a result of implemented measures. For example, the share of permeable land in urban areas, extent of protected areas. Finally, countries also need data on the resources used to implement the measures.

Most importantly, adaptation measurement is dependent on data that indicate climate impacts on the environment, economy and society to assess whether these impacts have decreased or not. Such data might include, for instance, rates of tree crown defoliation, annual economic damage from extreme weather events, percentage change in heat-related mortality, claims expenditure for property insurance, number of weather-related disruptions to power supply, and crop yield fluctuations. Ideally, impact data should be directly linked to climate change, such as heat-related mortality or economic damage induced by extreme weather events, instead of using proxy data that presume a relationship with climate change. Many countries lack the systematic documentation of climate-induced impact data, which explains the relatively low measurement of climate impacts described in Section 1.2.3. Countries also lack data on cascading and cross-sectoral impacts, such as the reduction of government finances due to lower tax revenues from impaired households and firms (EEA, 2022[22]; Financial Stability Board, 2021[60]).

Even where data exist, there can be gaps arising from limited spatial coverage or limited time series (EEA, 2015[5]; OECD, 2022[61]), or simply differences in reporting that render data less comparable. For example, regional disparities in climate risk and adaptation needs mean that sub-national jurisdictions report very different types of data and information, posing a methodological problem for countries in aggregating them in a relevant way at national level (Ellis, 2014[62]). For instance, in Costa Rica, 20 cantons established their own monitoring frameworks for tracking progress. Similarly, changes in the resources or methods devoted to data collection and administrative changes (e.g. staff turnover) can affect the continuity and quality of the data collected. In Austria, for instance, the information-gathering method was altered between the first and the second progress report, making it difficult to compare them, and to obtain an accurate evaluation of progress (BMK, 2021[37]). A prerequisite for addressing data gaps is an effective measurement agenda, with sufficient long-term funding.

OECD countries are making progress in assessing their data needs and gaps. Some countries (e.g. Germany, Norway and the UK) specifically assess data and information gaps in their measurement reports. For instance, Norway's auditor explored whether the transport ministry had enough data to assess the climate adaptation of transport infrastructure (Office of the Auditor General of Norway, 2022[63]). The UK CCC has flagged that nearly 40% of adaptation outcome measures lacked relevant and up-to-date datasets (e.g. either because they do not exist, or where they do exist, are not up to date, are not sufficiently comprehensive in scope or only provide a point-in-time snapshot) (see Chapter 2. United Kingdom).

Generating new evidence: collecting additional data and information

In addition to the use of existing available data (or data collected for other purposes), countries request and collect additional adaptation-specific information through the following methods:

- **Self-assessment:** Data and information, mainly qualitative information, is collected by a number of countries through self-assessments. Korea bases its adaptation measurement to a large extent on annual self-evaluations requested from all ministries and local governments. Each ministry conducts the self-evaluation using a standardised template for all adaptation projects for which they are responsible (286 projects are being reviewed for the 3rd NAP). The ministries assign scores to the performance of each action based on changes from the evaluation results from the previous year. They also look at other factors, such as compliance with the implementation schedule and budget disbursement, or the extent to which the target set out in the plan has been achieved.
- **Surveys and questionnaires:** Standardised surveys sent to local governments, sectoral representatives and national ministries can allow countries to collect new and harmonised information. In Ireland, for example, the Climate Action Regional Offices (CAROs) collect information on progress by sending a standardised survey to all 31 local authorities. Germany has conducted a one-off survey to assess the impact of the German Strategy for Adaptation to Climate Change on 249 municipalities across all 16 states. Finland's Ministry of Agriculture and Forestry conducted a national online survey addressed to non-government stakeholders (Ministry of Agriculture and Forestry Finland, 2020[45]).

- **Participatory approaches:** Another way of collecting data is to involve a wide range of stakeholders through interviews, consultations, workshops or the establishment of expert panels. For example, Austria conducted 10 thematic workshops to assess progress towards all of its 14 adaptation goals, guided by standard questions. The workshops were documented, with the reports commented on again by all participants and used as the basis for the evaluation of progress in all fields of action, as well as towards each adaptation goal set out in the NAP (BMK, 2021[37]).

To harness data and information on climate risks and on measures implemented from a broad range of non-government and public organisations, reporting mandates have also been set up. In the UK, the Adaptation Reporting Power gives the government a legal instrument to request direct public bodies and major infrastructure providers to report on climate risks and impacts they have faced and measures they have taken to prepare for them. Switzerland, in the revision of their current CO_2 law, specifically mandates its supervisory authorities to report on financial risks arising from climate impacts (Federal Council Germany, 2022[64]). Korea also systematically collects information on progress from each local authority, which is mandated in law. It uses a point system to present individual actions in relation to NAP, which enables comparison (Chapter 4. Korea).

To orientate data collection efforts, some countries also establish wish-list indicators for which data are not yet available, but that are deemed relevant to assess progress. Identifying a so-called indicator wishlist can help establish clarity on what needs to be measured and further encourage the development of methodologies and the generation of data. The UK, for instance, developed its indicator list using this approach, but 60% of its indicators remain on the wish-list because data are not yet available to populate them (Chapters 2 and 4).

1.3.2. Building adaptation indicators

In addition to collecting data, countries need to find ways of analysing them to report on their risk, impacts, needs and adaptation progress. Standardised indicators allow data to be presented in a simplified manner and synthesised, helping to facilitate communication and comparability (Ellis, 2014[62]). OECD countries highlight that indicators are particularly useful to i) clearly convey adaptation progress by showing trends or rates of change in implementation; ii) identify existing gaps and further adaptation needs; iii) show the extent to which measures have contributed to overarching targets and objectives; and iv) provide a comparable perspective across adaptation in different sectors, contributing to quality assurance and accountability (OECD, 2022[2]). However, developing indicators is also a resource-intensive and time-consuming process, which needs to be borne in mind when developing a measurement framework.

Indicators play a prominent role in adaptation measurement, as reflected by the large share of countries that use or intend to use indicators to measure progress in the implementation of adaptation policies (80% of responding countries). While around 30% of responding countries have developed indicators and are using them to measure progress, in others the process is still underway (OECD, 2022[2]).

Future OECD work on adaptation measurement will focus on establishing common indicators for different sectors that can report on climate hazards, exposure, vulnerability, implementation progress and inform adaptation effectiveness.

1.4. Fostering adaptation measurement and results use

This section presents an overview of legal and policy frameworks for adaptation measurement and analyses the main institutional actors and stakeholders responsible for adaptation measurement. It discusses how measurement results are used by policy makers, and how the use of the results is promoted at the national level, highlighting links and synergies between national and international adaptation measurement.

1.4.1. Institutional and policy frameworks for adaptation measurement

National legal frameworks for adaptation measurement

Legal mandates for measuring adaptation progress have been beneficial to ensure consistent reporting, increase data coverage, and help secure the capacities needed, including financial and human resources, to undertake adaptation measurement (Reckien et al., 2023[65]). An increasing number of countries anchor adaptation measurement in their climate laws (Table 1.5). Some of these laws require simple tracking of the implementation of adaptation policies, while others seek to evaluate the effectiveness of measures. Finland, for example, is one of the few countries whose law requires an analysis of whether their NAP has been effective overall in reducing climate risk (FINLEX, 2022[66]). In the UK, the existence of a statutory requirement to evaluate the NAP has been a driver of the extensive measurement activities undertaken by an independent statutory body (EEA, 2015[5]). These laws often determine the entity responsible for measuring adaptation progress (Table 1.5). In Norway the entity for reporting on implementation progress is the supreme legislature; in Finland and the UK it is the parliament.

Table 1.5. Mandating for adaptation measurement in climate laws

Selected countries with a legal mandate to review adaptation policies

Country	Laws and regulations mandating reviews	Elements to be measured and reported	Frequency of review	Responsible entity
Finland	Climate Law 2022	Assess **adequacy** and **effectiveness** of measures included in the NAP Review **implementation** of adaptation measures by administrative branch and regionally	n.a.	Government
Germany	Federal Climate Adaptation Act	Monitor observed climate change impacts and evaluate achievements of targets	Every four years	Federal government
Greece	National Climate Law on the Transition to Climate Neutrality and Adaptation to Climate Change 2022	Monitor adaptation **actions** and **policies** through indicators and other appropriate methods and tools	Every five years	National Observatory for Adaptation to Climate Change
Indonesia	Regulation 98 on the implementation of Carbon Pricing (2021)	Monitor and evaluate adaptation action at national, provincial and municipal level, as well as climate impacts on priority sectors in regions particularly exposed to climate change Develop climate resilience target and index of climate resilience to measure target achievement	n.a.	Respective ministries, provincial and municipal governments
Ireland	Climate Action and Low Carbon Development (Amendment) Act 2021	Review progress in **implementation** of adaptation policy measures under national adaptation framework and Sectoral Adaptation Plans, where they exist	At least every five years	Minister of the government
Japan	Climate Change Adaptation Act 2018	Understand progress in **implementation** of Climate Change Adaptation Plan, and develop an **evaluation method** Promote observation, monitoring, projection and assessment of **climate impacts**	Every five years	Government
Korea	Framework Act on Low Carbon and Green Growth 2010	Assess progress in implementing measures set out in the NAP and detailed implementation plans	Annually	Government
Mexico	General Law on Climate Change 2012 (amended in 2018)	Measuring, monitoring, reporting, verification (also applies to sectoral adaptation programmes) and evaluation, including effectiveness and compliance with objectives, of actions implemented under national **adaptation policy**	Every two years	The Inter-ministerial Commission on Climate Change

New Zealand	Climate Change Response (Zero Carbon) Amendment Act 2019	Evaluate **implementation** of NAP and its **effectiveness**, including: • progress in implementing strategies, policies and proposals • degree to which the **objectives** of the plan have been achieved • how well the plan responds to key climate risks • **barriers** to implementation and effectiveness and how to overcome them	Every two years	Climate Change Commission
Norway	Climate Change Act 2017	Take account of how Norway is preparing for and adapting to climate change	Annually	Government
Spain	Law on Climate Change and Energy Transition 2021	Define a system of indicators of **climate impacts** and adaptation to monitor and evaluate **public policies** and prepare risk reports	Every five years	Ministry for Ecological Transition & Demographic Challenge
UK	UK Climate Change Act 2008	Assess progress in **implementing** the objectives, proposals and policies set out in the adaptation programmes	Every two years	Committee on Climate Change

Source: (Federal Council Switzerland, 2021[67]); (Grantham Research Institute on Climate Change and the Environment, 2022[68]); (Ministry of Climate and Environment Norway, 2017[69]); (Ministry of Justice Japan, 2018[70]); (Mexico, 2023[71]); (Parliamentary Counsel Office New Zealand, 2019[72]); (The National Archives UK, 2008[73]); (FINLEX, 2022[66]); (Office of the Attorney General Ireland, 2021[74]); (Korea Legislation Research Institute, 2021[75]); (Government of the Republic of Indonesia, 2021[76]).

In the European Union (EU), the EU Climate Law provides a framework for promoting progress on implementing adaptation measures. It has also encouraged countries to consider anchoring adaptation measurement in national climate laws (EEA, 2022[22]; 2015[5]). Under the EU Regulation on the Governance of the Energy Union and Climate Action, Member States are required to report biennially to the European Commission on progress in national adaptation, which is summarised and documented by the European Environment Agency (EEA, 2022[22]) (EC, 2018[77]). Every five years from 2023 onwards, the European Commission will asses collective progress, including the consistency of relevant national measures, submit its conclusions to the EU Parliament and Council, and publicly issue recommendations if there are inconsistent actions by Member States.

At the sub-national level, some countries also mandate sub-national entities to assess progress in implementing state or local-level adaptation plans and measures (e.g. Indonesia, Korea, Mexico). Finland sets out sector-specific and regional reviews of adaptation. The laws in France, Ireland and Sweden mandate regional authorities to prepare climate risk assessments (see Section 1.2.1).

National adaptation strategies and plans

All 38 OECD member countries have either a National Adaptation Strategy (NAS), National Adaptation Plan (NAP) or both (Table 1.6). The OECD survey shows that 80% of responding countries include a specific section on monitoring and evaluation (M&E) in their NAPs (OECD, 2022[2]). This section tends to lay out the purpose of adaptation measurement, i.e. to monitor and evaluate the progress and effectiveness of adaptation policy implementation, and enhance the knowledge base, accountability, and/or learning in order to improve adaptation policies and practices. This stated purpose influences the way M&E is conducted, who might be involved in this process, the methodological approach, and even the extent to which the information produced can be used to support policy and practice (EEA, 2015[5]). While most countries are vague about the actual step-by-step process of measurement, some describe the steps in detail in their NAPS. Colombia, for example, has clearly set out the individual steps of the measurement process[4]. Czechia and Japan define what exactly needs to be measured and even suggest some indicators to be used for this purpose.

Table 1.6. Timeline of OECD countries' national adaptation policies

Country/year	'05	'06	'07	'08	'09	'10	'11	'12	'13	'14	'15	'16	'17	'18	'19	'20	'21	'22	'23
AUSTRALIA																			
AUSTRIA																			
BELGIUM																			
CANADA																			
CHILE																			
COLOMBIA																			
COSTA RICA																			
CZECHIA																			
DENMARK																			
ESTONIA																			
FINLAND																			
FRANCE																			
GERMANY																			
GREECE																			
HUNGARY																			
ICELAND																			
IRELAND																			
ISRAEL																			
ITALY																			
JAPAN																			
KOREA																			
LATVIA																			
LITHUANIA																			
LUXEMBOURG																			
MEXICO																			
NETHERLANDS																			
NEW ZEALAND																			
NORWAY																			
POLAND																			
PORTUGAL																			
SLOVAK																			
SLOVENIA																			
SPAIN																			
SWEDEN																			
SWITZERLAND																			
TÜRKIYE																			
UK																			
US																			

Note: Blue = NAS; Yellow = NAP; Orange = other framework; Green = both NAP + NAS; EU countries are marked in bold.

Eighteen responding countries have also developed sectoral adaptation plans. Most of them include an M&E section, which can help engage sectoral actors and data holders in adaptation measurement. Ireland, for example, has developed sectoral plans for nine different sectors, which include an M&E section (Department of the Environment Climate and Communications Ireland, 2023[78]).

Key actors and their responsibilities for adaptation measurement

The Ministry of Environment (MoE) (or the ministry which has a statutory responsibility for the environment) typically takes a lead role in adaptation measurement, either by conducting adaptation measurement itself (e.g. Greece) or through a co-ordinating function by centralising information from all other ministries and sub-national and sectoral authorities (e.g. Chile, Korea) (OECD, 2022[2]). The fact that all surveyed countries report that not only a ministry, but also a government agency (such as an environment agency), a statistical office, a scientific agency (e.g. meteorological institute) or an audit office are involved in the measurement effort shows the shared character of the task (Figure 1.11 and Table 1.7).

Figure 1.11. A range of institutions and organisations are involved in adaptation measurement

Country responses to "What are the roles and responsibilities of the following institutions or stakeholders in the process of measuring progress on adaptation?"

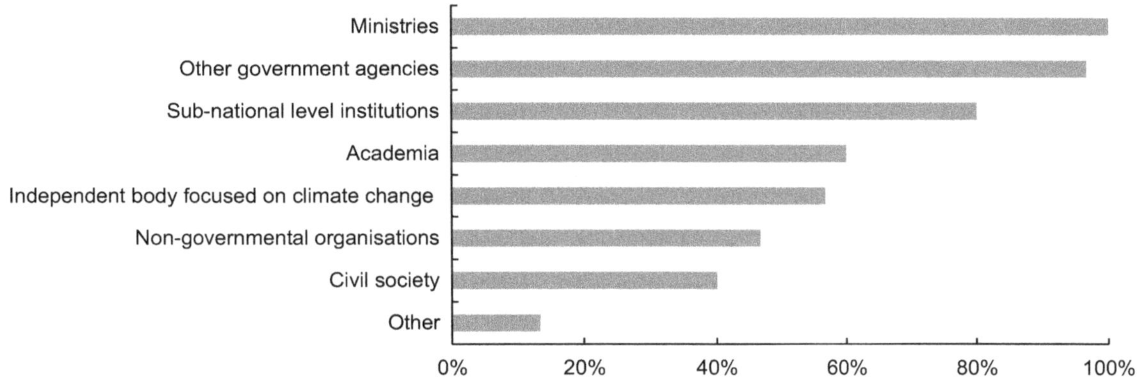

Note: As a share of respondents based on 30 responses received to the question 10: "What are the roles and responsibilities of the following institutions or stakeholders in the process of measuring progress on adaptation?" (multiple answers possible; open question). Examples given for "Ministries: include Ministry of Environment, Inter-ministerial working group. Examples given for "Other government agencies" include Environment Agency, National Office for Statistics, scientific agencies (e.g. meteorological institute), Audit Office, or similar. Examples given for "Independent body focused on climate change" include Climate Change Council, Committee, or Centre, or similar. Sub-national level institutions included those at the provincial/state, regional or municipal/city levels.
Source: (OECD, 2022[2]), *OECD Survey on Measuring Progress in Implementing National Adaptation Policies*. Details in Annex A.

Several countries have established inter-ministerial working groups (or councils of ministers, or committees) to co-ordinate meaurement tasks. In Germany, the Interministerial Working Group on Climate Change Adaptation regularly prepares a monitoring report of climate impact trends and implementation progress, and also sets out future priorities for measures to address identified implementation gaps. All federal ministries work together in this group under the leadership of the Federal Ministry for the Environment (BMUV) in order to update Germany's NAS every four years (OECD, 2023[79]).

Table 1.7. The role of national agencies in adaptation measurement

National body	Role	Country examples	Countries reporting involvement
Environment agency	• Support and inform ministry responsible for adaptation through knowledge generation, capacity building and decision support. • Store relevant environmental data and information. • May provide analysis of non-environmental impacts.	The Dutch Environment Assessment Agency monitors and assesses climate impacts and risks, identifies adaptation options, and their effectiveness The German Federal Environment Agency (UbA) develops adaptation targets, improves analysis of the effectiveness of measures, and is establishing a nationwide climate damage register	Chile, Australia, Czechia, France, Germany, Greece, Israel, Ireland, Sweden, Peru, the Netherlands
Other institutions (e.g. health, disaster management or fire departments)	• Provide specific information such as on fire risk and health-related issues (e.g. heat stress, allergies, or water quality) and adaptation measures taken to address them	Austria has the Competence Centre Health and Climate in the Austrian National Public Health Institute	Austria, Lithuania, the Netherlands, Indonesia
(Hydro-) Meteorological office and other scientific agencies	• Collect and provide climate- and water-related information and develop climate scenarios and models which then feed into adaptation reporting and CRAs. • Provide information on climate-related hazards, and conduct more advanced analysis of exposure and future climate risks	Australia's Climate Service (which includes the Bureau of Meteorology, Geoscience Australia, CSIRO, a scientific research organisation, and the Bureau of Statistics) assembles scientific information on climate risks to inform future adaptation measurement	Australia, Chile, Greece, Colombia, Costa Rica, UK, Israel, Lithuania, Netherlands, Slovak Republic, Spain, Croatia, Peru, Romania, Indonesia
National statistical office	• Store socio-economic and demographic data (e.g. on the economy, losses and damages, insurance, human health, energy use, land use and census data), which are increasingly used and further processed to assess climate impacts	UK's Office for National Statistics created a one-stop shop for statistics on climate change	Romania, Australia, Greece, Indonesia, UK
Audit office	• Scrutinise implementation of actions and spending on adaptation by public bodies in terms of adequacy and efficiency	Sweden's NAO has audited the efficiency of government efforts to support municipalities' adaptation of the built environment; Norway's NAO has assessed authorities' work in adapting infrastructure and buildings; In Australia, the NSW Audit Office has assessed how effectively the Department of Planning, Industry and Environment and Treasury have supported state agencies to manage climate risks to their assets and services	Norway, Sweden, Federal states: Australia (New South Wales, Canada (British Colombia), UK (Scotland)

Note: 30 responses received to question 10: "What are the roles and responsibilities of the following institutions or stakeholders in the process of measuring progress on adaptation?", i.e. all 30 respondents to the questionnaire. Countries listed in the right column include those that reported a role for the respective bodies in the survey, even if the body is not yet involved, but the intention stands.
Source: (OECD, 2022[2]); (NAO Sweden, 2022[80]); (The Office of the Auditor General Norway, 2021[81]); (Audit Office NSW Australia, 2021[82]).

Sub-national authorities (e.g. states, regions and cities) have a key role in adaptation measurement given their place-specific data and their direct role in implementation (OECD, 2023[36]). Indeed, 24 surveyed countries (80%) report that sub-national authorities contribute to adaptation measurement (OECD, 2022[2]). In France and Portugal, for instance, sub-national authorities communicate progress to the national government on the implementation of actions set out in the NAS or NAP. In Peru, sub-national governments are responsible for measuring their own adaptation policies and report progress to the national Ministry of Environment (OECD, 2022[2]). In Ireland, local authorities develop Local Authority Progress Reports and submit them to the national Department of Environment, Climate and Communications (Climate Action Regional Offices, 2022[83]). Sub-national authorities' differing priorities, resources and capacities to contribute to adaptation measurement may lead to uneven depths of reporting or integration of sub-national information into national adaptation measurement. Ensuring sub-national governments' responsibilities are clearly defined, such as in national adaptation policies or laws, could help secure the capacity required for adaptation measurement at sub-national level.

Reviews undertaken by independent non-government bodies provide a critical perspective on adaptation measurement. Just over half of responding countries indicate that there is an independent expert advisory body involved in adaptation measurement (OECD, 2022[2]). The UK's Climate Change Committee (CCC) is a good example: it has been carrying out an independent assessment of adaptation progress every two years (Box 1.2). The CCC demonstrates that having a clear statutory mandate, strong leadership and sufficient power to hold the government to account increases independent bodies' effectiveness in reviewing adaptation progress, provided they have resources to do so (Averchenkova, Fankhauser and Finnegan, 2018[84]). Some independent bodies, while not measuring adaptation progress themselves, identify adaptation gaps and develop recommendations. An example is the French *Haut Conseil pour le Climat*, which has done this every year since 2021 (High Council for Climate France, 2021[85]).

Box 1.2. The UK Climate Change Committee and its Adaptation Committee

Established by the UK Climate Change Act in 2008, the UK Climate Change Committee (CCC) is one of the oldest climate change advisory bodies in the world. Its design, as a body that includes provisions for feedback and evaluation of government progress, has been emulated by other countries (Nash and Steurer, 2019[86]). In terms of adaptation, its statutory duties are to monitor, evaluate and report on progress and advise policy makers in the UK Parliament and devolved legislatures (Scotland, Wales and Northern Ireland) on the risks and opportunities presented by climate change.

In 2009, the CCC established its Adaptation Committee. It is mandated to develop biennial adaptation progress reports of the UK's NAP and Scotland's Climate Change Adaptation Programme, as well as a five-yearly independent climate change risk assessment that identifies where additional adaptation actions are needed based on current and planned policies. The CCC also has an important role in independently developing suitable indicators to assess adaptation progress. Its assessments are based on data and information provided by or generated through consultations with government departments, industry representatives and non-government bodies, such as the British Red Cross, British Ports Association, Forestry Commission and Public Health England.

The CCC's work is a well-recognised and trusted source of information, benefitting from its position as an independent body holding the government to account. Its clear statutory mandate and strong leadership power offer a good practice model for other countries.

Note: The Adaptation Committee was previously called the Adaptation Sub-Committee.
Source: (Dudley, Jordan and Lorenzoni, 2022[87]); (Averchenkova, Fankhauser and Finnegan, 2018[84]).

Audit offices can scrutinise action and spending on adaptation by public bodies, and assess how well they are adapting and reporting publicly on the value for money that is being achieved from public investments. Audit offices may also assess the (state) government's implementation of adaptation measures (Table 1.7). Sweden's National Audit Office (NAO) has assessed whether central government efforts to support municipalities' climate adaptation of the built environment are efficient (NAO Sweden, 2022[80]). Similarly, Norway's NAO has assessed the Norwegian authorities' work on adapting infrastructure and buildings to climate change (The Office of the Auditor General Norway, 2021[81]). In Australia, the New South Wales (NSW) Audit Office has assessed how effectively the Department of Planning, Industry and Environment and NSW Treasury have supported state agencies to manage climate risks to their assets and services (Audit Office NSW Australia, 2021[82]).

Academia, NGOs, civil society and the private sector can also have roles in the measurement process. Some countries have established scientific advisory committees to advise the MoE. In Chile, for example, the National Council for Sustainability and Climate Change, composed of representatives from civil society, academia, and the corporate sector, among others, issues its opinion and makes proposals on adaptation measures, their progress, and the effects of their implementation (OECD, 2022[2]). Academic institutions or researchers commonly provide data, often focused on climate impacts, risks, and vulnerabilities, analyses of adaptation progress and sometimes advice on the adaptation measurement framework. In some countries academic institutions have representatives in a (scientific) committee involved in adaptation measurement. The OECD survey shows that in 60% of responding countries, academic institutions are involved in the measurement process. In 40% of countries NGOs and/or civil society are involved (OECD, 2022[2]).

The private sector can also act as an information provider and can assess its own progress in adapting to the climate impacts they face. The private sector can benefit from engaging in adaptation measurement as a way to increase its transparency and accountability in managing climate risk and potential ambition in financing and implementing actions (UNEP, 2021[16]). At present, relevant private sector data and information gathered for national adaptation measurement focuses on understanding the level of companies' awareness of their climate risks. There is less information on the actual climate impacts they face or their progress in addressing them. Due to the growing importance of climate risk management, as well as sometimes mandatory climate-related corporate disclosures (e.g. for environmental, social, and governance or in the context of the Task Force on Climate-related Financial Disclosures), the private sector's interest in assessing climate risks and resilience levels is increasing. How private sector information is integrated into national adaptation measurement differs between countries. Some countries use specific indicators. For example, Korea monitors whether a manual for adaptation has been developed for all industries vulnerable to climate change (Chapter 4. Korea). The UK monitors the percentage of FTSE100 companies evaluating climate risks to their supply chains, and surveys businesses to assess the proportion reporting on adaptation, in line with TFCD recommendations (CCC, 2021[52]).

1.4.2. Fostering the use of adaptation measurement results

Adaptation measurement generates evidence for policy decisions that feed into the learning process of the adaptation policy cycle (Figure 1.2). The majority (80%) of survey responding countries publish their adaptation measurement findings in a monitoring, evaluation or progress report (OECD, 2022[2]). The reports often include information on the methodology used and process followed to assess progress, adaptation objectives, and evolving climate risks and impacts. The frequency with which countries publish their measurement reports vary. The OECD survey shows that most responding countries (70%) publish measurement reports every one to five years, while some (10%) publish them in the middle and/or at the end (20%) of the implementation period of their NAS or NAP (Figure 1.12). Few countries publish reviews on an ad hoc basis. More than half of responding countries make their adaptation measurement reports publicly available (Figure 1.13) (OECD, 2022[2]).

Figure 1.12. Most countries publish adaptation measurement reports every one to five years

Country responses to "At what frequency are reports published?"

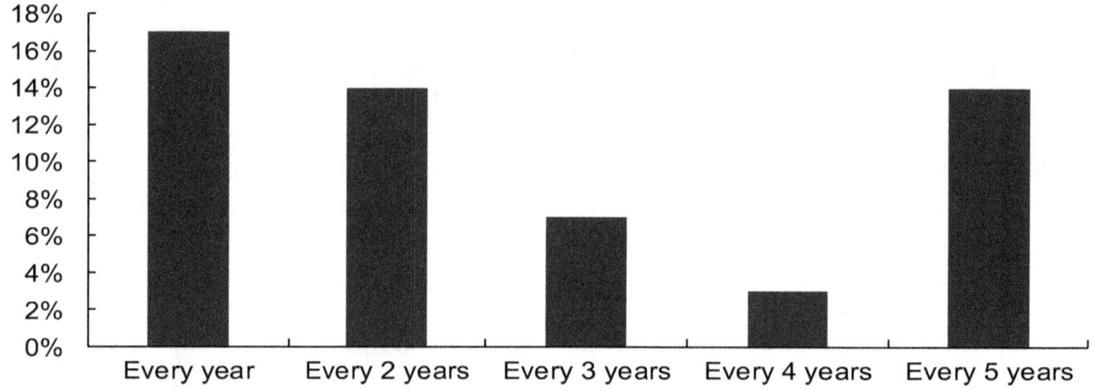

Note: As a share of respondents that publish reports on adaptation measurement, based on 30 responses received to questions 13: "Is progress on the implementation of adaptation policies documented in a report?" and 25 responses received to question 14: "If yes, at what frequency are they published?" out of a total of 30 respondents to the questionnaire. Few countries (e.g. Costa Rica) that state that they do not document progress in a report have still reported the frequency set out in their national adaptation policy.
Source: based on (OECD, 2022[2]), *OECD Survey on Measuring Progress in Implementing National Adaptation Policies*. Details in Annex A.

Figure 1.13. Progress reports are made public at the national and international levels

Country responses to "how can results be accessed?"

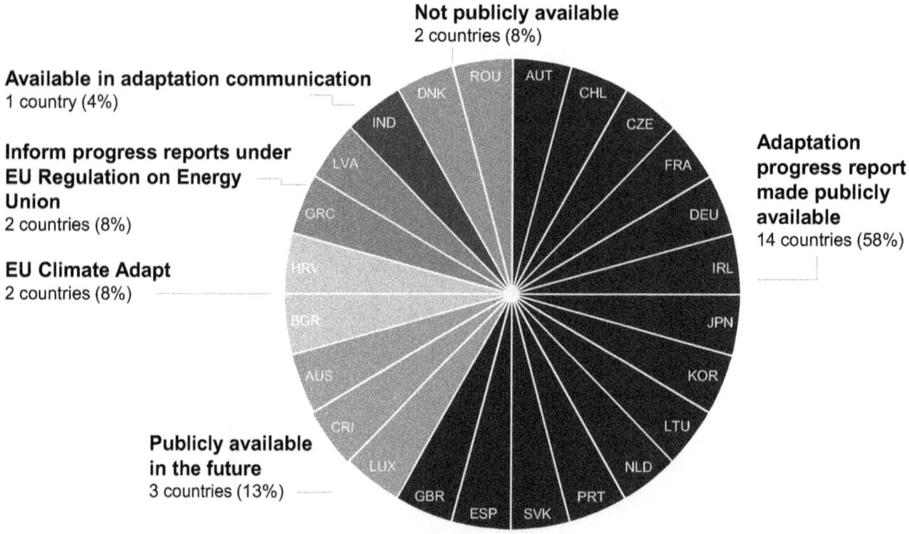

Note: 24 responses were received to the open-ended question 15: "If yes, how can results be accessed?", of a total of 30 respondents to the questionnaire. Only respondents that answered positively to question 13 were able to answer question 15. 21% of countries responding to question 13 did not answer question 15. In countries colour-coded with light to dark orange the results inform supranational mechanisms of adaptation-related reporting, notably the UNFCCC adaptation communication, regular progress reports under the EU Regulation on the Energy Union and on the EU Climate Adapt Platform, which also informs EU adaptation progress reports.
Source: (OECD, 2022[2]), *OECD Survey on Measuring Progress in Implementing National Adaptation Policies*. Details in Annex A.

The OECD survey shows that nearly all responding countries undertake adaptation measurement to inform policy making (OECD, 2020[88]), with 60% of responding countries stating that the results inform priorities for action in subsequent adaptation policies (Figure 1.14). In Korea, the 2021 Framework Act on Low Carbon and Green Growth requires poor performance or areas that need improvement to be addressed in the future NAS (Korea Environment Institute, 2023[89]). Switzerland's second NAS (2020-25) was developed based on the assessment of the first NAS (2012), including the impacts of implemented actions as well as changes in the adaptation framework conditions (Federal Office for the Environment Switzerland, 2014[90]). Similarly, France states that its second NAP (2018-22) has been developed based on the recommendations of the evaluation of the first NAP (2011-15) (Ministry of Ecological and Solidarity Transition France, 2018[91]).

Figure 1.14. Almost all country respondents use measurement results in policy making

Country responses to "How do the results inform policy-making?"

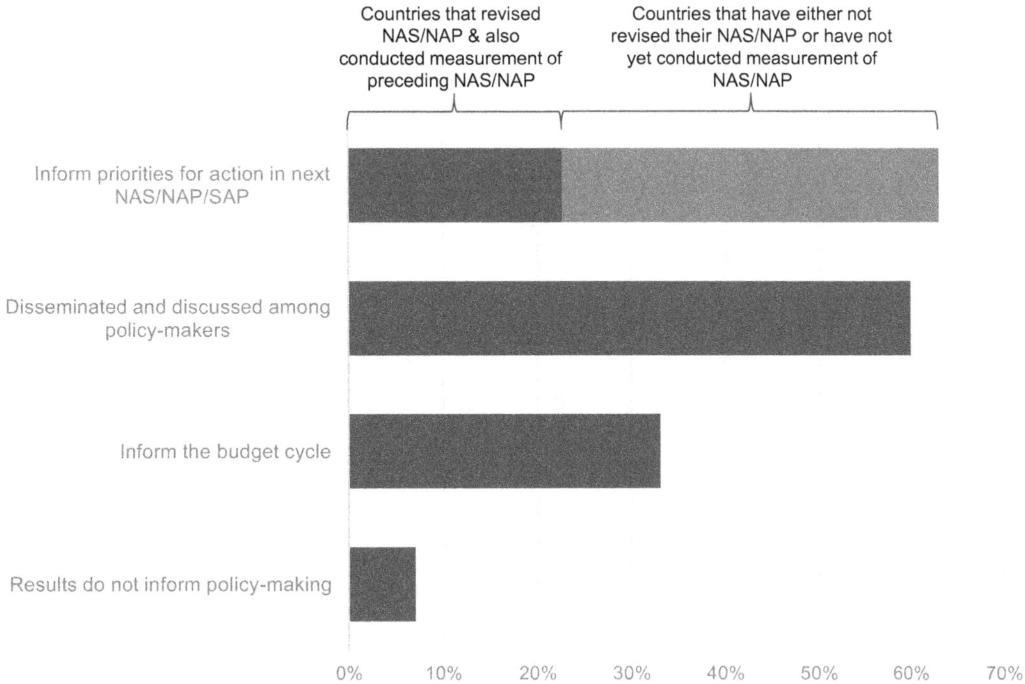

Note: Share of respondents based on 24 responses received to the multiple answer question 16: "If yes, how do the results inform policy-making?", out of a total of 30 respondents to the questionnaire. Responding countries that have adopted a revised NAS or NAP and also conducted an implementation assessment of the preceding NAS or NAP (first row, left bar) are Austria, France, Germany, Korea, Portugal, Spain and the UK.
Source: (OECD, 2022[2]), *OECD Survey on Measuring Progress in Implementing National Adaptation Policies.* Details in Annex A.

The findings from adaptation measurement can also inform adaption budgeting decisions by identifying areas where funding has been insufficient or where resources have been misallocated (see Section 1.2.1). Ten surveyed countries (30%) state that the measurement results inform budgeting decisions (OECD, 2022[2]). The Netherlands' evaluation of its Delta Programme, for example, identified the need to improve freshwater supplies. Consequently an additional EUR 100 million were allocated to improve freshwater supply for the period 2022-27, in addition to the EUR 150 million that had already been set aside (National Delta Programme, 2021[92]). Korea measures the budget execution rate for each action set out in its NAP, indicating how much of the foreseen budget has been spent at the time of the assessment (as a percentage), and whether the level is in line with the foreseen budget spending plan (Korea Environment Institute, 2023[89]).

References

Adaptation Committee (2021), *Approaches to reviewing the overall progress made in achieving the global goal on adaptation: Technical Paper*, UNFCCC, https://unfccc.int/sites/default/files/resource/ac2021_tp_gga.pdf. [8]

Adger, W., I. Brown and S. Surminski (2018), "Advances in risk assessment for climate change adaptation policy", *Philosophical Transactions of the Royal Society A: Mathematical, Physical and Engineering Sciences*, Vol. 376/2121, p. 20180106, https://doi.org/10.1098/rsta.2018.0106. [58]

Audit Office NSW Australia (2021), *Managing Climate Risks to Assets and Services*, https://www.audit.nsw.gov.au/our-work/reports/managing-climate-risks-to-assets-and-services. [82]

Averchenkova, A., S. Fankhauser and J. Finnegan (2018), *The role of independent bodies in climate governance: the UK's Committee on Climate Change*, https://www.lse.ac.uk/granthaminstitute/wp-content/uploads/2018/10/The-role-of-independent-bodies-in-climate-governance-the-UKs-Committee-on-Climate-Change_Averchenkova-et-al.pdf. [84]

Berrang-Ford, L. et al. (2019), "Tracking global climate change adaptation among governments", *Nature Climate Change*, Vol. 9, pp. 440–449, https://doi.org/10.1038/s41558-019-0490-0. [10]

BMK (2021), *Zweiter Fortschrittsbericht zur Österreichischen Strategie zur Anpassung an den Klimawandel [Second Progress Report on the Austrian Strategy for Adaptation to Climate Change]*, https://www.bmk.gv.at/themen/klima_umwelt/klimaschutz/anpassungsstrategie/publikationen/oe_strategie.html (accessed on January 2023). [37]

CCC (2021), *Cross-sector-adaptation indicators*, https://www.theccc.org.uk/wp-content/uploads/2021/06/Cross-sector-adaptation-indicators.xlsx (accessed on 2022). [52]

CCC (2021), *Independent Assessment of UK Climate Risk*, Climate Change Committee, https://www.theccc.org.uk/publication/independent-assessment-of-uk-climate-risk/. [23]

CCC (2021), *Progress in adapting to climate change: 2021 Report to Parliament*, Climate Change Committee, https://www.theccc.org.uk/publication/2021-progress-report-to-parliament/. [53]

CCC (2021), *Second National Adaptation Programme Monitoring Action Tracker (excel sheet)*, https://www.theccc.org.uk/wp-content/uploads/2021/06/CCC-Second-NAP-Monitoring-Action-Tracker.xlsx (accessed on January 2022). [33]

Climate Action Regional Offices (2022), *Local Authority Climate Change Adaptation Strategy / Climate Change Action Plans: Annual Progress Report 2022*, https://www.caro.ie/getattachment/Local-Authority-Climate-Action/Local-Authority-Adaptation-Progress-Reports/LA-Adaptation-Strategy_Annual-Progress-2022_i01.pdf.aspx?lang=en-GB. [83]

Climate Change Advisory Council Ireland (2022), *Annual Review 2022*, https://www.climatecouncil.ie/media/climatechangeadvisorycouncil/contentassets/publications/CCAC-ANNUAL-REVIEW-2022.pdf. [56]

Defra (2023), *Third National Adaptation Plan: Annex 1: Climate risks and opportunities: The 61 climate risks and opportunities, and planned actions to address them by government departments*, https://assets.publishing.service.gov.uk/government/uploads/system/uploads/attachment_data/file/1171134/NAP3_Annex_1_Climate_risks_and_opportunities.pdf. [34]

Defra (2018), *The National Adaptation Programme and the third strategy for climate adaptation reporting*, https://www.gov.uk/government/publications/climate-change-second-national-adaptation-programme-2018-to-2023 (accessed on January 2023). [29]

Department of the Environment Climate and Communications Ireland (2023), *Sectoral Adaptation Planning*, https://www.gov.ie/en/collection/51df3-sectoral-adaptation-planning/#. [78]

Dottori, F. et al. (2023), "Cost-effective adaptation strategies to rising river flood risk in Europe", *Nature Climate Change*, Vol. 13, pp. 196–202, https://doi.org/10.1038/s41558-022-01540-0. [48]

Dudley, H., A. Jordan and I. Lorenzoni (2022), "Advising national climate policy makers: A longitudinal analysis of the UK Climate Change Committee", *Global Environmental Change*, Vol. 76/102589, https://doi.org/10.1016/j.gloenvcha.2022.102589. [87]

EC (2023), *Guidelines on Member States' adaptation Strategies and Plans*, https://climate.ec.europa.eu/system/files/2023-07/Guidelines%20on%20MS%20adaptation%20strategies%20and%20plans.pdf. [54]

EC (2018), *Regulation (EU) 2018/1999 of the European Parliament and of the Council of 11 December 2018 on the Governance of the Energy Union and Climate Action*, https://eur-lex.europa.eu/legal-content/EN/TXT/?toc=OJ:L:2018:328:TOC&uri=uriserv:OJ.L_.2018.328.01.0001.01.ENG. [77]

EC & EEA (2019), *Assessing climate change risks and vulnerabilities: Conducting risk and vulnerability assessments*, https://climate-adapt.eea.europa.eu/en/knowledge/tools/urban-ast/step-2-4/index_html. [25]

EEA (2022), *Advancing towards climate resilience in Europe: status of reported national adaptation actions in 2021*, https://climate-adapt.eea.europa.eu/en/metadata/publications/advancing-towards-climate-resilience-in-europe-status-of-reported-national-adaptation-actions-in-2021 (accessed on April 2023). [22]

EEA (2015), *National monitoring, reporting and evaluation of climate change adaptation in Europe*, https://www.eea.europa.eu/publications/national-monitoring-reporting-and-evaluation. [5]

Ellis, J. (2014), *Climate Resilience Indicator Literature Review*, http://datacat.cbrdi.ca/sites/default/files/attachments/ClimateAdaptation_LitReview_15-03-15%5B1%5D.pdf. [62]

Environment Agency Portugal (2019), *Presidência Conselho de Ministros: Resolução do Conselho de Ministros n.º 130/2019 [Presidency of the Council of Ministers: Council of Ministers Resolution No. 130/2019]*, https://climate-adapt.eea.europa.eu/en/news-archive/portuguese-national-adaptation-plan-for-climate-change-2019-2030-adopted (accessed on January 2023). [32]

Federal Council Germany (2022), *Klimapolitik: Bundesrat verabschiedet Botschaft zum revidierten CO2-Gesetz [Climate policy: Federal Council adopts dispatch on revised CO2 Act]*, https://www.admin.ch/gov/de/start/dokumentation/medienmitteilungen.msg-id-90389.html#:~:text=Mit%20dem%20revidierten%20CO2%2DGesetz,Zeit%20von%202025%20bis%202030. [64]

Federal Council Switzerland (2021), *Climate policy: Federal Council adopts message on revised CO2 law*, https://www.admin.ch/gov/de/start/dokumentation/medienmitteilungen.msg-id-90389.html#:~:text=Mit%20dem%20revidierten%20CO2%2DGesetz,Zeit%20von%202025%20bis%202030. [67]

Federal Office for the Environment Switzerland (2014), *Anpassung an den Klimawandel in der Schweiz - Aktionsplan 2014–2019 [Adaptation to climate change in Switzerland - Action plan 2014-2019]*, https://www.bafu.admin.ch/bafu/de/home/themen/klima/publikationen-studien/publikationen/anpassung-klimawandel-schweiz-2014.html. [90]

Federal Parliament Germany (2023), *Bundes-Klimaanpassungsgesetz [Federal Climate Adaptation Law]*, https://www.recht.bund.de/bgbl/1/2023/393/VO. [41]

Financial Stability Board (2021), *The Availability of Data with Which to Monitor and Assess Climate-Related Risks to Financial Stability*, https://www.fsb.org/wp-content/uploads/P070721-3.pdf. [60]

FINLEX (2022), *Climate Change Act (Finland)*, https://www.finlex.fi/fi/laki/alkup/2022/20220423. [66]

Government of Canada (2023), *Canada's National Adaptation Strategy: Building Resilient Communities and a Strong Economy*, Environment and Climate Change Canada, https://publications.gc.ca/collections/collection_2023/eccc/en4/En4-544-2023-eng.pdf. [35]

Government of Ireland (2022), *Climate Action Plan 2021: Progress Report Q4 2021 and Q1 2022*, https://www.gov.ie/en/press-release/dd9b4-first-climate-action-plan-2021-progress-report-highlights-impactful-delivery-across-key-sectors-but-challenges-remain/. [42]

Government of the Republic of Indonesia (2021), *Regulation of the President of the Republic of Indonesia Number 98 of 2021 on the Implementation of Carbon Pricing to achieve the Nationally Determined Contribution Target and Control over Greenhousgas Emissions in the National Development*, https://jdih.menlhk.go.id/new/uploads/files/abstrak/LLPERPRESNO98TH2021_pdf_menlhk_abstrak_05182022104603.pdf. [76]

Grantham Research Institute on Climate Change and the Environment (2022), *National Climate Law 4936/2022 on the transition to climate neutrality and adaptation to climate change*, https://climate-laws.org/geographies/greece/laws/national-climate-law-4936-2022-on-the-transition-to-climate-neutrality-and-adaptation-to-climate-change. [68]

Heo, S. et al. (2019), "The use of a quasi-experimental study on the mortality effect of a heat wave warning system in Korea", *Int. J. Environ. Res. Public Health*, Vol. 12/16, https://doi.org/10.3390/ijerph16122245. [47]

High Council for Climate France (2021), *Rapport annuel 2021 – Renforcer l'atténuation, engager, l'adaptation [Annual Report 2021 – Strengthening mitigation, engaging adaptation]*, https://www.hautconseilclimat.fr/publications/rapport-annuel-2021-renforcer-lattenuation-engager-ladaptation/. [85]

INECC (2017), *Evaluación Estratégica del Programa Especial de Cambio Climático 2014-2018 [Strategic Evaluation of the Special Program Climate Change 2014-2018]*, Instituto Nacional de Ecología y Cambio Climático, https://cambioclimatico.gob.mx/evaluacion-estrategica-del-programa-especial-de-cambio-climatico-2014-2018-2017/. [50]

IPCC (2022), *Climate Change 2022: Impacts, Adaptation, and Vulnerability. Contribution of Working Group II to the Sixth Assessment Report of the Intergovernmental Panel on Climate Change*, Cambridge University Press, https://www.ipcc.ch/report/ar6/wg2/. [1]

IPCC (2018), *Strengthening and implementing the global response*, In Press, https://pure.rug.nl/ws/portalfiles/portal/168495473/SR15_Chapter4_Low_Res.pdf. [7]

ISO (2021), *ISO 14091:2021: Adaptation to climate change: Guidelines on vulnerability, impacts and risk assessment*, https://www.iso.org/standard/68508.html. [20]

ISO (2019), *ISO 14090:2019: Adaptation to climate change: Principles, requirements and guidelines*, https://www.iso.org/standard/68507.html. [19]

Jandaghian, Z. and H. Akbari (2020), "Increasing urban albedo to reduce heat-related mortality in Toronto and Montreal, Canada", *Energy and Buildings*, Vol. 237/110697, https://doi.org/10.1016/j.enbuild.2020.110697. [49]

Jeudy-Hugo, S., S. Errendal and I. Kotani (2022), *Adaptation in the global stocktake: Options to deliver on its mandate*, https://doi.org/10.1787/396b5224-en. [13]

Korea Environment Institute (2023), *Measuring Progress in Implementing Adaptation Polices in Korea*. [89]

Korea Legislation Research Institute (2021), *Framework Act on Low Carbon and Green Growth*, https://elaw.klri.re.kr/eng_service/lawView.do?hseq=53039&lang=ENG,%20date%20of%20search. [75]

Lamhauge, N., E. Lanzi and S. Agrawala (2012), "Monitoring and Evaluation for Adaptation: Lessons from Development Co-operation Agencies", *OECD Environment Working Papers*, No. 38, OECD Publishing, Paris, https://doi.org/10.1787/5kg20mj6c2bw-en. [4]

Leiter, T. (2021), "Do governments track the implementation of national climate change adaptation plans? An evidence-based global stocktake of monitoring and evaluation systems", *Environmental Science and Policy*, Vol. 125, pp. 179-188, https://doi.org/10.1016/j.envsci.2021.08.017. [3]

Mexico (2023), *General Law on Climate Change (2023 Amended Text)*, https://climate-laws.org/documents/general-law-on-climate-change-2023-amended-text_3db4?id=general-law-on-climate-change_14c5. [71]

Ministry for the Environment New Zealand (2022), *Aotearoa New Zealand's first national adaptation plan*, https://environment.govt.nz/publications/aotearoa-new-zealands-first-national-adaptation-plan/ (accessed on January 2023). [30]

Ministry of Agriculture and Forestry Finland (2020), *Implementation of Finland's National Climate Change Adaptation Plan 2022 - A mid-term Evaluation*, https://julkaisut.valtioneuvosto.fi/bitstream/handle/10024/162461/MMM_2020_9.pdf. [45]

Ministry of Climate and Environment Norway (2017), *Act relating to Norway's climate targets (Climate Change Act)*, https://lovdata.no/dokument/NLE/lov/2017-06-16-60#:~:text=Section%201.-,Purpose,and%20progress%20of%20this%20work. [69]

Ministry of Ecological and Solidarity Transition France (2018), *Le plan national d'adaptation au changement climatique [National climate change adaptation plan]*, https://www.ecologie.gouv.fr/sites/default/files/2018.12.20_PNACC2.pdf. [91]

Ministry of Ecological Transition and Territorial Cohesion & Ministry of Energy Transition France (2023), *Trajectoire de réchauffement de référence : ouverture de la consultation publique [Reference warming trajectory: opening of the public consultation]*, https://www.ecologie.gouv.fr/trajectoire-rechauffement-reference-ouverture-consultation-publique. [28]

Ministry of Ecology, Sustainable Development and Energy France (2015), *Evaluation du plan national d'adaptation au changement climatique [Evaluation of the national climate change adaptation plan]*, https://cgedd.documentation.developpement-durable.gouv.fr/documents/Affaires-0009000/010178-01_rapport.pdf. [43]

Ministry of Environment and Energy Costa Rica (2022), *Plan Nacional de Adaptación al Cambio Climático 2022-2026 [National Climate Change Adaptation Plan 2022-2026]*, https://cambioclimatico.go.cr/wp-content/uploads/2022/04/NAP_Documento-2022-2026_VC.pdf. [39]

Ministry of Environment Chile (2020), *Mapas de Riesgo Climático [Climate Risk Maps]*, https://arclim.mma.gob.cl/index/. [59]

Ministry of Environment Chile (2017), *Plan de Acción Nacional de Cambio Climático 2017-2022 (PANCC-II) [National Climate Change Action Plan 2017-2022]*, https://mma.gob.cl/wp-content/uploads/2016/04/Anteproyecto-PANCC-2017-2022-FINAL-2016-04-18.pdf. [38]

Ministry of Justice Japan (2018), *Climate Change Adaptation Act (Act No. 50 of 2018)*, https://www.japaneselawtranslation.go.jp/en/laws/view/3212/en. [70]

Ministry of the Environment Czechia (2021), *Národní akční plán adaptace na změnu klimatu [National Climate Change Adaptation Action Plan]*, https://www.mzp.cz/cz/narodni_akcni_plan_zmena_klimatu (accessed on January 2023). [31]

NAO Sweden (2022), *Central government efforts to adapt the built environment to climate change*, https://www.riksrevisionen.se/download/18.10b506a2185b30c547e2e980/1673853455568/RiR_2022_29_summary.pdf. [80]

Nash, S. and R. Steurer (2019), "Taking stock of Climate Change Acts in Europe: living policy processes or symbolic gestures?", *Climate Policy*, Vol. 8/19, pp. 1052–1065, https://doi.org/10.1080/14693062.2019.1623164. [86]

National Delta Programme (2021), *Sizeable investment in Delta Plan on Freshwater Supply*, https://english.deltaprogramma.nl/news/news/2021/09/21/sizeable-investment-in-delta-plan-on-freshwater-supply (accessed on April 2023). [92]

Noltze, M. et al. (2021), “Monitoring, evaluation and learning for climate risk management”, *OECD Development Co-operation Working Papers*, No. 92, OECD Publishing, Paris, https://doi.org/10.1787/58665de0-en. [18]

OECD (2023), “Adaptation measurement: Assessing municipal climate risks to inform adaptation policy in the Slovak Republic”, *OECD Environment Policy Papers*, No. 35, OECD Publishing, Paris, https://doi.org/10.1787/dad34bb3-en. [24]

OECD (2023), “Climate adaptation: Why local governments cannot do it alone”, *OECD Environment Policy Papers*, No. 38, OECD Publishing, Paris, https://doi.org/10.1787/be90ac30-en. [36]

OECD (2023), *OECD Environmental Performance Reviews: Germany 2023*, OECD Publishing, https://doi.org/10.1787/f26da7da-en. [79]

OECD (2022), *OECD survey on Measuring Progress in Implementing National Adaptation Policies.* [2]

OECD (2022), *Virtual event: Developing meaningful adaptation policy indicators.* [61]

OECD (2021), *Managing Climate Risks, Facing up to Losses and Damages*, OECD Publishing, Paris, https://doi.org/10.1787/55ea1cc9-en. [46]

OECD (2020), *Common Ground Between the Paris Agreement and the Sendai Framework: Climate Change Adaptation and Disaster Risk Reduction*, OECD Publishing, Paris, https://doi.org/10.1787/3edc8d09-en. [12]

OECD (2020), *Improving Governance with Policy Evaluation: Lessons From Country Experiences*, OECD Public Governance Reviews, OECD Publishing, Paris, https://doi.org/10.1787/89b1577d-en. [88]

OECD (2015), *National Climate Change Adaptation: Emerging Practices in Monitoring and Evaluation*, OECD Publishing, Paris, https://doi.org/10.1787/9789264229679-en. [6]

Office of the Attorney General Ireland (2021), *Climate Action and Low Carbon Development (Amendment) Act 2021*, https://www.irishstatutebook.ie/eli/2021/act/32/enacted/en/print.html. [74]

Office of the Auditor General of Norway (2022), *The Office of the Auditor General’s investigation into government authorities’ effort to adapt infrastructure and built-up areas to a changing climate*, https://www.riksrevisjonen.no/globalassets/reports/en-2021-2022/document-3-6-2021-2022---investigation-into-government-authorities-effort-to-adapt-infrastructure-and-built-up-areas-to-a-changing-climate.pdf. [63]

Parliamentary Counsel Office New Zealand (2019), *Climate Change Response (Zero Carbon) Amendment Act 2019*, https://www.legislation.govt.nz/act/public/2019/0061/latest/LMS183736.html. [72]

Pearce-Higgins, J. et al. (2022), *A framework for climate change adaptation indicators for the natural environment*, http://doi.org/10.1016/j.ecolind.2022.108690. [51]

Prognos (2022), *Bezifferung von Klimafolgekosten in Deutschland [Quantification of costs of climate change impacts in Germany]*, https://www.prognos.com/de/projekt/bezifferung-von-klimafolgekosten-deutschland#allePDFs. [26]

Reckien, D. et al. (2023), *Quality of urban climate adaptation plans over time*, https://doi.org/10.1038/s42949-023-00085-1. [65]

Schipper, E. (2020), "Maladaptation: When adaptation to climate change goes very wrong", *One Earth*, Vol. 3/4, pp. 409-414, https://doi.org/10.1016/j.oneear.2020.09.014. [55]

Singh, C. et al. (2021), "Interrogating 'effectiveness' in climate change adaptation: 11 guiding principles for adaptation research and practice", *Climate and Development*, pp. 1-15, https://doi.org/10.1080/17565529.2021.1964937. [21]

The National Archives UK (2008), *Climate Change Act 2008 (UK)*, https://www.legislation.gov.uk/ukpga/2008/27/section/59. [73]

The Office of the Auditor General Norway (2021), *The Office of the Auditor General's investigation into government authorities' effort to adapt infrastructure and built-up areas to a changing climate*, https://www.riksrevisjonen.no/globalassets/reports/en-2021-2022/document-3-6-2021-2022---investigation-into-government-authorities-effort-to-adapt-infrastructure-and-built-up-areas-to-a-changing-climate.pdf. [81]

UBA (2021), *Klimawirkungs- und Risikoanalyse für Deutschland 2021 (Kurzfassung) [Climate impact and risk analysis for Germany 2021 (short version)]*, https://www.umweltbundesamt.de/publikationen/KWRA-Zusammenfassung. [27]

UBA (2019), *2019 Monitoring Report: on the German Strategy for Adaptation to Climate Change*, https://www.umweltbundesamt.de/sites/default/files/medien/421/publikationen/das_2019_monitoring_report_bf.pdf. [57]

UBA (2019), *Politikanalyse zur Evaluation der Deutschen Anpassungsstrategie an den Klimawandel (DAS) – Evaluationsbericht [Policy analysis for the evaluation of the German Strategy for Adaptation to Climate Change (DAS) - Evaluation report]*, https://www.umweltbundesamt.de/sites/default/files/medien/1410/publikationen/politikanalyse_zur_evaluation_der_deutschen_anpassungsstrategie_an_den_klimawandel_das_-_evaluationsbericht.pdf. [44]

UNEP (2021), *Adaptation Gap Report 2021: The Gathering Storm - Adapting to climate change in a post-pandemic world*, https://unepdtu.org/wp-content/uploads/2021/11/adaption-gap-report-2021.pdf. [16]

UNEP DTU Partnership (2018), *Adaptation metrics: perspectives on measuring, aggregating and comparing adaptation results*, Christiansen, L., Martinez, G. and Naswa, P. (eds.), https://resilientcities2018.iclei.org/wp-content/uploads/UDP_Perspectives-Adaptation-Metrics-WEB.pdf. [40]

UNFCCC (2023), *Decision -/CMA.5 Glasgow-Sharm el-Sheikh work programme on the global goal on adaptation referred to in decision 7/CMA.3*, https://unfccc.int/sites/default/files/resource/cma5_auv_8a_gga.pdf. [14]

UNFCCC (2023), *Workshops under the Glasgow–Sharm el-Sheikh work programme on the global goal on adaptation*, https://unfccc.int/sites/default/files/resource/sb2023_07.pdf. [17]

UNFCCC (2022), *Synthesis report for the technical assessment component of the first global stocktake: State of adaptation efforts, experiences and priorities*, UNFCCC, https://unfccc.int/sites/default/files/resource/Synthesis%20report%20on%20the%20state%20of%20adaptation%20efforts%2C%20experiences%20and%20priorities.pdf. [9]

UNFCCC (2021), *Glasgow–Sharm el-Sheikh work programme on the global goal on adaptation. Proposal by the President*, https://unfccc.int/documents/311109. [15]

UNFCCC (2012), *The Rio Conventions: Action on Adaptation*, https://unfccc.int/resource/docs/publications/rio_20_adaptation_brochure.pdf. [11]

Notes

[1] Other terms include climate risk and impact assessments (CRIA), climate change impact and vulnerability assessments (CCIV).

[2] Some countries and organisations use different classifications to measure adaptation progress. Most countries do not, for instance, distinguish between inputs and outputs, but consider both under one category. This may lead to inconsistent assessments of individual elements (e.g. inputs only being measured for some actions, but not for all).

[3] Damage caused by increasing exposure to heat in agglomerations, impairment of water use by increasing warming and summer droughts, damage to buildings and infrastructure by heavy rain and flash floods, damage to buildings and infrastructure by river flooding, damage to coastline by rising sea levels and storm surges, changes in species composition and natural development phases due to gradual rise in temperature.

[4] Such as develop the CRA, assess early implementation results, identifyhow resources can be optimised and barriers overcome, identify the impact that actions had on climate risks, extract lessons learned.

2. Measuring progress in adapting to a changing climate: the case of the United Kingdom

This chapter presents the results of the United Kingdom case study. It documents efforts, achievements and remaining gaps in the design and use of adaptation measurement frameworks in England, Scotland, Northern Ireland and Wales, and assesses the suitability of adaptation indicators to help gauge progress in building resilience to climate change.

2.1. Summary and key findings

The United Kingdom (UK) is well equipped to review progress on implementing national adaptation policies. The 2008 Climate Change Act required the UK to develop a regular UK-wide Climate Change Risk Assessment and a subsequent National Adaptation Programme (NAP) focused on England. The UK/England and devolved governments (Scotland, Wales and Northern Ireland) each have their own responsibilities for developing, implementing and reviewing adaptation policies, which all follow a five-year adaptation policy cycle, and are currently in their third cycle.

All devolved administrations already have or are developing monitoring and evaluation reports in line with their respective adaptation plans, which cover different sectors. Their publication frequency varies and are complemented by the work of the Climate Change Committee (CCC), which independently and regularly reviews adaptation progress in the UK as well as in all three devolved administrations. They all track progress in implementing actions, though the extent to which they evaluate the actions varies:

- **In the UK as a whole and England**, the CCC undertakes the progress measurement. To do so, it has developed monitoring maps that lay out a high-level goal for climate resilience for each assessed sector, followed by a list of outcomes, as well as the enabling and policy conditions that support the outcomes. Progress towards the outcomes, enabling and policy conditions are monitored by way of indicators. By embedding a theory of change approach, the maps are useful to address the challenge of attribution and, at least, understand the contribution of a specific policy action and associated enablers to the intended objectives.
- **In Scotland**, an overarching vision for adaptation is broken down into nine relatively broad objectives by three themes (nature, the build environment and society). Sectoral ministries must report annually on climate risk, adaptation actions and future priorities. These are also independently assessed by the CCC.
- **In Northern Ireland**, each of the nine government departments has a duty to report on adaptation progress against the objectives set out in Northern Ireland's adaptation plan. This is complemented by an independent progress assessment by the CCC.
- **In Wales**, a broad adaptation vision is broken down into actions in three cross-cutting areas: knowledge, capacity and resilience. It has developed a specific monitoring and evaluation framework relying on both quantitative and qualitative information. The Welsh Government requested an additional assessment by the CCC.

Local authorities only partly measure progress in implementing adaptation actions. In Northern Ireland, for example, local governments submit information on local climate risks and adaptation actions online to track progress against the Northern Irish plan. In England, local authorities are no longer required to report on adaptation progress, with their requirement to report on selected national adaptation indicators between 2008-2010 now discontinued. A mandate for all the UK's local authorities to report on implementation of adaptation policies would help feed local information into national reporting, enhance consistency in adaptation progress measurement across the devolved administrations and secure financial capacity.

The UK has a wealth of indicators that are relevant for adaptation. The CCC relies on a set of indicators to review progress in achieving adaptation outcomes, enablers, policies and plans as well as to assess climate risk and hazards, exposure and vulnerability. A sectoral indicator set was developed iteratively based on the indicators' suitability to demonstrate change over time, even if data are lacking for the large majority of indicators (in England, 40% of the adaptation outcomes cannot be assessed due to data gaps). Involving data owners from relevant ministries and statistical offices early in the process of defining adaptation indicators is key to increase the usability and actual reporting on progress through them.

2.2. Adaptation policy and institutional context

2.2.1. Actors and institutional arrangements

Main national/United Kingdom actors

The four devolved administrations of the UK (England, Scotland, Wales and Northern Ireland) share responsibilities for climate change adaptation.[1] The UK Government, led by the Department for Environment, Food and Rural Affairs (Defra), co-ordinates adaptation policy in England[2] and throughout the UK on a range of non-devolved matters such as energy resilience (Defra, 2019[1]; UK Government, 2020[2]).

Defra prepares and publishes the UK Climate Change Risk Assessment (CCRA) and the National Adaptation Programmes (NAP) for England. It reports to the UK Parliament in order to account for its work. In addition, Defra's Secretary of State has to approve the objectives and deadlines of various government and non-government executive bodies.[3] The Secretary of State allocates resources and monitors the performance and progress of the projects and policies implemented by these bodies. Defra also develops responses to progress reports and to independent risk assessments prepared by the Climate Change Committee (CCC), the independent statutory body. Defra's work is supported by expert analysis from government departments and independent bodies, such as the CCC and the Met Office (an Arm's Length Body of the Department for Science Innovation and Technology).

The CCC and its Adaptation Committee (AC) play a key role in informing adaptation policies in the UK. The 2008 Climate Change Act requires the AC to publish biennial progress reports on the UK Government's climate change adaptation programme and to develop an Independent Assessment of UK Climate Risk (CRIA). The AC's role is to advise national authorities on adaptation, to provide analysis for the CCRA, and to report to the UK Parliament on the UK Government's progress in implementing its NAP for England. It can also provide ad hoc advice upon request. For example, the Scottish Government sought advice from the UK CCC on recovery from COVID-19 in a way that increases resilience to climate impacts (Scottish Government, 2021[3]). The AC is jointly sponsored by Defra, the Northern Ireland Executive, the Scottish Government and the Welsh Government, notably to undertake the evidence analysis to inform the climate risk assessment and to provide independent and impartial advice.

Responsibility for implementing adaptation actions identified by the CCRA spans multiple sectors. While Defra oversees this process, individual risks and priority risk groups defined in the CCRA, along with corresponding actions in the NAP, are managed and owned by policy teams in departments across the UK Government.[4] NAP3, which covers England and UK reserved matters, identifies 12 government departments and other agencies responsible for implementation, often working alongside key partners in their policy areas. These include the Meteorological Office, Environment Agency, and other stakeholders such as Network Rail, the water services regulation authority, Natural England and local highway authorities (Defra, 2023[4]).

Defra works with the Department for Energy Security and Net Zero (DESNZ) to ensure that energy providers invest in climate resilience (e.g. flood risk proofing). The Department for Transport (DfT) has a key role in managing infrastructure, particularly to identify vulnerabilities in the transport network and to fund or promote technologies that can help to reduce the risk of damage (Defra, 2023[4]). The Environment Agency in England provides advice on climate resilience to organisations from key sectors in England. The Cabinet Office and Defra have also established a new Climate Resilience Steering Board involving senior officials from key government departments to oversee strategic, cross-cutting climate adaptation and resilience issues and enable more co-ordinated policy making in central government.

The UK Treasury and financial authorities are also involved in adaptation policy decisions by taking steps to assess the exposure of the financial system to climate impacts. The UK Treasury aims to ensure consistent implementation of climate-related financial disclosures, as laid out in the UK's Green Finance Strategy and in the Treasury's 2021 Green Finance Roadmap (UK Government, 2021[5]; UK Government, 2019[6]). The Bank of England has published its second climate change adaptation report examining how firms (including around 1 500 banks and insurance companies) regulated by the Prudential Regulatory Authority (PRA) are exposed to climate risks and are managing these risks. It is now working with the UK Government on its roadmap for mandatory reporting against the Task Force on Climate-Related Financial Disclosure (TCFD) framework (PRA, 2021[7]; Defra, 2023[8]).

Local government[5] policy decisions can influence adaptation through planning, public health and flood risk management (UK Government, 2020[2]). In 2011, Defra established the Local Adaptation Advisory Panel (LAAP), a forum bringing together selected local authorities from England, the UK Government and other relevant arms-length delivery bodies to inform the NAPs (notably the Local Government Chapter), the progress reports and the CCRAs (UK Government, 2016[9]). However, the absence of reporting and limited resources at the local level challenge the LAAP's capacity to have more impact on policy decisions and its ability to implement adaptation practices. At the city level, some institutional arrangements also exist to bring expertise in facilitating adaptation policy implementation. For example, Bristol has set up an Advisory Committee on Climate Change to guide the work of the Environmental Sustainability Board (Bristol City Council, 2021[10]).

Main actors in devolved administrations

Devolved responsibility for the development, implementation and monitoring of adaptation policy lies with the Cabinet Secretary for Net Zero, Energy and Transport in Scotland; the Department of Agriculture, Environment and Rural Affairs (DAERA) in Northern Ireland, and the Welsh Government in Wales (Defra, 2023[8]). Devolved administrations have their own co-ordination mechanisms to develop and implement adaptation policies. In Northern Ireland for instance, the Climate Change Adaptation Sub-Group of the cross-department working group on climate change, involving representatives from each department, was established to support risk assessments, deliver a cross-departmental adaptation programme, review cross-departmental action on an annual basis and ensure that Northern Ireland's legal obligations under the UK Climate Change Act 2008 are met (DAERA NI, 2019[11]). Additionally, a Local Government Climate Action Network (LGCAN) was set up to facilitate information exchange between local authorities (councils) in Northern Ireland and to provide them with access to adaptation tools and resources (Climate NI, 2021[12]).

Other bodies provide support for designing and implementing adaptation policies in devolved administrations. Climate Northern Ireland (Climate NI), funded by DAERA, is a network of external stakeholders who promote actions to address climate impacts to support the devolved government (Climate NI, 2021[13]). Adaptation Scotland provides advice and support to help the public sector, businesses and communities prepare for and build resilience to climate impacts. Adaptation Scotland is a programme funded by the Scottish Government, currently delivered by the sustainability charity Sniffer (Adaptation Scotland, 2020[14]). The centre of expertise ClimateXChange works with the Scottish Government to deliver evidence-based policies informed by independent climate research (ClimateXChange, 2021[15]).

The policy development process also relies on extensive stakeholder engagement through various co-ordination mechanisms. In Wales for example, the current NAP proposes developing an External Stakeholder Adaptation Group to facilitate exchanges between the government and external delivery partners. A Core Internal Adaptation Group facilitates co-ordination of climate adaptation policy across Welsh government departments, reporting to the Climate Change Portfolio Board (Welsh Government, 2020[16]). The Transboundary Adaptation Learning Exchange (TalX) is a collaborative research project that provides a learning network for climate adaptation across the UK's devolved administrations and the

Republic of Ireland, which are areas subject to similar climate risks but at different stages of maturity in adaptation planning and implementation (TalX, 2021[17]).

2.2.2. Adaptation policies in the United Kingdom

Legal framework and development process

The UK has a long history of government support for work on climate change adaptation. In 2008, the Climate Change Act (CCA) created the legal framework for adaptation in the UK. It requires the development of a UK-wide Climate Change Risk Assessment (CCRA) every five years, as well as a National Adaptation Programme (NAP) addressing climate change risks in England[6] following each CCRA. The act established the CCC to provide independent advice to the UK and devolved governments on progress made in adapting to climate change. The act requires the UK Government to take into account the advice of the CCC (UK Parliament, 2008[18]). The UK's domestic and international actions and ambitions on adaptation and resilience are reported to the United Nations Framework Convention on Climate Change (UNFCCC) in the form of an adaptation communication,[7] and in the UK's Nationally Determined Contribution (UK Government, 2020[2]; UK Government, 2020[19]; UK Government, 2021[20]).

The UK Parliament is consulted twice in the adaptation policy development process: i) the government is obliged to present the CCRA to parliament; and ii) the CCC has to report every two years on progress in adapting to climate change (CCC, 2023[21]). The UK's Environment Act 2021 includes provisions for biodiversity conservation and water management that are relevant to adaptation, and legally formed the Office for Environmental Protection (OEP) to hold public authorities accountable by reviewing and reporting on the government's progress in meeting environmental goals and targets (UK Government, 2021[22]).

Legal frameworks have also been developed in devolved administrations. The Climate Change (Scotland) Act 2009 requires the development of a Scottish Climate Change Adaptation Programme (SCCAP) to address the risks identified in the UK Climate Change Risk Assessment for Scotland. All public bodies, including local authorities, are required to help deliver the SCCAP. The Welsh Well-Being of Future Generations Act 2015 requires councils to take account of the impacts from climate change to ensure environmental well-being (Welsh Government, 2015[23]). Similarly, the Environment (Wales) Act 2016 sets further provisions for the establishment of a local evidence base for natural resources to determine risks, priorities and opportunities (Welsh Government, 2016[24]). In Northern Ireland, the Climate Change Act 2022 gives the CCC the mandate to undertake an independent assessment of progress towards implementing the latest NICCAP and to provide recommendations for improving the NICCAP, and requires DAERA to respond to the CCC's report (CCC, 2023[25]).

The UK/England, Scotland, Wales and Northern Ireland all follow a five-year adaptation policy cycle (Figure 2.1). A number of documents inform national adaptation policy development, notably the latest climate change risk assessments (CCRA), evidence reports,[8] evaluation/progress reports and the UK government's response.

Figure 2.1. The five-year adaptation policy cycle in the UK and devolved administrations

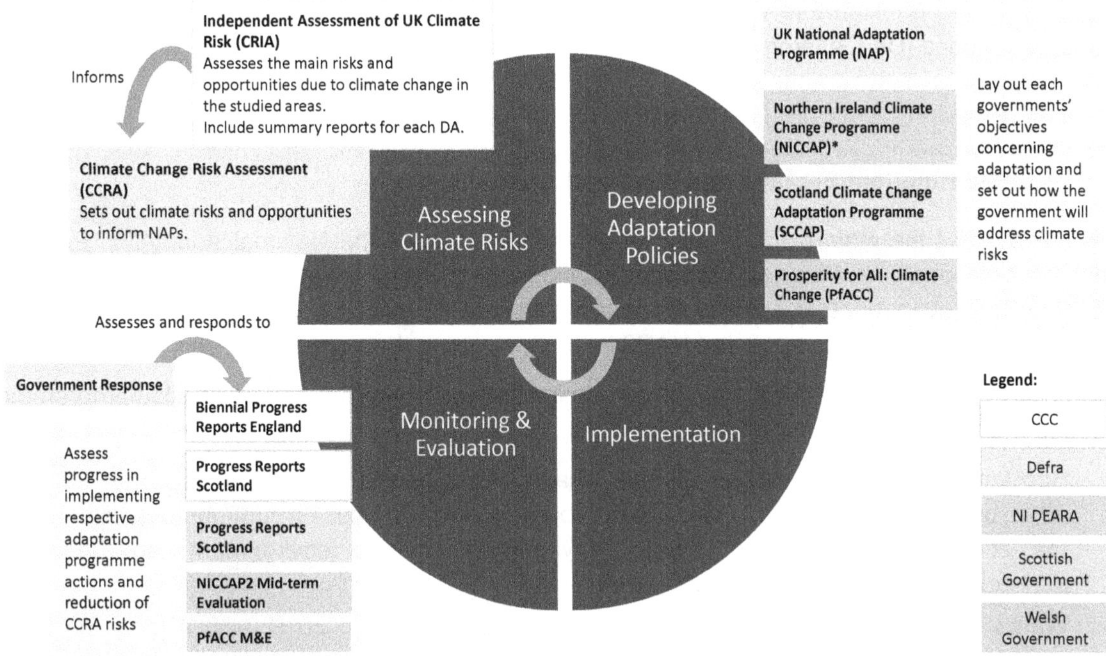

Note: *NICCAP2 (2019) comprises an evaluation of NICCAP (2014).
Source: Authors, based on documents listed in Annex 1.A.

The climate risk assessment process – the CCRA, Independent Assessment of UK Climate Risk (CRIA), and government's response– is the basis for developing the national adaptation programmes:

- The Independent Assessment of UK Climate Risk, published by the CCC,[9] considers where additional adaptation action is needed in the coming five years based on current and planned policies, as well as on sectors in which impacts are expected (natural environment, infrastructure, people and the built environment, and business and industry). The independent risk assessment is also funded by all three devolved administrations and Defra, as the UK Government adaptation policy lead.
- The CCRA, building on the Independent Assessment of UK Climate Risk, is a UK-wide risk assessment which informs the NAPs of the UK Government and the adaptation programmes of all three devolved administrations, by whom it is funded. Defra oversees this process for England and in reserved policy areas, but individual risks and priority risk groups, along with corresponding actions in the NAP, are owned by policy teams in departments across the UK Government. Adaptation programmes for Scotland, Wales and Northern Ireland are devolved to the respective devolved administrations, again with policy teams across departments responding to individual risks and risk groups.

There are also bridges built with the science community. The UK's Met Office is in charge of providing the necessary data on climate change. It publishes a *State of the UK Climate* report annually, including an assessment of UK climate trends, variations and extremes, based on the latest available high-quality climate observational datasets (Met Office, 2023[26]). In 2018, the Met Office's Hadley Centre Programme published the latest major update of UK Climate Projections (UKCP18), including regional scenarios (Met Office, 2021[27]) which offer unprecedented spatial detail to inform adaptation planning and decision making (Defra, 2019[1]; UK Government, 2020[2]). Policy development is also informed by universities and research institutes. For example, the UK Climate Resilience Programme is a research institute that helps inform the management of climate-related risks (UKRP, 2021[28]). In 2021, the UK Department for Business, Energy & Industrial Strategy (now the Department for Energy Security and Net Zero) launched the research programme CS-NOW (climate services) led by a consortium of research institutions to help inform policies on climate resilience (UK Government, 2021[29]).

National and local adaptation plans

United Kingdom/England and devolved administrations

Figure 2.2 lays out the main plans for all the UK's governments. The National Adaptation Programme outlines the UK Government's objectives for adaptation in England and certain reserved policy areas, and sets out how the government will address the risks highlighted in the CCRA. The UK Government published the first NAP in 2013, NAP2 in 2018 and NAP3 in 2023, covering the period 2023-28.

The governments of each of the UK's devolved administrations have their own adaptation programmes to respond to their respective climate change priorities:

- **Scotland** published its second Climate Change Adaptation Programme (SCCAP2, 2019-24) in 2019, building on the 2009 plan and 2014 programme with a focus on communities, climate justice, the economy, infrastructure, natural environment, marine environment, and international partnerships (Scottish Government, 2019[30]).
- **Wales** released its second climate change adaptation plan in 2019, with a focus on flooding, droughts, risks to ecosystems and agriculture businesses and risks to the historic environment (Welsh Government, 2019[31]).
- **Northern Ireland**'s first (NICCAP1, 2014-19) and second (NICCAP2, 2019-24) adaptation programmes both address five key priority areas, namely natural capital, infrastructure services, people and the built environment, disruption to business and supply chains, food security/global food production (DAERA NI, 2019[11]). NICCAP3 is due to cover the period 2024-29.

A number of sectoral policies mainstream adaptation – notably those related to flood and coastal erosion management, and water resources policy – within the National Infrastructure Strategy as well as environmental policies such as England's *25-Year Environment Plan* (25-YEP) (UK Government, 2020[2]). Similarly, in Wales the policy framework is supplemented at the sectoral level, for example by the 2015 *Water Strategy for Wales* and the 2018 *Woodlands Strategy for Wales*.

Figure 2.2. Key adaptation-related documents in the United Kingdom and devolved administrations

Climate change adaptation policies, risk assessment reports and evaluation reports

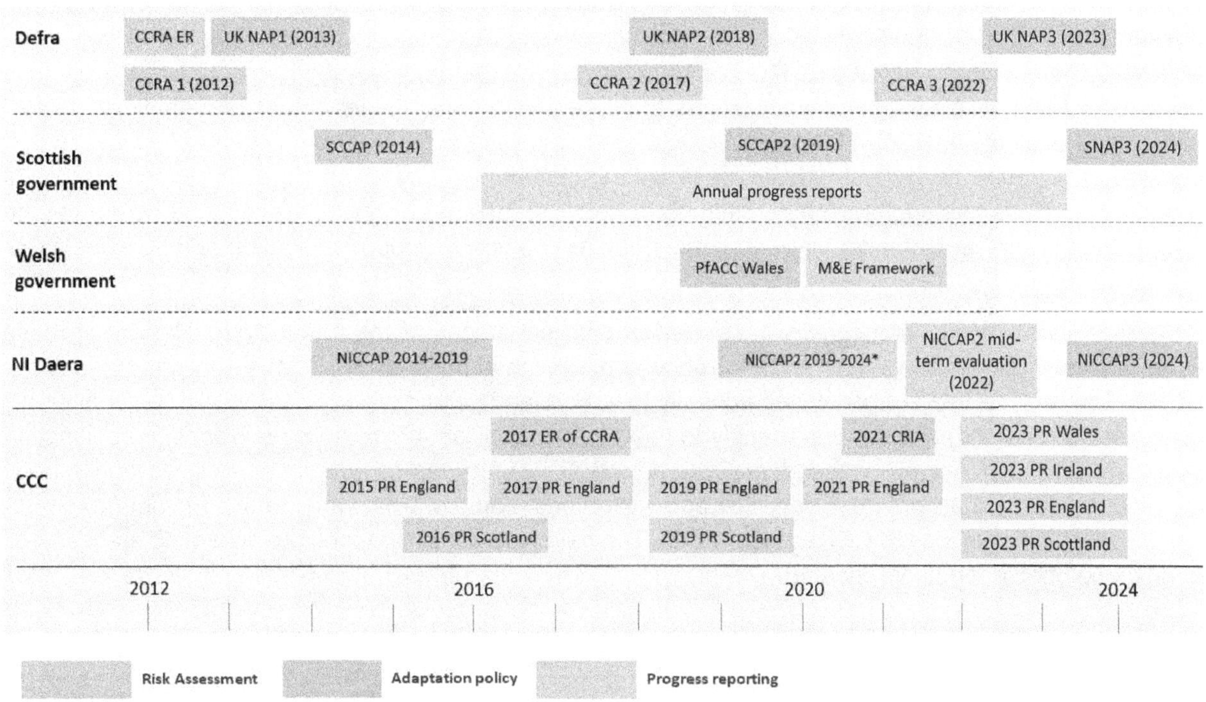

Note: ER = evidence report, PR = progress report. *Review of NICCAP1 is built into NICCAP2.
Source: Authors, based on documents listed in Annex 1.A.

Local adaptation plans

Where these exist, local adaptation policies usually build on risk assessments, which are critical for informing the priority setting process and creating a baseline for measuring progress towards adaptation. However, most local authorities have not undertaken risk assessments. There is no requirement to undertake risk assessments at the regional or city/council level and in addition, the development of risk assessments is often hindered by the limited funding, capacity and knowledge of which risks to assess. Below are some examples of where risk assessments have been undertaken.

The Mayor of London is required by the Greater London Authority Act 1999 to consider the impact of climate change and adaptation options. The mayor has developed a dedicated chapter on adapting to climate change for the 8.7 million Londoners in the 2018 London Environment Strategy (Greater London Authority, 2018[32]). Bristol (a Mayors Adapt member) has endorsed its 2020 strategy, building on a climate resilience assessment, and is now developing an action plan (Bristol City Council and ARUP, 2020[33]; Bristol City Council, 2021[10]). In Northern Ireland, Derry and Strabane District Council were the first to develop a local authority climate adaptation plan, building on a local risk assessment (Derry City & Strabane DC, 2018[34]). Climate NI have developed a five-step adaptation planning tool to support local councils and organisations in assessing current and future vulnerability to climate impacts, leading to the development of a risk register and adaptation plan (Climate NI, 2021[35]). Several other local authorities are developing adaptation plans and strategies (Cambridge City Council, Fermanagh & Omagh, and Derry City and Strabane District Council) (Belfast City Council, 2020[36]; Fermanagh & Omagh District Council, 2021[37]; Derry City & Strabane DC, 2018[34]; Cambridge City Council, 2018[38]). However, although around 300 councils have declared a climate emergency, less than 12% of them mention adaptation to climate change (LSE, 2021[39]).

2.2.3. Monitoring and reporting frameworks

The UK and all devolved administrations have or are developing monitoring and evaluation reports (Table 2.1). These are undertaken by the respective governments. Additional independent reviews are conducted by the CCC for Scotland and for Northern Ireland (UK Parliament, 2008[18]; UK Government, 2009[40]). The establishment of a CCC office for Scotland is under consideration. Although the CCC does not have a remit to assess progress in Wales at present, it provides informal advice on indicators, goal setting and evaluation (CCC, 2020[41]). The CCC's remit is wide compared to its internal capacity, which consists of five full-time analysts whose tasks are to conduct in-house research, analysis and drafting of reports, as well as managing external research to help increase its expertise. It should be noted that the CCC's capacity for work on adaptation is smaller than its capacity to support mitigation-related work (CCC, 2020[41]).

Progress reports/evaluations can be developed at different stages of the policy cycle. Results of these reviews allow policy makers to adjust and refine strategies and actions and to take account of the latest CCRA. The reviews that are conducted annually (e.g. Scotland), biennially (e.g. UK) or at regular intervals (e.g. Northern Ireland) are those that apply in most cases and can inform policy revisions in conjunction with the latest CCRA and independent CCC advice. The timelines of adaptation policies and related monitoring and evaluation across devolved administrations (some of which are statutory in nature) do not necessarily align with the UK CCRA (Figure 2.2). The devolved administrations are also at different stages of advancement in terms of reporting.

Table 2.1. Monitoring and evaluation frameworks for adaptation in the United Kingdom

Focus	Mandate / framework	Review	Frequency	Lead	Presented to
UK / England	2008 Climate Change Act	Report on assessing the UK Government's progress in preparing for climate change in England and in implementing the UK NAP	Biennially (2015 2017 2019 2021 2023)	AC	UK Parliament
		Government response to the CCC reports	Biennially (2015 2017 2019 2021 2023)	Defra	UK Parliament
Scotland	Climate Change (Scotland) Act 2009	Independent assessments of progress on the SCCAP	Twice every 5-year cycle (2016, 2019, 2022)	AC	Scottish Parliament
	Climate Change (Scotland) Act 2009	Annual progress reports	Annually since 2015	Scottish Government	Scottish Parliament
Northern Ireland	2008 Climate Change Act	Yearly reviews (senior managers)	Annually	DAERA	Director level within DAERA
		Mid-programme progress review (2022) + end-of-programme evaluation (2024)		DAERA	NI Ministers
	2022 Climate Change Act	Report on assessing progress in implementing the NICCAP2	Three years after NICCAP	CCC	DAERA
		DAERA response to CCC report	Within 6 months of receiving CCC report	DAERA	NI Assembly
Wales	*Prosperity for All: A Climate Conscious Wales*	Reporting on evidence of progress collected by relevant delivery leads representing sectors in Welsh Government's Climate Change Portfolio Governance Board (CCPG)	Annually	Welsh Government	Cabinet of Welsh Government, with publication every 2 years
		Welsh Government intends to work with the UK CCC to allow for independent evaluation		AC	

Source: Based on documents listed in Annex 1.A.

2.3. Measuring progress in implementing adaptation policies

2.3.1. Approaches to monitoring and reviewing progress on adaptation

United Kingdom/England

Clear objectives that address key climate risks, and associated actions to achieve them, are the basis for assessing progress. The priorities identified in the CCRA for the UK and devolved administrations are reflected in the respective national adaptation programmes and actions. The UK NAP1 and NAP2's overall goal on adaptation (focused on England and reserved matters) is: "A society which makes timely, far-sighted and well-informed decisions to address the risks and opportunities posed by a changing climate". The UK NAP2 contains a detailed action log listing adaptation policies, objectives and actions to be implemented, with its chapters reflecting the second CCRA evidence report (Defra, 2019[1]).

Similarly, NAP3 states that the UK Government's vision for adaptation is for a country that effectively plans for and is fully adapted to the changing climate, and which is resilient to each of the identified climate risks. The UK NAP3 has responded to the 61 risks and opportunities identified in CCRA3, grouped into five chapters (infrastructure, natural environment, healthy communities and built environment; business and industry, international dimensions), all of which include risk reduction goals, and actions to achieve those objectives (Defra, 2023[8]). It also often sets out timescales and responsible owners for the implementation of actions, although less consistently than in NAP2 (Table 2.2). Instead, it aims to develop an M&E framework for assessing the first NAP3 progress report, expected in 2025 (Table 2.2) (Defra, 2023[8]).

Table 2.2. Comparison between action logging in NAP2 and NAP3

Selected examples from NAP2 and NAP3

NAP2	Objective	Risks addressed	Action	Timing	Metric	Owner
	Manage all of England's soils sustainably	Risks to soils from increased seasonal aridity and wetness	Incentivise good soil management practices that enhance soil's ability to deliver environmental benefits through future environmental land management schemes to ensure soils are healthy and productive	By 2030	Soil health index at farm level to assess whether management practices have beneficial impact on soil health	Defra
NAP3	**Risk reduction goal**					
	Maintain and improve the resilience of water infrastructure to flooding despite the changing climate		Water companies will follow the National Flood and Coastal Erosion Risk Management Strategy for England, which includes developing plans for their infrastructure to be resilient to flooding and coastal change between now and 2030	By 2030 (not always stated)	Metric not set out	Not always available or clearly stated

Source: (Defra, 2018[42]); (Defra, 2023[8])

Under the Climate Change Act (2008), it is the CCC and AC's statutory duty to biennially assess the UK Government's progress in preparing for climate change and in implementing the NAP in England. The AC is responsible for providing advice to national authorities on climate change impacts and for reporting on progress to the UK Parliament (UK Parliament, 2008[18]). The AC first reported to parliament in 2015, and has done so every two years ever since (2017, 2019, 2021, 2023). Defra responds to these progress reports with inputs from the devolved administrations (Table 2.1).

The CCC's 2019 and 2021 UK progress reports mirror the themes outlined in NAP2. The 2021 report assesses clustered adaptation priorities within the 4 themes: 8 priorities for the natural environment, 12 for people and the built environment, 10 for infrastructure and 4 for business. The report assesses changes in policies regarding these adaptation priority areas; lists updated indicators related to vulnerability, exposure, adaptation actions and impact; and sets out 8 key messages and 50 specific recommendations to improve progress (CCC, 2021[43]).

In its advice to Government for the CCRA3, the CCC recommends the integration of ten principles for good adaptation into NAPs and devolved adaptation programmes (CCC, 2021[44]). The ten principles include: setting out a vision for a well-adapted UK; integrating adaptation into policies; adapting to 2°C and assessing the risks up to 4°C; avoiding lock-in; preparing for unpredictable extremes; assessing interdependencies; understanding threshold effects; addressing inequalities; considering opportunities from climate change; supporting the implementation of adaptation through resources and research (CCC, 2021[44]).

The CCC's latest progress report applies a new framework that assesses 13 sectors, structured around assets or systems impacted by climate risks. Most significantly it increases the focus on tangible changes in the economy and across society and the environment, by identifying a set of outcomes needed to deliver climate resilience within each sector (CCC, 2023[45]). It also strongly expands on the assessment of the enabling conditions necessary to achieve the outcomes, and the role of public policy to bring them about.

The UK CCC's evaluation method is based on a three-part framework (CCC, 2023[45]):

- **A monitoring map**: this lays out a high-level goal or vision for what climate resilience in each of the 13 sectors assessed might mean, as well as 45 tangible outcomes that need to be in place to help deliver the outcomes (Figure 2.3). Through the maps, the CCC also identifies policy and planning milestones that need to be in place to achieve the outcomes. Furthermore, it assesses a set of enabling and contextual factors (which are largely independent of policy action but will nonetheless affect the ability of the outcomes to be delivered).
- **Evaluation of delivery and implementation indicators:** Similar to the CCC's previous measurement framework, the framework presents a set of indicators to gauge progress in the different elements of the monitoring maps. In addition, the CCC uses indicators to assess the enabling factors in place based on hazards, exposure and vulnerability data (Section 2.3). However, in many instances there are important data gaps or indicators are not sufficiently up to date to provide a current understanding of trends.
- **An assessment of progress against policy and planning requirements:** As in its previous measurement methodology, the CCC documents recent developments in relevant policies and plans and assesses to what extent the relevant policy milestones identified on the monitoring maps are in place, to what extent they are appropriately ambitious, and whether there is appropriate monitoring and evaluation to allow them to function effectively.

The CCC assigns a score to the progress made for each sector's identified outcomes. Two summary scores are identified, one for delivery and implementation (Table 2.3) and one for policies and plans (Table 2.4) to distinguish between important policy developments and evidence that adaptation outcomes are being delivered on the ground. The scores are given based on a number of criteria that are synthesised through expert judgement (Table 2.3 and Table 2.4).

Table 2.3. Scoring criteria for delivery and implementation

Score	Criteria
Good progress	Indicators are moving in the right direction or being maintained at a high level
Mixed progress	Some indicators are moving in the right direction, others are stagnant at a low level or moving in the wrong direction
Insufficient progress	Indicators are stagnant at a low level or are moving in the wrong direction
Unable to evaluate	Limited or no available data

Source: (CCC, 2023[45]), *CCC Adaptation Monitoring Framework*, https://www.theccc.org.uk/publication/ccc-adaptation-monitoring-framework/#introduction.

Table 2.4. Scoring criteria for policies and plans

Score	Criteria for policy milestones
Credible policies and plans	• are almost entirely achieved or in place • are comprehensive and appropriately ambitious • include monitoring and evaluation
Partial policies and plans	• are achieved or in place for key milestones but some gaps remain • cover most important elements, could be more ambitious • include some monitoring and evaluation
Limited policies and plans	• are partially achieved or in place with some key milestones missing • cover some important elements, could be more ambitious • include some monitoring and evaluation
Insufficient policies and plans	• are mostly not achieved, only minor policies in place • lack important elements, do not cover key areas or lack ambition • have minimal monitoring and evaluation

Note: For policy and plans assessment, policies published up until March 2023 are included in the latest progress report
Source: (CCC, 2023[45]), *CCC Adaptation Monitoring Framework*, https://www.theccc.org.uk/publication/ccc-adaptation-monitoring-framework/#introduction.

The UK has made efforts to improve its monitoring and evaluation system. Efforts began as part of NAP2, following criticism that the first NAP for England and reserved policy areas required clearer adaptation priorities; that it needed objectives that would be outcome-focused, measurable, time bound and under clear ownership; and that it needed to prioritise a core set of policies and actions that would have the greatest impact (CCC, 2017[46]). However, the CCC's first review of NAP2 concluded that the "Government has failed to increase adaptation policy ambition and implementation through its latest National Adaptation Programme" (CCC, 2019[47]). The CCC's second progress review of NAP3 in 2023 still finds very limited evidence of the implementation of adaptation at the scale needed to fully prepare for climate risks facing the UK (CCC, 2023[21]). This suggests that despite the monitoring, reporting and evaluation progress, CCC's recommendations remain valid.

In its latest progress reports, the CCC flagged that NAP2 had limited objectives, targets or performance indicators that allowed the government or others to track progress in implementing the programme or its effects on exposure and vulnerability to climate change (CCC, 2023[21]). The third NAP has therefore set out a vision for a country that plans effectively for and is fully adapted to the changing climate, with clear risk reduction goals for addressing each risk identified in the latest CCRA (Defra, 2023[8]). Setting these risk reduction goals is a significant step forward, enabling an assessment of not only NAP3's action implementation, but also whether the actions have contributed to achieving the risk reduction goals.

To the extent possible, the UK applies a theory of change in developing its adaptation policy objectives, with the aim of attributing the achievement of an objective to the linked policy action (Box 2.1). This approach is embedded in the latest progress report in the monitoring maps (see Figure 2.3 for an example).

These maps specify tangible adaptation outcomes, a set of enablers, and policy milestones needed to deliver the outcomes and put in place the necessary enablers (CCC, 2023[45]). To develop the maps, the CCC organised workshops with relevant actors to test the adaptation pathways approach and separate out each intervention stage (policies, enablers, contextual factors, outcomes, and goals). The monitoring maps help to understand developments across all of these levels, providing a full picture of progress towards building climate resilience, and identifying key gaps in reaching adaptation goals. The maps also provide a degree of flexibility in the combinations of policies and actions possible to deliver effective adaptation and respond to changing contexts over time.

Box 2.1. A 'theory of change' to guide action towards final outcomes

The theory of change (ToC) is a framework that aims to determine how a given action impacts the level of risk. It maps out the logical sequence of a programme (project or policy) from inputs to impact, and provides a non-linear way to consider what will change, and the underlying dynamics and assumptions around how and why change will occur. This concept reflects the Magenta Book's guidance on establishing a project's logic chains to set the emphasis on the expected causal relationships, including potential unintended consequences. The book underlines the importance of this mapping stage in a context, like adaptation, where policy or its setting is complex. The UK has applied this ToC approach in its third NAP (Table 2.5).

Table 2.5. 'Theory of change' flowchart

Impact	What it means for broader and longer-term effects (for reducing climate risks but also on other impacts)	Continuous feedback loops from inputs to impacts (monitor, evaluate, report, revise plan)
Outcomes	What is achieved: Results of or change resulting from the intervention that are an intermediate prerequisite for meeting the government's overarching policy goals	
Outputs	What is delivered through the activity: Legislation, change in assets or capability	
Activities*	What we do: analysis/engagement. A given project can comprise many discrete and interrelated actions or activities. This could be physical (e.g. a new floodwall), experiential (e.g. workshop attended by stakeholders) or virtual (e.g. an online tool)	
Input	Resources needed: investment; hours/week	

Note: *The activities category was added to the third NAP.
Source: (HM Treasury, 2020[48]); (Power et al., 2018[49]); (Defra, 2023[8]); (CCC, 2023[45]).

The CCC continues to find large gaps in the capacity to monitor and evaluate adaptation progress at the UK level. In 2019, the CCC published a set of adaptation indicators for Defra to populate, however, lack of capacity has meant that little progress had been made (CCC, 2021[43]). In 2021, the CCC urged the UK Government to improve its datasets and establish new ones where necessary, and to develop a detailed monitoring and evaluation framework to assess the effectiveness of adaptation actions to reduce the risks determined in the CCRA3 in NAP3 (CCC, 2021[43]). The latest progress assessment in 2023 reiterates the data gaps issue, notably for assessing adaptation outcomes (see Indicator frameworks in the United Kingdom/England). The CCC is urging the UK Government to introduce an effective adaptation monitoring and evaluation programme, with sufficient long-term funding, as a prerequisite to fill important data gaps (CCC, 2023[21]). To address the CCC's recommendations, the third NAP sets out to develop new process and outcome indicators which will form part of a forthcoming monitoring and evaluation framework to evaluate the success of NAP3, and which will inform the CCC's next progress report in 2025.

Figure 2.3. Example of the monitoring map for water supply

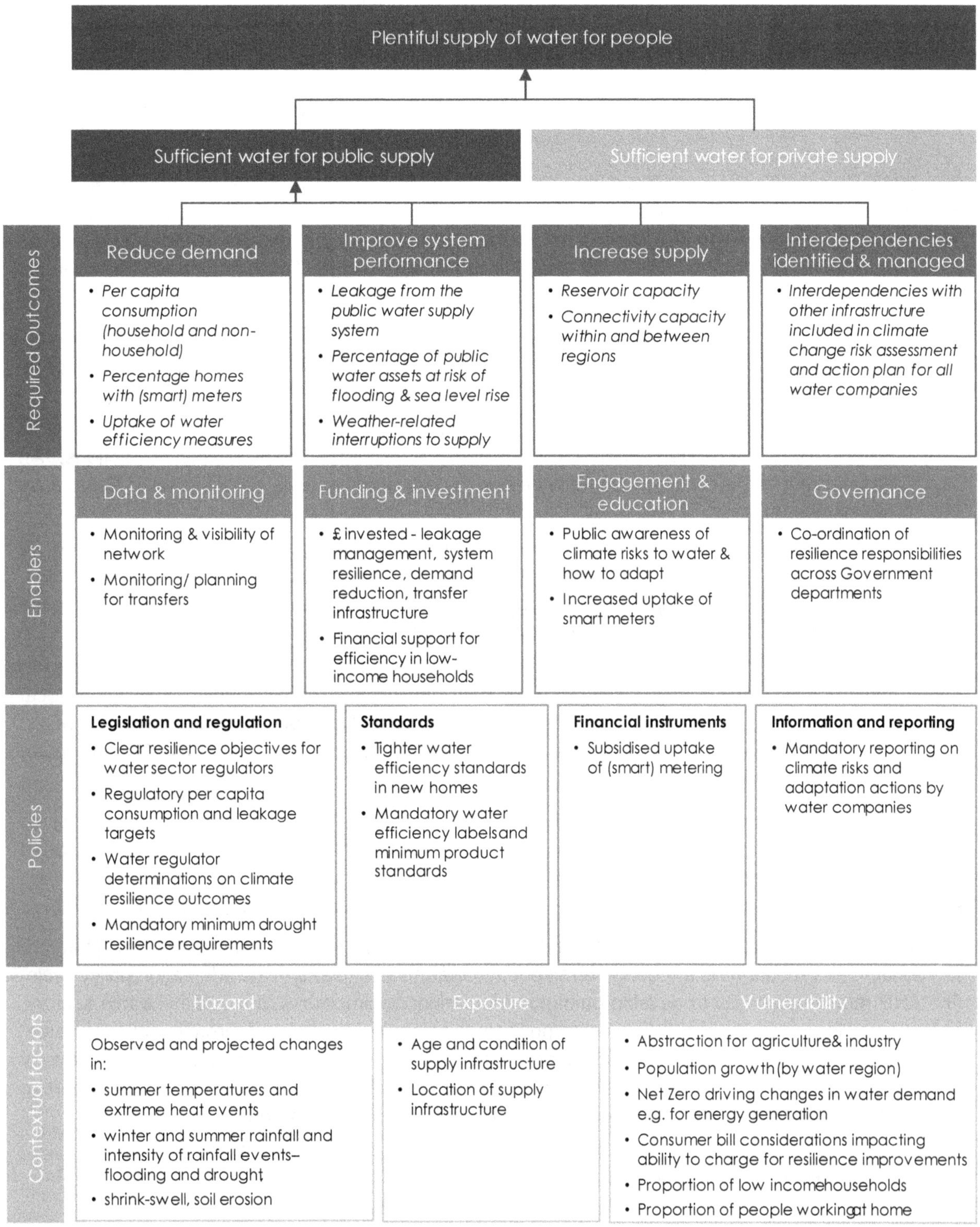

Source: (CCC, 2023[21]), *Progress in Adapting to Climate Change: 2023 report to Parliament*, https://www.theccc.org.uk/publication/progress-in-adapting-to-climate-change-2023-report-to-parliament/

As a way to address data and information gaps and continue raising awareness, the UK 2008 Climate Change Act prescribed Adaptation Reporting Power (ARP) to the UK Government and Welsh Ministers, which allows the UK Secretary of State and Welsh Ministers to direct organisations to report on how they are addressing current and future climate impacts (UK Parliament, 2008[18]). This unique mechanism to enable a national government to collect data on public and private organisations can bring value to organisation and government reporting (Box 2.2).

Box 2.2. Collecting information on actions using the Adaptation Reporting Power

The 2008 Climate Change Act gives the UK Government and Welsh Ministers the power to ask organisations, such as those responsible for public services and infrastructure (e.g. energy and transport companies), to produce reports on the current and predicted impacts of climate change on their organisation, and their proposals for adapting to climate change. There have been three rounds of reporting since its introduction, with a fourth underway during 2024:

- In the first round of reporting (2010-12), over 100 organisations, primarily from the energy, transport and water sectors, reported on their risks, which were evaluated by a third party organisation (Defra, 2012[50]; Defra, 2012[51]).
- The second round (2014-16) relied on a voluntary approach. This saw a lower level of participation and limited evidence of increased resilience from adaptation actions. An assessment of the costs and benefits of reporting for organisations was developed to increase stakeholder buy-in.
- The third ARP reporting round (2019-21), also conducted on a voluntary basis, invited 89 organisations from a range of infrastructure sectors (water, energy, transport, environment, heritage, health and finance) and public bodies. While reporting improved, there remained gaps in coverage, with 20% of organisations still missing (CCC, 2022[52]).
- Reports for the fourth round of reporting are due by the end of 2024, in time to be reflected in the CCRA. Over 130 organisations have been invited to report, including a group of local authorities to pilot reporting in the local government sector. Defra advises organisations to report on how climate risks will affect the delivery of their functions, in line with ISO 14090 on climate adaptation management.

The ARP is currently not employed by Ministers in Wales and does not apply to the devolved administrations of Scotland or Northern Ireland. In England, not all relevant organisations have reported under the ARP. For instance, certain organisations responsible for critical infrastructure and services, such as canals and food supply chains, were not covered in previous reporting rounds (CCC, 2021[43]).

The reports are reviewed by the CCC to understand the readiness of the various sectors. They are shared with relevant teams in the UK Government and thereby aim to inform the adaptation policy cycle. The ARP requires capacity to develop guidance on monitoring processes, co-ordinate within sectors, evaluate and learn from the reports. Its use in policy making could be enhanced through more consistent reporting across organisations on quantified risks and closer monitoring of actions and their benefits. It could consider the potential trade-offs between ensuring comparability and ownership by the reporting organisations when opting for a certain degree of standardisation in the reports.

Source: (CCC, 2017[53]; Defra, 2012[50]; Defra, 2013[54]; Defra, 2017[55]; Defra, 2021[56]; Defra, 2022[57]; EEA, 2020[58]; Street, Hayman and Wilkins, 2017[59]; Street and Jude, 2019[60]; UK Government, 2020[2]).

Devolved administrations

Scotland

The Scottish Government's overarching vision for adaptation is to ensure that Scotland is a place where "built and natural places, supporting infrastructure, economy and societies are climate-ready, adaptable and resilient to climate change" (Scottish Government, 2019[30]). Scotland's SCCAP sets out nine objectives for adaptation across three themes: natural environment (e.g. support a healthy and diverse natural environment with capacity to adapt); buildings and infrastructure networks (e.g. provide the knowledge, skills and tools to manage climate change impacts on buildings and infrastructure); and society (e.g. increase the awareness of the impacts of climate change to enable people to adapt to future extreme weather events). All three themes aim to understand the effects of climate change and impacts on the natural environment, buildings and infrastructure and society.

In viewing adaptation as a process, Scotland expects the country to be flexible and able to manage the uncertainty of climate change impacts. The nine objectives were developed through a consultation process involving 58 organisations during the preparation of SCCAP2, which also emphasised the need for an outcomes-based approach and the development of a monitoring and evaluation framework. The outcomes-based approach is driven by both the UN Sustainable Development Goals and Scotland's National Performance Framework. The programme outlines policies, proposals and research for each of seven high-level outcomes (understood as overarching aims, which describe what the programme ambitions to achieve at the highest level), each split into sub-outcomes (Scottish Government, 2019[30]) (see Section 2.4.3).

As laid out in the Scottish Climate Change Act 2009, Scottish Ministers must provide an annual report on progress towards achieving the objectives and implementing the proposals and policies set out in the SCCAP. Under the act, public bodies are also required to provide annual reports on climate risk, adaptation action and future priorities, and – as of reporting year 2021-22 – what contribution the public body has made to help deliver SCCAP2, where applicable (Scottish Government, 2021[3]; UK Government, 2020[61]). The act also requires the government's progress to be independently assessed, which was first done by the CCC in 2016, then in 2019, 2022 and 2023 (Scottish Government, 2021[3]; CCC, 2022[62]).

Scotland's current SCCAP2 aims to capture the effect of actions over many years, understand how actions are driving outcomes, and make it easier to adjust adaptation in response to changes (Scottish Government, 2019[30]). Its progress report – covering Scotland's communities, businesses and natural environment as well as their engagement with international partners – is structured to reflect the seven SCCAP2 high-level outcomes and sub-outcomes (e.g. progress towards our communities being inclusive, empowered, resilient and safe in response to the changing climate) and includes examples of progress in implementing the policies (Scottish Government, 2021[3]).

The progress report also notes that further work is needed to develop a monitoring framework for tracking progress towards achieving the SCCAP2 outcomes (Scottish Government, 2021[3]). ClimateXChange (CXC), a research centre that provides independent advice to the Scottish Government, has recommended a set of principles for the design and development of the SCCAP's monitoring and evaluation framework, which is not yet operational. For example, it recommended that the framework links the adaptation process to adaptation outcomes and aims to discourage the listing of policies and actions without considering their potential effectiveness (Moss, 2019[63]). The CCC's 2022 independent assessment criticised the annual reports for lacking a sufficiently in-depth assessment of what has and has not been achieved. It recommends that the Scottish Government sets specific and more ambitious objectives and actions, and develops appropriate indicators to best measure the achievement of these objectives (rather than only using indicators for which data are available) (CCC, 2022[62]).

The framework used for the CCC's independent assessment of the SCCAP has evolved in line with the one used for the UK/England (see Section 2.3.1). The CCC's latest progress report for Scotland applies the monitoring map, evaluation of delivery and implementation indicators and an assessment of progress against policy and planning requirements. This independent assessment complements Scotland's progress by investigating the effectiveness of implemented actions in reducing climate risks, resulting in a more comprehensive measurement of progress (CCC, 2023[64]). The CCC concludes that since 2022 monitoring and evaluation of adaptation has been slowly improving (for example, the analysis of public body reporting), but remains limited, with insufficient data collection hampering adaptation efforts in many areas. For the next adaptation policy (SNAP3), due in 2024, the CCC highlights the need to ensure that there are quantified targets for climate resilience; that there are clear linkages between activities and outcomes, with clear ownership of delivery; and that an effective monitoring and evaluation system is implemented.

Northern Ireland

In Northern Ireland, the aim of "a resilient Northern Ireland, which will take timely and well-informed decisions to address the socio-economic and environmental impacts of climate change", was agreed in the NICCAP2 following extensive central government and non-government stakeholder engagement exercises (DAERA NI, 2019[11]). The Northern Ireland Environment Link (NIEL), a network and forum for organisations interested in the natural and built environment, was commissioned by DAERA to work with stakeholders outside of government through the Climate NI project. The NICCAP2's aim is backed by five priority areas and seven outcome objectives (DAERA NI, 2019[11]).

Each of the nine government departments in Northern Ireland is responsible for reporting on progress towards the objectives set out in NICCAP2 for which they are the responsible risk owners. The Climate Change Adaptation Sub-group led by DAERA reviews progress against NICCAP2 objectives across all departments annually. It is currently undertaking its Year 2 progress review.

In its NICCAP2, Northern Ireland has incorporated lessons learnt from an ex-post review of NICCAP1, in line with the requirement of Section 60 of the UK Climate Change Act 2008 (DAERA NI, 2019[11]). At the end of 2022, DAERA also conducted the Mid-programme Progress Review of NICCAP2, which provides a progress update on actions contained in the implementation plan (DAERA NI, 2022[65]). The review also developed 36 new measures to be included in NICCAP2 to address gaps identified.

In addition to the "stocktake" type review, DAERA also commissioned the CCC to carry out an independent review of NICCAP2 and provide recommendations for NICCAP3 (CCC, 2023[25]). As for Scotland, the CCC applied its latest measurement framework to this review of Northern Ireland's progress in adapting to climate change. This complements DAERA's mid-term review by assessing whether risk reduction objective outcomes have been achieved. The CCC finds that for two-thirds of the adaptation outcomes, the lack of relevant indicator data prevents the CCC from making a judgement on progress in delivery and implementation. The CCC recommends that the NICCAP3 closes these critical data gaps.

Wales

The 2030 vision of Wales is to be "a country which has the resources and is prepared, has the knowledge to understand the risk and challenges ahead and has the capacity to adapt to the impact of climate change" (Welsh Government, 2019[31]). It measures its success based on actions in three key areas: increasing knowledge, capacity and resilience to respond to climate change risk. The Welsh Government's approach to developing actions in its climate change adaptation plan – *Prosperity for All: A Climate Conscious Wales* (PfACCW) – has been to use a theory of change to understand what is intended by each action and to determine the best way to monitor and evaluate progress (Welsh Government, 2020[16]).

The Welsh Monitoring and Evaluation Framework (MEF) has been developed to support the delivery of the PfACCW. It outlines a governance structure to monitor the plan's delivery, as well as the interventions, outputs, outcomes and timelines for completion (Welsh Government, 2020[16]). Based on the MEF, in 2022 Wales published a report that assesses progress across eight sectors and indicates additional actions to respond to the CCC's updated climate risk advice (Welsh Government, 2022[66]). The report outlines research activities and actions undertaken and next steps to fully implement the PfACCW. While the MEF recommends using a combination of qualitative and quantitative indicators to demonstrate the role of adaptation in addressing complex multi-causal risks, the progress report follows a predominantly qualitative stocktaking approach, without assessing outputs or outcomes of the actions implemented.

As with the governments of Northern Ireland and Scotland, the Welsh Government has asked the CCC to provide an independent assessment of progress in Wales (CCC, 2023[67]). Referring to the qualitative stocktaking approach of the Welsh Government's own progress report, the CCC's 2023 review concludes that for more than 50% of adaptation outcomes, the limited or absence of indicator data prevents it from conducting a full assessment of progress.

2.3.2. Measuring progress at local and international levels

Measuring adaptation at the local level

As highlighted above, a growing number of local authorities have established local adaptation strategies and plans, and some monitor and evaluate their plans (Box 2.3). A number of cities have also voluntarily signed up to Mayors Adapt, or to the EU Covenant of Mayors for Climate and Energy (e.g. Glasgow, Greater Manchester, Edinburgh and Leicester) (Covenant of Mayors, 2021[68]), thereby committing to reporting on adaptation progress every two years across the range of activities in their cities.

In Northern Ireland, civil society and local governments contribute to tracking progress on implementing the NICCAP2 actions, including for the mid-term evaluation. An online submission form on climate risks and adaptation measures was developed by Climate NI, as a deliverable of their contract with DAERA, to track methods, programmes and outcomes of adaptation actions by local councils (Climate NI, 2019[69]). As set out above, in Scotland, public bodies including local authorities are required to report annually on any relevant contributions to the SCCAP.

However, there is a disconnect between information gathered from local plans and reviews, and the national level, despite the substantive inputs they could provide into national monitoring. Between 2008 and 2010, all English local authorities were required to report against a performance indicator related to adaptation (National Indicator 188). They had to self-report their level of action, ranking it from level 0 (climate risks not assessed) to level 4 (adaptation action plan implemented and process for monitoring and review established) (UK Government, 2010[70]; EAC and House of Commons, 2010[71]; UK Government, 2013[72]). Although it was largely process-oriented, it helped to demonstrate progress before it was discontinued. As of 2021, there is no UK-wide level assessment of adaptation at city/local county level, which reflects the general limited nature of the evidence of local-level adaptation measurement (EEA, 2020[58]). Local authorities have no reporting requirement under the 2008 Climate Change Act, despite local-level work and knowledge-sharing within and across sectors being useful for developing consistent and robust adaptation plans (UK Government, 2020[2]).

Box 2.3. Keeping resilience on track in the county of Hampshire

Hampshire County Council (HCC), which includes close to 2 million inhabitants, has developed a climate change strategy and a framework for strategic programmes (2020-25). The aim is for the county to be carbon neutral and to build resilience to a 2 degrees Celsius rise in temperature by 2050 (Hampshire County Council, 2020[73]). In addition, an action plan lists 200 actions across departments, along with indicators and outcomes for each action. Progress on the implementation of the plan is reviewed qualitatively and reported on annually. The first progress report was published in 2021 (Hampshire County Council, 2021[74]).

In parallel, HCC has developed decision-making support tools, rolled out across the county since 2021, to assess climate impacts on individual council projects. They set a vulnerability score which can be applied across all the council's diverse services. They aim to provide a clear, robust, and transparent way of assessing how projects, policies and initiatives contribute towards HCC's climate change targets and mainstream climate considerations into the local authority's activities. The tools have helped to increase awareness and understanding of how decisions contribute to climate change mitigation, and how climate change will affect decisions.

Source: (Hampshire Country Council, 2021[75]; South East Climate Alliance, 2021[76]).

International monitoring, evaluation and reporting

The UK is party to several international agreements, including the Paris Agreement, the Sendai Framework for Risk Reduction, Agenda 2030 for Sustainable Development, the Ramsar Convention and the Convention on Biological Diversity (UK Government, 2020[2]; GIZ, 2017[77]). These frameworks set objectives to achieve sustainable development, reduce disaster risk, and conserve environmental habitats and species. They all have synergies with or address the need for adaptation to climate variability and change (UNFCCC, 2012[78]; OECD, 2020[79]). The UK reports on its activities for achieving the objectives under all these agreements. For instance, it conducts a Voluntary National Review of Progress on the Sustainable Development Goals (SDGs).

In 2017, the UK submitted its 7th National Communication to the United Nations Framework Convention on Climate Change (UNFCCC) (a four-yearly binding requirement) and its first Adaptation Communication in 2020, followed by an update in 2021 (UK Government, 2020[2]; UK Government, 2021[20]; BEIS, 2017[80]; UNFCCC, 2017[81]). In advance of COP26, the Scottish Government published an indicative Nationally Determined Contribution document, including a summary of the approach to adaptation in Scotland (Scottish Government, 2021[82]).

The UK also aligns particular areas of adaptation with respective international frameworks. Most notably, biodiversity indicators are reviewed to fit with the Post-2020 Global Biodiversity Framework of the Convention on Biological Diversity. The Sendai Framework for Disaster Risk Reduction has established a monitoring process, including indicators (UNDRR, 2021[83]).

2.3.3. Addressing specific measurement challenges

Like many other countries, the UK faces difficulties in overcoming certain measurement challenges, notably linking greater resilience to specific policy actions (attribution), aggregating information across scales, and dealing with the uncertainty surrounding adaptation interventions (OECD, 2021[84]).

Attribution

While there is growing experience of tracking progress across OECD countries, including the UK, there is a need to move towards understanding the outcomes and impacts of policies and actions. Attribution aims to evaluate the contribution of an adaptation policy or action to a certain outcome. It is, however, difficult to identify the factors that shape adaptation outcomes, notably because of the long timescales of adaptation interventions. Adaptation is an ongoing process that is mainstreamed across various policy areas and unfolds in a changing context. As a result, adaptation outcomes are intertwined with other drivers (e.g. population growth) (Bours, McGinn and Pringle, 2014[85]). It is also difficult to distinguish inter-annual variability from long-term trends. Thus, being able to attribute impacts to actions requires constant monitoring. It is important to understand the role of formalised attribution study following an event for developing and attributing impact indicators to track changes in impacts. The disaggregation of the data is also a challenge because the evidence available on risks cannot always be broken down into specific actions. It is therefore important to understand the context of the action and how non-adaptation factors (e.g. natural variability) influence its success (Bours, McGinn and Pringle, 2014[85]). In Scotland, for example, non-domestic water consumption has continued to decrease, but it is not possible to assess whether the decrease is attributable to water efficiency actions (based on the indicator CXC 2018 Indicators Non-domestic water usage) (CCC, 2019[86]).

Defra, in its NAP3, acknowledges the challenges of tracking progress to a moving target in a system with interacting and cascading climate and socio-economic risks, the mismatch between short evaluation cycles and the time needed to effect change. The NAP therefore recommends that policy officials identify accompanying process and outcome indicators when developing policy responses for the 61 risks or opportunities (Defra, 2023[8]). The CCC has also made efforts to produce new indicators of impacts (e.g. prevalence of flooding impacts, deaths from overheating, or monetary impacts of climate-related water shortages). In cases where explicit policy goals exist, the AC considers how likely these are to be met in the face of climate change (CCC, 2020[41]). There are ways to provide a clear description of the system being monitored and hypotheses or causal chains outlining how policies and actions are likely to contribute to an intended objective (Klostermann et al.[87]; Price-Kelly et al., 2015[88]). The CCC's adaptation monitoring maps, developed as part of its new measurement methodology (described above, see Figure 2.3), illustrate how sectoral goals can be linked with outcomes needed to deliver the goals, as well as policies, enablers and contextual factors to achieve the outcomes. This is a positive step to begin to address the uncertainty around how much change can be attributed to the effectiveness of actions (OECD, 2021[84]).

Aggregation

The measurement framework in the UK and devolved administrations is cross-sectoral (natural environment, people and built environment, business and infrastructure), and thus related to the remits of a number of government departments. The number of sectors involved and the diversity of the dimensions of the expected outcomes can make it difficult to aggregate the results at the UK level. Metrics used in certain sectors may not be appropriate at the aggregate level due to the context specificity of climate risk and adaptation interventions (Christiansen, Martinez and Naswa, 2018[89]). Although monitoring and reviewing can help support policy making at different levels of government, the international, national and local levels may have different scopes and objectives in their reviews. However, certain topics can be aggregated or connected through indicators (EEA, 2020[58]). The four devolved administrations have their own monitoring and evaluation frameworks. The CCC's recent efforts in assessing progress of all four devolved administrations by applying the same methodology is a strong enabler for aggregating progress at the UK level. Nevertheless, different indicators may be required to evaluate progress towards the same outcome in different parts of the UK because some datasets do not have UK-wide coverage (CCC,

2023[45]). For example, the Environment Agency collects data on flood risk in England, whereas other organisations collect flood risk data in other parts of the UK.

Uncertainty and complexity

Another inherent complexity in measuring progress on adaptation is due to uncertainty over how climate will unfold in a particular location. To address this, the CCC scores the quality of plans and whether actions demonstrably reduce either vulnerability or exposure to two possible temperature scenarios. It reviews actions across all sectors to see whether they are adequate in a 2°C world, and whether adaptation to a 4°C world has been considered (CCC, 2020[41]). As it can be unclear what policy makers need to be measuring, regular reviews of indicators to ensure that the measurement and indicator frameworks are still relevant are key. This is done by the CCC, as well as the Defra team when reviewing the indicator framework attached to the 25-Year Environment Programme (YEP).

Cross-sector interactions can become significant drivers of overall risk. The CCC has highlighted that the vulnerability of interconnected systems may be significantly underestimated. The wide-ranging nature of the linkages within and across sectors lays the foundation for potential cascading failures caused by the climate hazards identified in the third CCRA (e.g. from flooding, reduced water availability, increased temperatures and wildfire, as well as potential increases in storms) (CCC, 2021[44]). The effects of climate change adaptation will interact with other pressures, such as population and demographic transition, economic dynamics, or land use change. For these reasons, the CCC has adapted its measurement methodology to assess contextual factors affecting sectors' exposure and vulnerability to climate hazards (e.g. population growth by region, age) (CCC, 2023[21]). Furthermore, the CCC has made efforts to assess inter-dependencies among different areas and systems, such as infrastructure, nature and socio-economic factors.

2.4. Development and use of adaptation indicators

2.4.1. Overview of indicator frameworks

The UK and its three devolved administrations have each developed specific indicator frameworks for tracking progress to accompany their adaptation policy cycle. The indicators usually cover topics identified in the risk assessment and in the adaptation plans (Table 2.6).

Table 2.6. A summary of adaptation indicators across the United Kingdom

	Number of indicators	Topics covered	Development
UK/England	599 indicators on outcomes, enablers, policies, vulnerability, exposure and hazards	Natural environment Land & seas, transport, business, towns & cities, telecommunications & ICT, community response & preparedness, health, buildings, finance, water supply, energy, food security	First set of indicators published over a decade ago and iterative research updated the list
Scotland	105 baseline indicators presented in 13 narratives (i.e. type of risk/impact addressed by indicator)	Natural environment Buildings and infrastructure networks Society	Populated through research by 80 academics and agency staff of 25 organisations; developed in partnership and consultation with 50+ policy makers and stakeholders
Northern Ireland	13 indicators across the Key Priority Areas	Natural capital Infrastructure services People & built environment Disruption to businesses & supply chains Food security/Global food production	Statistical datasets were developed after discussions with all government departments and DAERA's Analytical and Services Branch
Wales	A couple for each objective	Adaptive Nature & the Rural Economy, Protecting our Coasts and Seas, Staying Healthy, Safe Homes and Places, Caring for the Historic Environment, Successful Businesses, Resilient Infrastructure and Transport	Indicators from the CCC, Defra and Welsh Government National Indicators were considered

Source: (ClimateXChange, 2016[90]; ClimateXChange, 2021[91]; Ffoulkes et al., 2021[92]; Welsh Government, 2020[16]; DAERA NI, 2019[11]; CCC, 2021[93]).

2.4.2. Indicator frameworks in the United Kingdom/England

Up until the 2023 progress report, the CCC used two sets of indicators for reporting on adaptation on a two-year cycle: i) a cross-sector indicator framework; and ii) the NAP monitoring tracker to monitor the 253 actions listed in England's NAP2. In its 2023 framework, and with the development of monitoring maps, the CCC has expanded and targeted indicators to capture progress towards each identified outcome across 13 sectors. This now involves close to 600 indicators (Table 2.6). This evolved set of indicators has allowed the CCC to significantly increase its focus on outcome-related indicators. The complete set is the result of an iterative research process in which the CCC has regularly updated and added indicators (2017, 2019, 2021, 2023), in line with its role to review indicator frameworks based on the most recent CCRA (CCC, 2021[43]).

As discussed above, the CCC's monitoring maps (Figure 2.3) showcase indicators related to outcomes, as well as enablers, plans and policies, and climate risks (or contextual factors) (Figure 2.4). Based on these, the CCC assigns a three-level score (good, mixed, insufficient) to each of the 13 sectors' objectives (see United Kingdom/England section). The enablers, which correspond to 30% of all indicators (Figure 2.4), are elements that need to be in place to achieve the outcomes. They include funding and investment, research, engagement and education, and are different to policies or plans. In previous assessments, these were considered as input indicators. An additional 20% of indicators relate to policies and plans to help track whether key roles and milestones for public policy and planning are in place. These include the adoption of regulations, standards or plans, or the mainstreaming of topics or targets into relevant plans, policies or financial instruments (CCC, 2023[21]). While neither enabler or policy indicators show whether vulnerability has been reduced, they can be used to analyse climate change preparedness (Klostermann et al., 2015[87]).

The CCC scores progress made in implementing key policies and plans individually based on a four-point scale: credible, partial, limited, and insufficient policies considered to be in place (Table 2.4) (CCC, 2023[45]). This aims to assess the overall strength of policies and plans in place to achieve each sector's objectives, and also aims to close the gap identified in NAP2 in which risk magnitude was growing despite progress on completing actions. With the publication of NAP3, it will remain important to have a clear and assigned monitoring tool in place to assess the implementation of the plan's actions. Previous annual progress reports indicate that half of the 370 actions included in the UK NAP were completed in 2017, while 35% were on track for completion (CCC, 2017[46]; 2019[47]).

The majority of the monitoring maps' indicators are defined as outcome indicators (Figure 2.4). They indicate whether actions have increased resilience or reduced climate risks, climate impacts, economic damage or negative effects on human health. They include factors such as a reduction in building permits issued for high flood-risk areas; or whether adaptation measures have reduced the magnitude of infrastructure service disruptions caused by extreme weather; or a reduction in flooding damage recorded. There are overall outcome indicators that are often measured by more than one sub-indicator. For example, the outcome "Protected and resilient habitats" is measured by two sub-indicators: the state of priority habitats for biodiversity in England, and the proportion of terrestrial Sites of Special Scientific Interest (SSSIs) in England classed as "recovering" (Table 2.7). The sub-indicators used to measure the outcomes might not be listed in the monitoring maps, but are available in the progress report.

Compared to its previous framework, the CCC's new framework comprises both immediate changes to the environment, society and economy, as well as longer-term climate impacts. It also includes direct outputs, such as the level of achievement of risk reduction measures, which classify as tracking adaptation actions. There are both shorter-term outcomes, such as trends in restored habitats or species abundance, and longer-term outcomes that indicate a climate impact (i.e. change in climate-related losses and damages).

These might include weather-related delays and incidents on rail networks or in ports; annual damage from coastal and river flooding; agricultural losses from drought or heat-related mortality.

Figure 2.4. Outcome indicators make up the largest share of indicators in CCC's monitoring maps

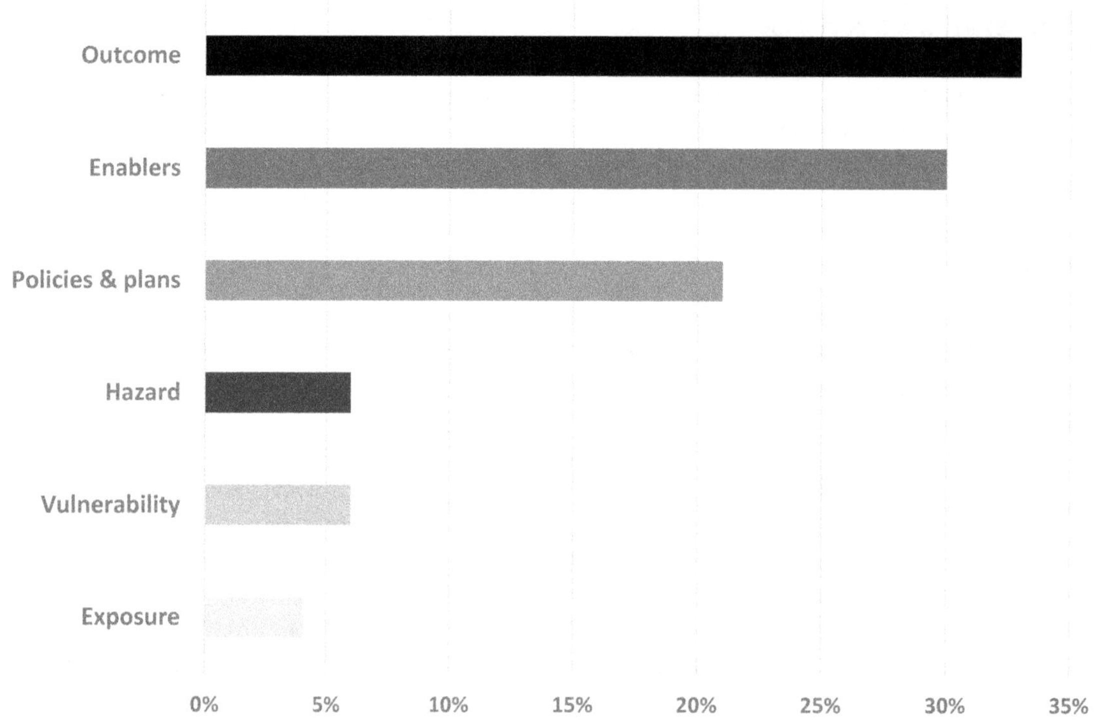

Note: The indicators developed as part of the monitoring maps are indicative. Not all of them are measured in practice due to lack of data availability. Some indicators are used to assess multiple sectors but are not counted twice.
Source: Authors, based on (CCC, 2023[21]), *Progress in Adapting to Climate Change: 2023 report to Parliament*, https://www.theccc.org.uk/publication/progress-in-adapting-to-climate-change-2023-report-to-parliament/

However, it is difficult to rely on outcome, or climate impact, indicators for assessing adaptation progress because of the challenges of disentangling year-to-year variability from long-term trends. It is also difficult to attribute results to drivers, which could be a change in hazard levels, or socio-economic factor or the result of adaptation actions. For climate impact indicators to be robust, they would need to have a sufficiently long record (multi-decade at least) and one needs to be able to isolate the effects of climate change from other pressures, an area in which the science is improving. The CCC considers these indicators to have great potential use in the long term, once attribution becomes more feasible (CCC, 2019[47]). The CCC assesses quantitative data where possible, but for some important aspects that are difficult to measure quantitatively, such as the mental health impacts of climate change, the CCC uses a qualitative approach, often referring to academic studies or expert judgement.

Table 2.7. The use of selected outcomes and their indicators for measuring adaptation progress

Overall outcomes	Indicators measured
Protected and resilient habitats	• State of priority habitats for biodiversity in England [outcome] • Proportion of terrestrial Sites of Special Scientific Interest (SSSIs) in England classed as 'recovering' [outcome]
Asset and system level reliability of rail network	• Delay minutes per heat, flood and storm incidents in England [outcome] • Proportion of railway stations and tracks at 'significant' risk of surface water flooding (1/30 chance or greater of occurrence) [impact; exposure] • Train Accident Risk Reduction (TARR) measures achievement of key risk reduction activities planned [output]
Protect population health from the impacts of climate change and utilise potential benefits	• Heat-related mortality [impact] • Vector abundance of different species [outcome] • Number of people living with chronic respiratory conditions [impact] • Proportion of properties with access to private outdoor space; average distance to public park or public garden in England [output]
Public and private adaptation measures are implemented to minimise risks to business sites	• Number of non-residential buildings at risk of surface water and river and sea flooding [impact] • Non-household consumption from the public water supply in England [output]
Reduced vulnerability of energy assets to extreme weather	• Proportion of critical electricity substations that are considered flood-proofed [output] • Age and condition of overhead poles [impact]

Note: Only indicators that can be measured are listed; however, additional "wishlist" indicators exist.
Source: (CCC, 2023[21]), *Progress in Adapting to Climate Change: 2023 report to Parliament,* https://www.theccc.org.uk/publication/progress-in-adapting-to-climate-change-2023-report-to-parliament/

Each of the 13 sectors are assigned a number of outcome, enabler and policy indicators, as well as climate risk indicators on hazard, sector-specific indicators on exposure and vulnerability. While some sectors are associated with a high number of outcome indicators (e.g. the natural environment, working land and seas, transport, and urban areas), sectors such as food security, telecommunications and ICT, community preparedness, energy, and water supply only use a few outcome indicators to assess progress (Figure 2.5). Sectoral differences also exist for policies and enabling factors. The maps cover climate risk indicators to a smaller extent; these are considered as contextual factors (see Figure 2.4 and Table 2.8 for examples). For five sectors, the framework does not assess climate risk indicators at all (Figure 2.5).

Figure 2.5. The number and type of indicators used vary across the 13 sectors assessed

Number of indicators

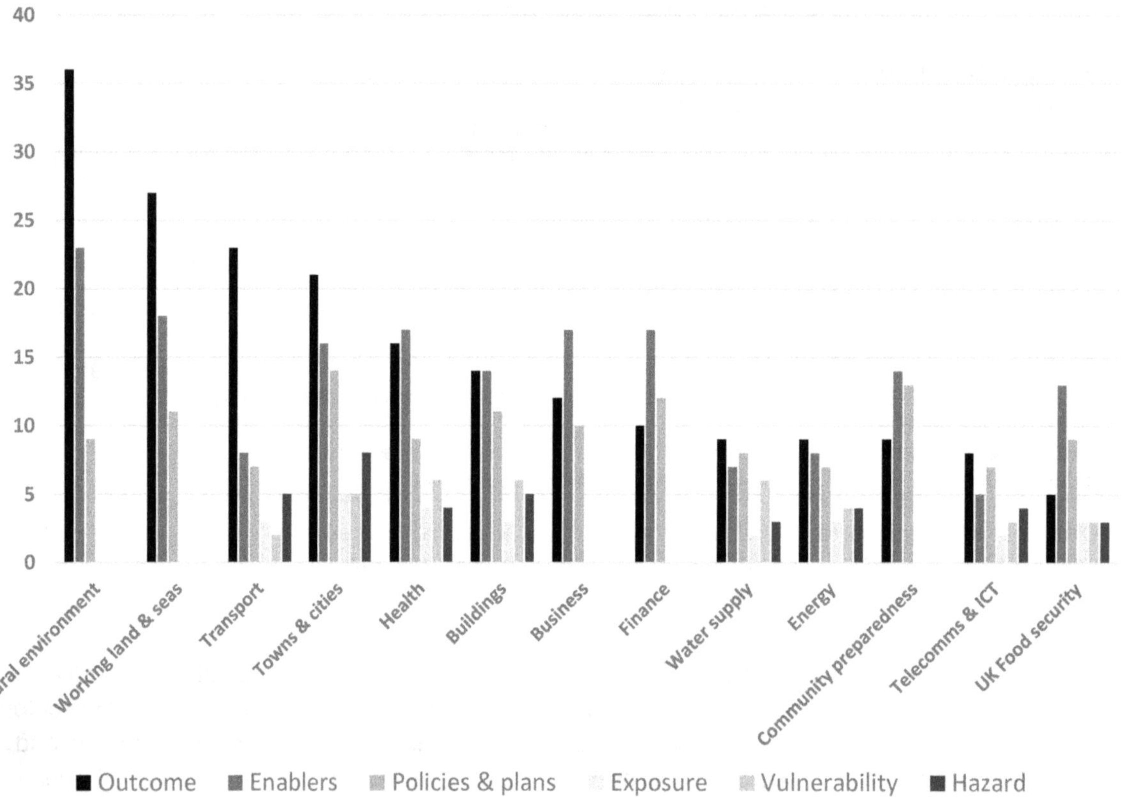

Note: Some indicators are used to assess multiple sectors, but are not counted twice.
Source: Authors, based on (CCC, 2023[21]), *Progress in Adapting to Climate Change: 2023 report to Parliament*, https://www.theccc.org.uk/publication/progress-in-adapting-to-climate-change-2023-report-to-parliament/

Table 2.8. Examples of climate-related risks indicators

Type	Examples of climate-related risks indicators
Hazard	Extent of flooding; droughts; length and intensity of heatwaves; storms, soil erosion
Vulnerability	Population growth by region; net zero driving change in transport mode demand; water abstraction for agriculture and industry; proportion of low-income households; health conditions; social isolation; growing dependence on digital infrastructure; reliance on imported food; changing dietary preferences
Exposure	Location of transport infrastructure; hospitals and acre of houses; access to local green space; urban heat islands

Source: (CCC, 2023[45]), CCC Adaptation Monitoring Framework, https://www.theccc.org.uk/publication/ccc-adaptation-monitoring-framework/#introduction

The indicators were selected based on their relevance, practicality, and replicability over time, even if no data were available. The monitoring maps include indicators considered important, including for which data availability is insufficient or whose time series is too short to be meaningful. This approach began with the addition of "wishlist" indicators in the CCC 2021 progress report. For nearly 40% of adaptation outcomes, the lack of relevant and up-to-date indicator datasets prevents an assessment of outcomes. The sectors with the largest data gaps are telecommunications and ICT; food security; buildings (e.g. data tracking the overall scale of property flood resilience implementation); finance (e.g. data on financial exposure to climate risks are limited); transport (e.g. incomplete data on ports and airports); energy; and business (e.g.

exposure and vulnerability of business assets, business access to credit and insurance, and worker productivity is largely unquantified, supply chains) (CCC, 2023[21]). There are also gaps in data for assessing the ecosystem health of land and seascapes, the implementation of nature-based solutions, and the size and connectivity of habitats.

Through this indicative approach of showing what outcomes need to be assessed, the CCC's monitoring maps provide a useful way to highlight the data gaps for evaluating outcomes, including whether the datasets are partial, geographically incomplete, out-of-date, or lack sufficient measurement history to allow a trend in progress over time to be estimated (CCC, 2023[45]). Going one step further, the CCC also urges specific agencies to generate additional data and indicators where needed. For example, the CCC has asked Defra to develop a set of indicators for monitoring the impacts of weather and climate on telecommunication and ICT services (CCC, 2023[21]).

Progress in populating wishlist indicators, notably to assess outcomes, appears to have been made since the CCC's 2021 progress report, when close to 60% of the indicators included were on the wishlist (CCC, 2021[94]). The CCC's 2021 assessment concluded that current indicators for measuring progress and the effectiveness of adaptation actions were insufficient. Indicators did not necessarily align with the measurements needed to identify tangible reductions in climate risk or improvement in resilience. Instead they were more relevant to measure progress towards policy targets or legal requirements (CCC, 2021[43]). In 2023, the assessment concluded that 40% of the outcomes could not be assessed due to gaps in data availability. Defra, in the lead up to its third NAP, conducted a series of sector-specific workshops that brought together data owners, holders and users to share best practice and discuss challenges in developing adaptation indicators in response to the CCC's 2021 assessment (Defra, 2023[8]) (CCC, 2021[95]; CCC, 2021[43]). Nonetheless the 2023 assessment still finds that the absence of relevant robust data is a key barrier to assessing adaptation outcomes.

In light of the shortage of indicators to enable a consistent assessment of the effectiveness of adaptation interventions over time, the CCC has identified areas that would benefit from future work to fill methodological and data gaps on outcome indicators, as follows (CCC, 2023[21]):

- Natural environment: indicators to assess outcomes related to the effectiveness of restoring ecosystem health and improving climate resilience. Specifically, data and information to measure climate-resilient native species; future UK wildfire risks; effectiveness of nature-based solutions for adaptation; impacts of acidification, temperature and salinity on marine species; impacts on agriculture from unpredictable and unseasonal weather, such as yield and profit changes; crop/livestock losses due to flooding/heatwaves; and fish losses due to sea temperature rises or changes to ocean chemistry.
- Working land and seas: data on exposure and vulnerability of the sector to climate change; impact of agricultural policies.
- Transport: climate impacts on ports and airports.
- Water supply: catchment storage capacity.
- Buildings: effectiveness of property-level installations and how well they have worked in a flood event; number of buildings at risk of groundwater flooding.
- Food security: climate risk of food companies' supply chains; data on how the productivity of the agriculture sector is changing in relation to climate change.
- Energy: exposure to hazards other than flooding.
- Health: effectiveness of interventions to reduce overheating in health and social care facilities.
- Community preparedness & response: effectiveness of different types of behaviour changes for adaptation.

- Business: exposure and vulnerability of business assets; effectiveness of business actions to reduce climate risks; resilience of essential goods supply chains; impact of adaptation measures on size of insurance pay-outs; impacts on worker productivity.
- Finance: key data on financial exposure to climate risks; impact of financial institutions incorporating physical risks into financial decision making; impact of investment portfolios on adaptation outcomes.

In addition, as part of the efforts to define the indicators, along with a timeline comes the difficulty of setting baselines. The most appropriate timing of a baseline might vary depending on the topic (e.g. start of the policy, average at some point in the past). For instance, the 25-YEP Outcome Indicator Framework (described below), used the launch year of the 25 Year Environment Plan (2018) as its indicator baseline, and considers additional frames of reference where relevant and appropriate (e.g. for indicators that relate to long-term trends such as changes in bird populations).

Synergies with other frameworks, and the use of proxies

In parallel to the CCC's efforts to develop indicators, several other institutions have established or are developing data and indicators that are relevant to adaptation. As they are already available, the CCC's framework uses several of the data and indicators from these institutions. However, since many of these were originally designed for purposes other than to measure changes in climate risk, they can only be used as proxies (Box 2.4) (CCC, 2021[43]; CCC, 2023[21]).

In 2019, Defra published a set of indicators as part of the Outcome Indicator Framework to evaluate the effectiveness of policies and interventions in the 2018 25-Year Environment Plan (25-YEP). Updated in 2021, the framework contains 66 indicators, categorised into 10 environmental themes and following 16 headlines to help communicate progress towards the goals of the 25 YEP. It includes indicators that could suggest successful adaptation (e.g. enhancement of green/blue infrastructure), the need for adaptation (e.g. status of mammals, birds and fish) and that show the resilience of natural assets to climate change (e.g. state of the water environment). Other adaptation-relevant areas in the Outcome Indicator Framework include communities resilient to flooding and coastal erosion; quantity, quality and connectivity of habitats; water bodies achieving sustainable abstraction criteria; and health and wellbeing benefits. The review of progress occurs annually based on existing datasets from across relevant departments, and the indicator framework is reviewed every five years (Defra, 2018[42]; Defra, 2019[96]; Defra, 2021[97]).

Box 2.4. Proxy indicators as a second-best option

Proxy indicators are often used to measure the outcomes and impacts of adaptation actions. Indicators are referred to as proxies when they are used as an alternative measure of progress on adaptation to fill a gap in the absence of relevant and accurate data, despite not directly measuring the impact of adaptation actions.

The CCC uses many indicators in the natural environment sector as proxy measures for adaptation, drawn from the annual UK Biodiversity Indicators report. For example, indicators related to the natural environment, such as peatland condition and species abundance, can be used as proxy indicators for the vulnerability of a habitat to climate change, where better condition and higher abundance can be interpreted as higher resilience. Similarly, the water and wetland bird index can give an indication of a habitat's level of resilience, but does not reveal to what extent wetland restoration or lack of restoration have contributed to the index level, for instance.

In general, the use of proxies needs to be accompanied by caveats to avoid simplistic assessments of progress that can ultimately inaccurately classify adaptation actions as effective because proxies usually do not address the causal relationship between an adaptation policy and its outcomes and impacts. Choosing a proxy indicator may introduce a discrepancy between the measured proxy level and the actual impact of individual adaptation measures. The CCC acknowledges in its current measurement framework that multiple indicators need to be considered together to provide a full picture.

Source: (CCC, 2021[43]); (CCC, 2023[45])

Stakeholder engagement is an important part of the measurement process. It can help identify the suitability of existing data (What evidence will we need in order to know what is working?), source relevant quantitative and qualitative data, and also interpret the available data and derive relevant messages (Moss, 2019[63]). Defra has engaged with stakeholders and industry representatives to develop further indicators in response to the CCC's recommendation to bring together expertise to identify, develop and source data for new indicators, create a framework for using them, and co-ordinate ongoing work to ensure indicators remain appropriate and relevant for helping streamline various processes (CCC, 2021[43]).

Institutions that are involved in the process of developing and using indicators that are relevant for adaptation include:

- The Office for Environmental Protection, which is to conduct an independent scrutiny of the government's progress towards meeting the 25-YEP goals.
- The British Ecological Society (BES), which is investigating how a set of indicators may be developed to assess the effectiveness of adaptation actions in the natural environment.
- The Environment Agency, which is exploring the design and use of indicators to measure progress towards the adaptation objectives set out in its Flood and Coastal Erosion Risk Management Strategy (CCC, 2021[43]). The Environment Agency has also initiated a project to design a new outcome-based corporate monitoring and reporting framework for adaptation to review progress in achieving adaptation outcomes (covering flood risk and other adaptation issues) across the organisation.
- A new one-stop shop for statistics on climate change, developed in 2021 by the Office of National Statistics together with partners from across the UK Government. It showcases climate change statistical indicators in six areas (including climate and weather, impacts on nature and society) and aims to inform policy making (OSR, 2021[98]). The portal is expected to evolve through an iterative process to broaden the indicators included, providing a more comprehensive picture of

climate change. Adaptation-related indicators cover woodland area, water leakage and pollinator species (UK Government, 2021[99]). There would be scope to align with the CCC's indicator framework.

2.4.3. Indicator frameworks in devolved administrations

The Scottish Government has begun the process of developing their own adaptation indicator framework for the current SCCAP2. The framework is intended to include action and impact indicators for some of the high-level outcomes (Figure 2.6). Research supporting SCCAP2 set out potential baseline information and existing trends to assess how well Scotland is doing against the nine objectives of the SCCAP across three of seven themes (natural environment, buildings and infrastructure networks, and society).

Scotland's full list contains 105 indicators, presented in 13 narratives, driven by policy need (ClimateXChange, 2016[90]). While just over one-third of the indicators indicate a trend (38 indicators), the majority either provide baseline data without a trend (44 indicators), or data over time but with no discernible trend (23 indicators) (Mäkinen et al., 2018[100]). They are presented along with the rationale for selecting them and the conclusions that may be drawn from them. They also come with baseline information to enable assessment over time and to document the nature and effectiveness of adaptation interventions (ClimateXChange, 2021[91]). For instance, excess deaths due to extremely cold temperatures are measured against the first available records, from 1951/52. They follow a framework to understand how they can lead to certain outcomes.

They were developed in consultation with 80 academic researchers and staff from 25 organisations and over 50 policy makers and stakeholders (ClimateXChange, 2016[90]). The SCCAP2 research programme aims to address specific evidence gaps outlined in the CCC's progress report, for instance to measure soil health (Neilson et al., 2020[101]) and recovery from extreme events (Orr et al., 2020[102]).

The CCC's independent assessment of the SCCAP applies a similar evaluation approach to its evaluation of England (see section on United Kingdom/England) (CCC, 2016[103]). Where possible, the CCC's Scotland evaluation is based on the indicator set developed by ClimateXChange to assess progress on the SCCAP. For the independent assessments, the CCC gathered additional information through stakeholder interviews, and from public bodies' duty reports and a wider literature review. In the 2019 assessment, the CCC concluded that key data and evidence gaps were hampering progress assessments for a number of priorities. It also recommended Scotland to improve the measurement of vulnerability. In 2022, the CCC assessed progress on indicators for which data were available and recommended that the Scottish Government rely more on the most relevant, adaptation-related indicators recently or soon to be developed as part of other environmental frameworks, such as the Environment Strategy 2021 or Scotland's Forestry Strategy Implementation Plan 2020-22.

Figure 2.6. Scotland's indicator framework (SCCAP 2019-24)

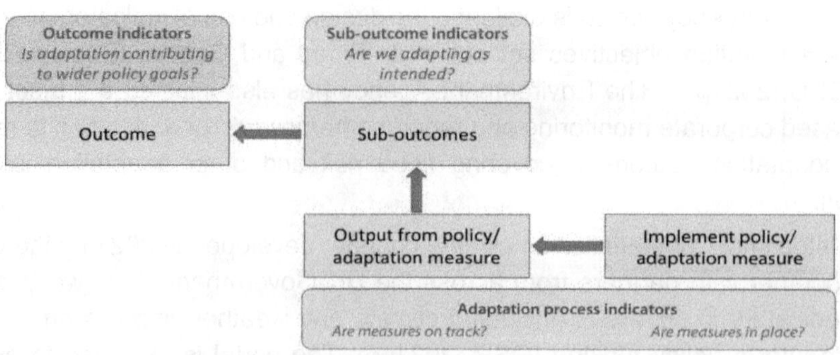

Source: (Scottish Government, 2019[30]), *Climate Ready Scotland: Second Scottish Climate Change Adaptation Programme 2019-2024*

Indicators in other devolved administration programmes are less detailed. In Wales, a largely qualitative approach is taken to monitor and evaluate progress, as the Welsh Government considered the quantitative indicators would provide limited insights into implementation in the context of the methodologies available at the time. It does however consider the use of quantitative indicators where the action is clearly reflected in the indicator, and where resources are available for measuring them (Welsh Government, 2020[16]). The Welsh Government intended to develop adaptation indicators for the level of uptake, and the subsequent performance of adaptation planning across Wales, such as the number of Health Board Plans which focus on planning for climate risks. It also intends to develop multi-faceted strategy-level indicators to cover the level of adaptive capacity, and the degree to which key tasks described in the guidance have been implemented (Welsh Government, 2013[104]). Indicators from the CCC, Defra and Welsh Government National Indicators are taken into consideration in its framework (Welsh Government, 2020[16]).

In Northern Ireland, an initial set of indicators has been developed in consultation with all government departments and DAERA's Analytical and Services Branch (DAERA NI, 2019[11]). They have been assigned, where possible, to relevant NICCAP2 outcome objectives (Table 2.9). They aim to provide a mechanism to evaluate the progress made towards delivering the objectives (Defra, 2019[1]).

Table 2.9. Northern Ireland's objectives and indicators in NICCAP2

Key priority areas	NICCAP 2 outcome objectives	Examples of NICCAP2 indicators
Natural capital	NC1: We will have species, habitats and water bodies that are resilient to the impacts of climate change	% of terrestrial and marine protected area under favourable management % of water bodies at 'good' status (published every 3 years)
	NC2: We have coastal communities, habitats, landforms and infrastructure that are resilient to impacts of climate change	Area of in-shore water protected for nature conservation % of sea wall in each structural condition code
	NC3: We have soils and woodland that are resilient to the impacts of climate change	Area of new woodland planted
Infrastructure services	IF1: We have transport & network services that are resilient to the impacts of flooding & extreme weather	Number of properties removed from the 'Out of Sewer Flooding' Register % uptake of sustainable drainage systems Amount spent on structural drainage
People & built environment	P1: We have people, homes, buildings and communities that are resilient to the impacts of flooding & extremes of weather	% uptake of Sustainable Drainage Systems % of properties at risk of flooding in NI Number of Local Development Plans taking adaptation into account in line with the Strategic Planning Policy Statement

Source: (DAERA NI, 2019[11]), *Northern Ireland Climate Change Adaptation Programme 2019-2024.*

References

Adaptation Scotland (2020), *About Us*, https://www.adaptationscotland.org.uk/about-us. [14]

BEIS (2017), *7th National Communication*, UK Dept. for Business, Energy and Industrial Strategy, https://unfccc.int/sites/default/files/resource/19603845_United%20Kingdom-NC7-BR3-1-gbr%20NC7%20and%20BR3%20with%20Annexes%20%281%29.pdf. [80]

Belfast City Council (2020), *Resilient Belfast*, https://www.belfastcity.gov.uk/resilientbelfast. [36]

Bours, D., C. McGinn and P. Pringle (2014), *Guidance note 1: Twelve reasons why climate change adaptation M&E is challenging*, Seachange and UKCIP, https://www.ukcip.org.uk/wp-content/PDFs/MandE-Guidance-Note1.pdf. [85]

Bristol City Council (2021), *Council action on climate change*, https://www.bristol.gov.uk/policies-plans-strategies/council-action-on-climate-change. [10]

Bristol City Council and ARUP (2020), *Bristol One City Climate Strategy - Preliminary Climate Resilience Assessment*, https://www.bristolonecity.com/wp-content/uploads/2020/02/Preliminary-climate-resilience-assessment.pdf. [33]

Cambridge City Council (2018), *Climate Change Adaptation Plan*, https://www.cambridge.gov.uk/media/5996/climate-change-adaptation-plan.pdf. [38]

CCC (2023), *Adapting to Climate Change: Progress in Northern Ireland*, https://www.theccc.org.uk/publication/adapting-to-climate-change-progress-in-northern-ireland/. [25]

CCC (2023), *Adapting to Climate Change: Progress in Scotland*, https://www.theccc.org.uk/wp-content/uploads/2023/11/Adapting-to-climate-change-Progress-in-Scotland-Web.pdf. [64]

CCC (2023), *Adapting to Climate Change: Progress in Wales*, https://www.theccc.org.uk/publication/adapting-to-climate-change-progress-in-wales/. [67]

CCC (2023), *CCC Adaptation Monitoring Framework*, https://www.theccc.org.uk/publication/ccc-adaptation-monitoring-framework/?chapter=3-how-we-monitor-progress-on-preparing-for-climate-change#a-monitoring-maps. [45]

CCC (2023), *Progress in Adapting to Climate Change: 2023 report to Parliament*, https://www.theccc.org.uk/publication/progress-in-adapting-to-climate-change-2023-report-to-parliament/. [21]

CCC (2022), *Is Scotland Climate Ready? 2022 Report to Scottish Parliament*, https://www.theccc.org.uk/publication/is-scotland-climate-ready-2022-report-to-scottish-parliament/. [62]

CCC (2022), *Understanding Climate Risks to UK Infrastructure: Evaluation of the third round of the Adaptation Reporting Power*, https://www.theccc.org.uk/publication/understanding-climate-risks-to-uk-infrastructure-evaluation-of-the-third-round-of-the-adaptation-reporting-power/. [52]

CCC (2021), *Cross-sector-adaptation indicators*, https://www.theccc.org.uk/wp-content/uploads/2021/06/Cross-sector-adaptation-indicators.xlsx (accessed on 2022). [94]

CCC (2021), *Independent Assessment of UK Climate Risk*, https://www.theccc.org.uk/wp-content/uploads/2021/07/Independent-Assessment-of-UK-Climate-Risk-Advice-to-Govt-for-CCRA3-CCC.pdf. [44]

CCC (2021), *Joint Recommendations 2021 Report to Parliament*, https://www.theccc.org.uk/wp-content/uploads/2021/06/CCC-Joint-Recommendations-2021-Report-to-Parliament.pdf. [95]

CCC (2021), *Progress in Adapting to Climate Change: 2021 Report to Parliament*, Climate Change Committee, https://www.theccc.org.uk/publication/2021-progress-report-to-parliament/. [43]

CCC (2021), *Second National Adaptation Programme Monitoring Action Tracker (excel sheet)*, https://www.theccc.org.uk/wp-content/uploads/2021/06/CCC-Second-NAP-Monitoring-Action-Tracker.xlsx. [93]

CCC (2020), *Assessing Progress in Preparing for Climate Change in the UK*, https://www.theccc.org.uk/wp-content/uploads/2020/10/CCC-Insights-Briefing-7-Assessing-progress-preparing-for-climate-change.pdf. [41]

CCC (2019), *Final Assessment - The first Scottish Climate Change Adaptation Programme*, https://www.theccc.org.uk/publication/final-assessment-of-scotlands-first-climate-change-adaptation-programme/. [86]

CCC (2019), *Progress in Preparing for Climate Change*, https://www.theccc.org.uk/publication/progress-in-preparing-for-climate-change-2019-progress-report-to-parliament/. [47]

CCC (2017), *Adaptation Reporting Power: second round review*, https://www.theccc.org.uk/wp-content/uploads/2017/03/Adaptation-Reporting-Power-Second-round-review-Committee-on-Climate-Change-March-2017.pdf. [53]

CCC (2017), *Progress in Preparing for Climate Change*, https://www.theccc.org.uk/wp-content/uploads/2017/06/2017-Report-to-Parliament-Progress-in-preparing-for-climate-change.pdf. [46]

CCC (2016), *Scottish Climate Change Adaptation Programme: An independent assessment for the Scottish Parliament*, https://www.theccc.org.uk/wp-content/uploads/2016/09/Scottish-Climate-Change-Adaptation-Programme-An-independent-assessment-CCC-September-2016.pdf. [103]

Christiansen, L., G. Martinez and P. Naswa (2018), *Adaptation metrics: perspectives on measuring, aggregating and comparing adaptation results*, UNEP DTU Partnership, https://resilientcities2018.iclei.org/wp-content/uploads/UDP_Perspectives-Adaptation-Metrics-WEB.pdf. [89]

Climate NI (2021), *Climate Northern Ireland - Embedded Researcher Pitch*, https://www.ukclimateresilience.org/climate-northern-ireland-embedded-researcher-pitch/. [12]

Climate NI (2021), *NI Adapts: Planning Toolkit*, https://www.climatenorthernireland.org.uk/NIAdapts/. [35]

Climate NI (2021), *What we do*, https://www.climatenorthernireland.org.uk/aboutus/. [13]

Climate NI (2019), *Civil Society and Local Government Adapts: Supporting Document*, [69]
https://climatenorthernireland.org.uk/site/wp-content/uploads/2022/02/NICCAP-Civil-Society-and-Local-Government-Adapts.pdf.

ClimateXChange (2021), *Indicators and trends*, [91]
https://www.climatexchange.org.uk/research/indicators-and-trends/ (accessed on September 2021).

ClimateXChange (2021), *Who we are*, https://www.climatexchange.org.uk/. [15]

ClimateXChange (2016), *Climate Change in Scotland: Risks, Impacts and Actions*, [90]
https://www.climatexchange.org.uk/media/1372/cxc_adaptationguide_hyperlinks.pdf.

Covenant of Mayors (2021), *Plans & Actions*, https://www.covenantofmayors.eu/plans-and-actions/action-plans.html. [68]

DAERA NI (2022), *Northern Ireland Climate Change Adaptation Programme 2019-2024: Mid-programme Progress Review 2022*, https://www.daera-ni.gov.uk/publications/northern-ireland-climate-change-adaptation-programme-2019-2024-mid-programme-progress-review-2022. [65]

DAERA NI (2019), *Northern Ireland Climate Change Adaptation Programme 2019-2024*, Department of Agriculture, Environment and Rural Affairs (DAERA), https://www.daera-ni.gov.uk/sites/default/files/publications/daera/Northern%20Ireland%20Climate%20Change%20Adaptation%20Programme%202019-2024%20Final-Laid.PDF. [11]

Defra (2023), *Annex 1: Climate risks and opportunities: The 61 climate risks and opportunities, and planned actions to address them by government departments*, https://assets.publishing.service.gov.uk/media/65d47d9b0f4eb10064a981ae/NAP3_Annex_1_Climate_risks_and_opportunities.pdf. [4]

Defra (2023), *The Third National Adaptation Programme (NAP3) and the Fourth Strategy for Climate Adaptation Reporting*, Defra, https://assets.publishing.service.gov.uk/media/64ba74102059dc00125d27a7/The_Third_National_Adaptation_Programme.pdf. [8]

Defra (2022), *Collection: Climate change adaptation reporting: third round reports*, https://www.gov.uk/government/collections/climate-change-adaptation-reporting-third-round-reports. [57]

Defra (2021), *Outcome Indicator Framework for the 25 Year Environment Plan: 2021 Update*, https://assets.publishing.service.gov.uk/government/uploads/system/uploads/attachment_data/file/992970/Outcome_Indicator_Framework_for_the_25_Year_Environment_Plan_2021_Update.pdf. [97]

Defra (2021), *Policy paper: List of organisations reporting under adaptation reporting power: third round*, https://www.gov.uk/government/publications/climate-change-adaptation-reporting-third-round/list-of-organisations-reporting-under-adaptation-reporting-power-third-round. [56]

Defra (2019), *2019 UK report on Climate Change Adaptation Actions under Art. 15 of the European Union's Monitoring Mechanism Regulation (MMR)*, http://cdr.eionet.europa.eu/gb/eu/mmr/art15_adaptation/envxiwda/2019_UK_response_under_article_15_of_EU_MMR.pdf. [1]

Defra (2019), *Measuring Environmental Change: Outcome indicator framework for the 25 Year Environment Plan*, https://assets.publishing.service.gov.uk/government/uploads/system/uploads/attachment_data/file/925779/25-yep-indicators-2019.pdf. [96]

Defra (2018), *UK's National Adaptation Programme and the Third Strategy for Climate Adaptation Reporting 2018-2023*, UK Government, https://www.gov.uk/government/publications/climate-change-second-national-adaptation-programme-2018-to-2023. [42]

Defra (2017), *Collection: Climate change adaptation reporting: second round reports*, https://www.gov.uk/government/collections/climate-change-adaptation-reporting-second-round-reports#full-publication-update-history. [55]

Defra (2013), *Adapting to Climate Change: Ensuring Progress in Key Sectors: 2013 Strategy for exercising the Adaptation Reporting Power and list of priority reporting authorities*, https://assets.publishing.service.gov.uk/government/uploads/system/uploads/attachment_data/file/209875/pb13945-arp-climate-change-20130701.pdf. [54]

Defra (2012), *Adaptation Reporting Power: received reports*, https://www.gov.uk/government/publications/adaptation-reporting-power-received-reports. [50]

Defra (2012), *Evaluating the Risk Assessment of Adaptation Reports under the Adaptation Reporting Power: Final Summary*, https://assets.publishing.service.gov.uk/government/uploads/system/uploads/attachment_data/file/183427/annex-b-cranfield-uni-report-arp.pdf. [51]

Derry City & Strabane DC (2018), *Climate: Adapting to Change*, https://www.derrystrabane.com/climate. [34]

EAC and House of Commons (2010), *Adapting to Climate Change: Sixth Report of Session 2009-10*, https://publications.parliament.uk/pa/cm200910/cmselect/cmenvaud/113/113.pdf. [71]

EEA (2020), *Monitoring and Evaluation of National Adaptation Policies Throughout the Policy Cycle*, European Environment Agency, https://www.eea.europa.eu/publications/national-adaptation-policies. [58]

Fermanagh & Omagh District Council (2021), *Restore ReviveThrive Our Environment: Climate Change and Sustainable Development Action Plan*, https://www.fermanaghomagh.com/app/uploads/2021/10/Restore-Revive-Thrive-5.pdf. [37]

Ffoulkes, C. et al. (2021), *Research to review and update indicators of climate-related risks and actions in England*, Climate Change Committee, https://www.theccc.org.uk/publication/research-to-review-and-update-indicators-of-climate-related-risks-and-actions-in-england-adas/. [92]

GIZ (2017), *Climate Change Policy Brief: Synergies in monitoring the implementation of the Paris Agreement, the SDGs and the Sendai Framework*, https://www.adaptationcommunity.net/wp-content/uploads/2017/11/giz2017-en-cc-policy-brief-synergies-PA_SDG_SF.pdf. [77]

Greater London Authority (2018), *London Environment Strategy*, https://www.london.gov.uk/sites/default/files/london_environment_strategy_0.pdf. [32]

Hampshire Country Council (2021), *Climate Change Adaptation Tool*, https://www.youtube.com/watch?v=wp2vqALkmHo (accessed on 2022). [75]

Hampshire County Council (2021), *Climate Change Annual Report 2020 - 2021*, https://democracy.hants.gov.uk/documents/s85115/Climate%20Change%20Annual%20Report%202020-21%20-%20Appendix%202-2021-10-12-Cabinet.pdf. [74]

Hampshire County Council (2020), *Responding to Climate Change*, https://www.hants.gov.uk/landplanningandenvironment/environment/climatechange/whatarewedoing/climatechangestrategy. [73]

HM Treasury (2020), *Magenta Book 2020: Handling Complexity in Policy Evaluation*, https://assets.publishing.service.gov.uk/government/uploads/system/uploads/attachment_data/file/879437/Magenta_Book_supplementary_guide._Handling_Complexity_in_policy_evaluation.pdf. [48]

Klostermann, J. et al. (2015), "Towards a framework to assess, compare and develop monitoring and evaluation of climate change adaptation in Europe", *Mitigation and Adaptation Strategies for Global Change*, Vol. 23, pp. 187-209, https://doi.org/10.1007/s11027-015-9678-4. [87]

LSE (2021), *We've declared a climate emergency – now what?*, Blog, London School of Economics and Political Science, https://www.lse.ac.uk/research/research-for-the-world/sustainability/weve-declared-a-climate-emergency-now-what. [39]

Mäkinen, K. et al. (2018), *Indicators for adaptation to climate change at national level - Lessons from emerging practices in Europe*, ETC/CCA, https://doi.org/10.25424/CMCC/CLIMATE_CHANGE_ADAPTATION_INDICATORS_2018. [100]

Met Office (2023), *State of the UK Climate 2022*, https://www.metoffice.gov.uk/research/climate/maps-and-data/about/state-of-climate. [26]

Met Office (2021), *UK Climate Projections (UKCP)*, https://www.metoffice.gov.uk/research/approach/collaboration/ukcp/index (accessed on 2021). [27]

Moss, A. (2019), *A Monitoring and Evaluation Framework for the Second SCCAP*, ClimateXChange, https://www.climatexchange.org.uk/media/3913/cxc-a-monitoring-and-evaluation-framework-for-the-second-sccap.pdf. [63]

Neilson, R. et al. (2020), *Measuring the Vulnerability of Scottish Soils to a Changing Climate*, ClimateXChange, https://doi.org/10.7488/era/546. [101]

OECD (2021), *Discussions at the OECD event - measuring progress in implementing national adaptation policies*, https://www.oecd.org/environment/cc/climate-adaptation/Summary-record-Measuring-progress-in-implementing-national-adaptation-policies.pdf. [84]

OECD (2020), *Common Ground Between the Paris Agreement and the Sendai Framework: Climate Change Adaptation and Disaster Risk Reduction*, OECD Publishing, Paris, https://doi.org/10.1787/3edc8d09-en. [79]

OECD (2015), *National Climate Change Adaptation: Emerging Practices in Monitoring and Evaluation*, OECD Publishing, https://doi.org/10.1787/9789264229679-en. [105]

Orr, P. et al. (2020), *Measuring Recovery from Extreme Weather Events*, ClimateXChange, https://doi.org/10.7488/era/1240. [102]

OSR (2021), *Accessibility and coherence of UK climate change statistics*, Office for Statistics Regulation, https://osr.statisticsauthority.gov.uk/publication/accessibility-and-coherence-of-uk-climate-change-statistics/. [98]

Power, K. et al. (2018), *Adaptation Actions in Cities: What works?*, Committee on Climate Change, https://www.theccc.org.uk/wp-content/uploads/2018/11/Adaptation-actions-in-cities-what-works-final.pdf. [49]

PRA (2021), *Climate-related financial risk management and the role of capital requirements: Climate Change Adaptation Report 2021*, Bank of England, Prudential Regulation Authority, https://www.bankofengland.co.uk/-/media/boe/files/prudential-regulation/publication/2021/october/climate-change-adaptation-report-2021.pdf?la=en&hash=FF4A0C618471462E10BC704D4AA58727EC8F8720. [7]

Price-Kelly, H. et al. (2015), *Developing National Adaptation Monitoring and Evaluation Systems: A guidebook*, German Federal Ministry for Economic Cooperation and Development, https://www.adaptationcommunity.net/download/uploads/giz2015_Developing_national_adaptation_M&E_systems_-_A_guidebook.pdf. [88]

Scottish Government (2021), *Scotland's Contribution to the Paris Agreement – an indicative NDC*, https://www.gov.scot/binaries/content/documents/govscot/publications/strategy-plan/2021/07/scotlands-contribution-paris-agreement-indicative-ndc/documents/scotlands-contribution-paris-agreement-indicative-ndc-july-2021/scotlands-contribution-paris-agreeme. [82]

Scottish Government (2021), *Second Annual Progress Report on Climate Ready Scotland: Scotland's Climate Change Adaptation Programme 2019 to 2024*, Energy and Climate Change Directorate, https://www.gov.scot/publications/scottish-climate-change-adaptation-programme-progress-report-2021/. [3]

Scottish Government (2019), *Climate Ready Scotland: Second Scottish Climate Change Adaptation Programme 2019-2024*, Energy and Climate Change Directorate, https://www.gov.scot/publications/climate-ready-scotland-second-scottish-climate-change-adaptation-programme-2019-2024/documents/. [30]

South East Climate Alliance (2021), *Embedding Climate Change in Decision-making: The Hampshire Toolbox*, https://seclimatealliance.uk/hampshire_toolbox/. [76]

Street, R., V. Hayman and T. Wilkins (2017), *Understanding the value of the Adaptation Reporting Power process to the reporting organisations involved*, Report prepared for Defra by the ARCC network, https://www.arcc-network.org.uk/wp-content/pdfs/ARP-report-for-Defra-04-2017.pdf. [59]

Street, R. and S. Jude (2019), "Enhancing the value of adaptation reporting as a driver for action: lessons from the UK", *Climate Policy*, Vol. 19/10. [60]

TalX (2021), *Transboundary Adaptation Learning Exchange*, https://talx.ie/. [17]

UK Government (2021), *Climate change statistics*, https://climate-change.data.gov.uk/. [99]

UK Government (2021), *Environment Act 2021*, https://www.legislation.gov.uk/ukpga/2021/30/contents/enacted. [22]

UK Government (2021), *Government boosts UK resilience against climate change*, https://www.gov.uk/government/news/government-boosts-uk-resilience-against-climate-change. [29]

UK Government (2021), *Greening Finance: A Roadmap to Sustainable Investing*, https://assets.publishing.service.gov.uk/government/uploads/system/uploads/attachment_data/file/1031805/CCS0821102722-006_Green_Finance_Paper_2021_v6_Web_Accessible.pdf. [5]

UK Government (2021), *United Kingdom Adaptation Communication Update 2021*, https://unfccc.int/sites/default/files/resource/United%20Kingdom%20Update%20to%20the%20Adaptation%20Communication.pdf. [20]

UK Government (2020), *The Climate Change (Duties of Public Bodies: Reporting Requirements) (Scotland) Amendment Order 2020*, https://www.legislation.gov.uk/ssi/2020/281/made?view=plain. [61]

UK Government (2020), *United Kingdom of Great Britain and Northern Ireland's Adaptation Communication to the United Nations Framework Convention on Climate Change*, https://unfccc.int/sites/default/files/resource/UK_adcom.pdf. [2]

UK Government (2020), *United Kingdom of Great Britain and Northern Ireland's Nationally Determined Contribution*, https://www4.unfccc.int/sites/ndcstaging/PublishedDocuments/United%20Kingdom%20of%20Great%20Britain%20and%20Northern%20Ireland%20First/UK%20Nationally%20Determined%20Contribution.pdf. [19]

UK Government (2019), *Green Finance Strategy: Transforming Finance for a Greener Future*, https://assets.publishing.service.gov.uk/government/uploads/system/uploads/attachment_data/file/820284/190716_BEIS_Green_Finance_Strategy_Accessible_Final.pdf. [6]

UK Government (2016), *Remit & Terms of Reference of the Local Adaptation*, https://www.adeptnet.org.uk/system/files/documents/Local%20Adaptation%20Advisory%20Panel_Terms%20of%20Reference.pdf. [9]

UK Government (2013), *Climate Change Adaptation: Information for local authorities*, https://www.gov.uk/guidance/climate-change-adaptation-information-for-local-authorities. [72]

UK Government (2010), *NI 188 - Planning to adapt to climate change*, https://data.gov.uk/dataset/172a4386-b95f-469e-bad5-c4f9a5668afe/ni-188-planning-to-adapt-to-climate-change. [70]

UK Government (2009), *Climate Change (Scotland) Act 2009*, https://www.legislation.gov.uk/asp/2009/12/contents. [40]

UK Parliament (2008), *Climate Change Act 2008*, https://www.legislation.gov.uk/ukpga/2008/27/data.pdf. [18]

UKRP (2021), *The UK Climate Resilience Programme*, https://www.ukclimateresilience.org/. [28]

UNDRR (2021), *Measuring Implementation of the Sendai Framework*, https://sendaimonitor.undrr.org/. [83]

UNFCCC (2017), *United Kingdom. Biennial Reports (BR). BR 3. National Communication (NC). NC 7.*, https://unfccc.int/documents/198292. [81]

UNFCCC (2012), *The Rio Conventions: Action on Adaptation*, https://unfccc.int/resource/docs/publications/rio_20_adaptation_brochure.pdf. [78]

Welsh Government (2022), *Prosperity for All: A climate conscious Wales: Progress report 2022*, https://www.gov.wales/sites/default/files/publications/2022-12/prosperity-for-all-a-climate-conscious-wales-progress-report.pdf. [66]

Welsh Government (2020), *Prosperity for all: A Climate Conscious Wales: Monitoring and evaluation framework*, https://gov.wales/prosperity-all-climate-conscious-wales-monitoring-and-evaluation-framework. [16]

Welsh Government (2019), *Prosperity for All: A Climate Conscious Wales*, https://gov.wales/sites/default/files/publications/2019-11/prosperity-for-all-a-climate-conscious-wales_0.pdf. [31]

Welsh Government (2016), *Overview of the Environment (Wales) Act*, https://gov.wales/sites/default/files/publications/2019-05/environment-wales-act-2016-overview.pdf. [24]

Welsh Government (2015), *Well-being of Future Generations (Wales) Act 2015*, https://www.legislation.gov.uk/anaw/2015/2/contents. [23]

Welsh Government (2013), *Welsh Government Policy Statement: Preparing for a changing climate*, https://gov.wales/sites/default/files/publications/2019-04/preparing-for-a-changing-climate-policy-statement.pdf. [104]

Annex 2.A. Key policies and documents

Table 1.A1. Key adaptation-related policies and documents

	UK/ England and UK reserved matters	Wales	Northern Ireland	Scotland
National Adaptation Strategies (legislation)	Climate Change Act 2008 Environment Act 2021	Well-being of Future Generations Act (2015) Environment (Wales) Act 2016	Section 60 of the UK Climate Change Act 2008 Climate Change (No. 2) Bill	Climate Change (Scotland) Act 2009
National Adaptation Plans	First Second National Adaptation Programme (2018 to 2023) The Third National Adaptation programme (NAP3)	Adaptation Delivery Plan (2010) Prosperity for All: A Climate Conscious Wales (2019)	Northern Ireland Climate Change Adaptation Programme (2014) Northern Ireland Climate Change Adaptation Programme 2019-2024	First 2014 SCCAP 2019 Scottish Climate Change Adaptation Programme Consultation on Second Programme
Impacts, vulnerability and adaptation assessment	UK CCRA2 2017 UK CCRA3 2021	National Summary for Wales	National Summary for Northern Ireland	National Summary for Scotland
CCC reviews and progress reports	2015 CCC Progress Report 2017 CCC Progress Report 2019 CCC Progress Report 2021 CCC Progress Report 2023 CCC Progress Report	Adapting to climate change: Progress in Wales 2023	Northern Ireland Climate Change Adaptation Programme 2019-2024: Mid-Programme Progress Review 2022 Adapting to climate change: Progress in Northern Ireland 2023	ASC's first independent assessment of the first SCCAP (2016) Final assessment of the first SCCAP (2019) Adapting to climate change: Progress in Scotland 2023
Government progress reports & government response	Government response to the CCC 2021 Government response to the CCC 2019 Government response to CCC 2017 Government response to the CCC 2015		NICCAP2 (including the review of NICCAP1)	SCCAP2 : First annual progress report 2020 SCCAP1 : Fifth annual progress report 2019 Fourth annual progress report 2018
Monitoring, indicators and methodologies		Climate Change Adaptation Plan for Wales: Monitoring and Evaluation Framework (2019)	NICCAP2 subject to a mid-programme review and an end of programme evaluation.	ClimateXChange M&E

Notes

[1] Adaptation policy in the UK is a devolved matter. The UK Parliament has transferred a range of powers to the Scottish Parliament, National Assembly for Wales and the Northern Ireland Assembly and Executive. Matters that remain the responsibility of the UK Parliament are referred to as "reserved matters", and include national security and defence, insurance, aspects of the infrastructure/energy network, and food/energy supply.

[2] The UK National Adaptation Programme covers England and some reserved matters.

[3] Such as the Environment Agency and Natural England, an executive non-departmental body.

[4] Some risks are owned by private sector bodies (e.g. water companies).

[5] Local government systems are different in each of the four devolved administrations, and can be responsible for a range of community services, including environmental matters, firefighting, housing, planning, etc.

[6] Adaptation policy is a devolved matter in the UK.

[7] Article 7 of the Paris Agreement requires parties to submit and update periodically an adaptation communication, which may include information on its priorities, implementation and support needs, plans and actions. The UK submitted its first adaptation communication in December 2020 and updated it in October 2021.

[8] 2021 UK Climate Risk Independent Assessment (CRIA) for CCRA3 (previously called the Evidence Report for CCRA2 in 2017).

[9] The first evidence report (2012) was prepared by Defra, while the subsequent reports (2017, 2021) were independently prepared by the Adaptation Committee.

3. Measuring progress in adapting to a changing climate: the case of Chile

This chapter presents the results of the country case study of Chile. It documents the policy and institutional context for adaptation in Chile and discusses the efforts, achievements, and remaining gaps for measuring progress on adaptation. It also reviews Chile's adaptation indicator frameworks.

3.1. Summary and key findings

For over a decade now, Chile has developed robust adaptation policies, recently underpinned by its 2022 Climate Change Law. Much of the experience gained helped establishing these elements in the law and, as a result, a sophisticated legal and institutional framework that guides adaptation efforts across national, regional and local levels. Under this framework, Chile improved its adaptation measurement framework to assess progress in the implementation of national, sub-national and sectoral adaptation plans. The current development of Chile's second National Adaptation Plan aims to address gaps in Chile's understanding of progress and effectiveness in implementing adaptation policies.

The measurement framework is designed to better understand sectoral and sub-national adaptation progress. It is based on a system of annual and biennial reporting by the Ministry of Environment that collects data from institutions responsible for implementing adaptation measures. The annual reviews focus on the implementation status of adaptation actions, measuring the extent to which these actions have been executed relative to their planned objectives and the financial resources invested. The biennial Climate Change Action Reports provide an overview of adaptation progress, covering the Long-Term Strategy, the Nationally Determined Contributions, and sectoral as well as regional plans. Under the Climate Change Law, Chile has institutionalised a series of feedback mechanisms designed to uphold transparency and accountability across implementing agencies and ensure that findings guide the strategic direction of future adaptation efforts. Chile has also developed a roadmap setting out the use of a theory of change approach and the development of further indicators to strengthen its measurement framework and to better understand how the actions that are implemented enable to achieve policy outcomes.

To support its adaptation measurement efforts, Chile has created information systems that communicate climate risk assessment information and that guide the prioritisation of adaptation measures. The cornerstone of this is the Climate Risk Atlas (ARClim), through which Chile presents current and projected climate threats according to the worst-case scenario of the IPCC and assesses 80 current and projected climate risks and impacts at communal level. The platform is being expanded to become a comprehensive adaptation information system covering indicators and additional information on sub-national and sectoral adaptation progress. Chile is looking to integrate the adaptation platform with further information systems on climate change research and citizen participation to facilitate easy and comprehensive access to climate information, thereby enhancing informed decision making. Driven by the Climate Change Law, which sets ambitions to further develop sub-national indicators, several regions in Chile are including and assessing sub-national progress indicators in their regional adaptation plans. The platform is publicly available, enabling stakeholders to assess risks based on their exposure and vulnerability and provides data that can be used, among other applications, to meet the current obligation to incorporate the evaluation of climate risks in the projects presented to the Environmental Impact Assessment and the Strategic Environmental Assessment.

Adaptation-related indicators have been included to differing extents in Chile's adaptation policies. Currently, Chile assesses implementation by indicating the percentage level of achievement of each measure in the Climate Change Action Plan. As part of ARClim, Chile has established so-called impact indicators (such as the impact of temperature rise on transmission lines or productivity change in crops). Furthermore, Chile is looking to build a comprehensive set of cross-sector climate risks to better understand the interconnection between sectors and to avoid maladaptation. Chile is planning to expand indicator coverage in its second National Adaptation Plan, with a view to assessing progress across sectors and different levels of government.

3.2. Chile's adaptation institutional and policy context

3.2.1. Chile's Climate Change Framework Law, the Long-term Strategy and the NDC

In 2022, Chile adopted the Climate Change Framework Law (Law 21.455) (the Climate Change Law), which establishes the framework for adaptation policies, institutional arrangements, as well as information systems related to climate change at the national, regional and local levels. In addition, the Long-Term Strategy sets out directions for adaptation and mitigation over a 30-year horizon (Government of Chile, 2021[1]). It was developed through a multi-stakeholder, multi-level and transparent participatory process to build an inclusive and representative vision. The Long-Term Strategy acknowledges that the adaptation process is an iterative cycle. It contains long-term objectives and goals for 11 of the 12 adaptation sectors in the Climate Change Law, which were developed by the sectors themselves (Table 3.1). The Climate Change Law stipulates that the Long-Term Strategy will be updated every ten years. The Climate Change Law also states that the milestones and intermediate targets for achieving Chile's long-term objectives will be set out in the Nationally Determined Contribution (NDC). Chile presented its updated NDC in 2020, which included an adaptation component of developing, updating and implementing, as appropriate, sectoral plans and regional action plans. The NDC also committed to developing an adaptation monitoring and reporting system (Government of Chile, 2020[2]).

The Climate Change Framework Law outlines clear obligations and sets deadlines for the development and updating of policies and tools for the 12 priority sectors, 16 administrative regions, and 346 municipalities. It also creates the enabling conditions for a more sustainable and robust adaptation measurement system. It notably requires the Long-Term Strategy to include criteria for monitoring, reporting, and verifying the compliance of actions with the goals and measures, and to ensure transparency in the monitoring, quality and consistency of the data reported.

3.2.2. Climate plans, NAPs and sectoral plans

At the national level, the first climate policy cycle started with the National Climate Change Action Plan I (2008-12) (hereafter referred to as CC Action Plan I), which was structured around 3 pillars of action: mitigation, adaptation, and capacity building. In terms of adaptation, it established the commitment to develop a National Adaptation Plan (NAP) and 7 sectoral plans. In response to this, the first milestone was the publication of the adaptation plan in 2014. The NAP's established new institutional arrangements, now recognised by the law (the Technical Inter-Ministerial Committee on Climate Change at a national level and the Regional Climate Change Committees, at a regional level) and called for the elaboration and implementation of the sectoral plans and the enhancement of the country's capacities to prepare for climate risks.

A mid-term evaluation of the CC Action Plan I in 2011 and an external evaluation (built on expert consultations) in 2015 contributed to the development of the CC Action Plan II (2017-22). The CC Action Plan II aimed to strengthen the foundations laid by the NAP 2014, regarding the assessment of vulnerability and the implementation of actions, and expanded to nine the number of sectoral plans (Table 3.1). The CC Action Plan II also included measures to develop metrics and progress indicators to assess the effectiveness of adaptation processes, as well as to establish a reporting system for adaptation. However, capacity and resource limitations hindered the achievement of this objective. The Climate Change Framework Law does not include the CC Action Plan as part of its climate change management instruments, making this policy obsolete.

A second National Adaptation Plan is currently being developed, expected for 2024, with the aim to address the gaps and needs that were identified during an external evaluation of the first NAP carried out in 2021. These include the monitoring, reporting, and evaluation system. It is planned to develop a more user-friendly, transparent, and robust measurement system, to be integrated into the information systems established by the Climate Change Law (Section 3.4).

In addition, the Climate Change Law requires the development of a series of sectoral and sub-national adaptation plans within the next three years, as follows:

- Sectoral Adaptation Plans: These should be in line with the Long-Term Strategy, be developed by the respective sectoral ministries and updated every five years. The plans should assess the sector's climate risks and impacts, outline measures, identify barriers and spell out indicators.
- Climate Change Regional Action Plans: The Climate Change Law requires the Regional Climate Change Committee to develop plans for the 16 administrative regions. Covering mitigation, adaptation and means of implementation, they need to be aligned with the Long-Term Strategy, the sectoral plans for mitigation and adaptation, communal plans for mitigation and adaptation, as well as strategic water resource plans for basins, where they exist (there are also 101 main water basins considered in different plans related to climate change adaptation).
- Climate Change Communal Action Plans: The Climate Change Law requires municipalities to develop plans for all 346 communes. They need to outline vulnerability and potential impacts of climate change, mitigation and adaptation measures, as well as measures related to means of implementation and indicators.

The Climate Change Law further instructs national policy documents to be developed in line with Chile's international commitments and encourages the mainstreaming of adaptation within policies and instruments in land-use planning, disaster risk management and environmental impact assessments.

Table 3.1. Overview of adaptation policies in Chile

	Name and year of adoption
National Climate Adaptation Policies	2008: National Climate Change Action Plan I (2008-12) covering mitigation and adaptation 2014: First National Adaptation Plan 2017: National Climate Change Action Plan II (2017-22)* Under preparation: Second National Adaptation Plan
Sectoral Adaptation Plans**	2013: Agricultural and livestock sector 2014: Biodiversity 2015: Fisheries and aquaculture 2016: Health 2017: Infrastructure (focus on public infrastructure) 2018: Cities; Energy 2019: Tourism All sectoral plans undergoing updating processes to comply with the law Under development: Coastal zones, mining, transport and water resources***
Climate Change Regional Action Plans	Adopted: Atacama, O´Higgins, Los Ríos, Los Lagos **** Under development: Arica y Parinacota, Tarapacá, Antofagasta, Coquimbo, Valparaíso, Metropolitan Maule, Ñuble, Biobío, Araucanía, Aysén, and Magallanes
Climate Change Communal Action Plans	The communal plans must be developed within a period of three years of the publication of the Climate Change Law, i.e. by June 2025.

Note: * Now obsolete with the adoption of the Climate Change Law. ** Twelve sectors are included in the Climate Change Law. *** The sectoral plan on water resources was delayed due to some complexities, primarily institutional co-ordination. **** as of May 2024.
Source: (Ministry of Environment of Chile, 2014[3]); (Ministry of Environment of Chile, 2020[4]); (Ministry of Environment of Chile, 2008[5]).

3.2.3. Institutional arrangements

The Climate Change Law defines the responsibilities of the various actors and institutionalises national and sub-national co-ordination bodies. Figure 3.1 presents the institutional arrangements at the national and regional levels.

At the national level, the Ministry of Environment oversees the development and implementation of environmental and climate policies, and prepares, reviews and updates the Long-Term Strategy and the NDC. It co-ordinates the adaptation policy process in close collaboration with the sectoral ministries, supported by an inter-sectoral and multi-level governance body. The Ministry of Environment ensures the coherence of the different instruments at sectoral, national and regional levels. It also ensures compliance with international conventions on climate change (the Ministry of Foreign Affairs is Chile's National Focal Point to the UNFCCC). In terms of adaptation measurement, the Ministry of Environment centralises information on progress on the sectoral plans and manages the Climate Adaptation Platform.

The Climate Change Law defines the following national co-ordination bodies and functions:

- Technical Inter-Ministerial Committee on Climate Change (ETICC): has the main responsibility for adaptation measurement. It is a technical body composed of representatives of public sector institutions. The ETICC collaborates with the Ministry of Environment on the design, development, implementation, monitoring and updating of climate change policies by providing analysis for actions and measures. It also provides technical assistance to other national administration bodies and public services.
- Council of Ministers for Sustainability and Climate Change:[1] a political body that guides the country's national climate agenda. It takes decision on the Long-Term Strategy, NDC, National Adaptation Plan and the sectoral mitigation and adaptation plans, and ensures coherence among them. The council is chaired by the Minister of the Environment and made up of the sectoral ministers.[2]
- Scientific Advisory Committee for Climate Change (SACCC): a scientific body that provides advice to the Ministry of Environment based on scientific knowledge to design, implement and update climate change management instruments. The Secretary of the SACCC is the Ministry of Science, Technology, Knowledge, and Innovation.
- National Council for Sustainability and Climate Change: a multi-sectoral body that issues opinions on climate management instruments, their progress, and the effects of their implementation. The council is made up of two scientists, two representatives of environmental NGOs, two representatives of independent academic centres in environmental matters, two business representatives, two workers' representatives, one representative of the President of the Republic, and two representatives of youth organisations for environmental protection.

At both the national and regional levels, citizen participation plays a key role in the development of climate policy. The development of all instruments, policies, plans and programmes involves robust participation mechanisms that reduce uncertainty while promoting public consensus. A period of citizen participation and public consultation is a requirement for the approval of regional plans, as well as the opinion of the Regional Consultative Council of the Ministry of the Environment. The scientific work involves an exchange with the knowledge of the communities and their territories, as well as with indigenous people, providing a more comprehensive vision of progress in adaptation to climate change. A growing group of scientists supports various processes, including capacity building.

Including the private sector and civil society in adaptation measurement is a key challenge. It notably requires improving capacities and technologies, while ensuring transparency helps strengthen ownership of the information collected. ARClim is a tool that was designed for adaptation measurement purposes, as well as for making climate information more accessible to the private sector and citizens. Public-private information integration, increasing citizen science (i.e. participatory or voluntary monitoring) and environmental education are desirable goals for adaptation progress that have been included as part of the goals for the NAP updating.

Figure 3.1. Institutional arrangements for climate change in Chile

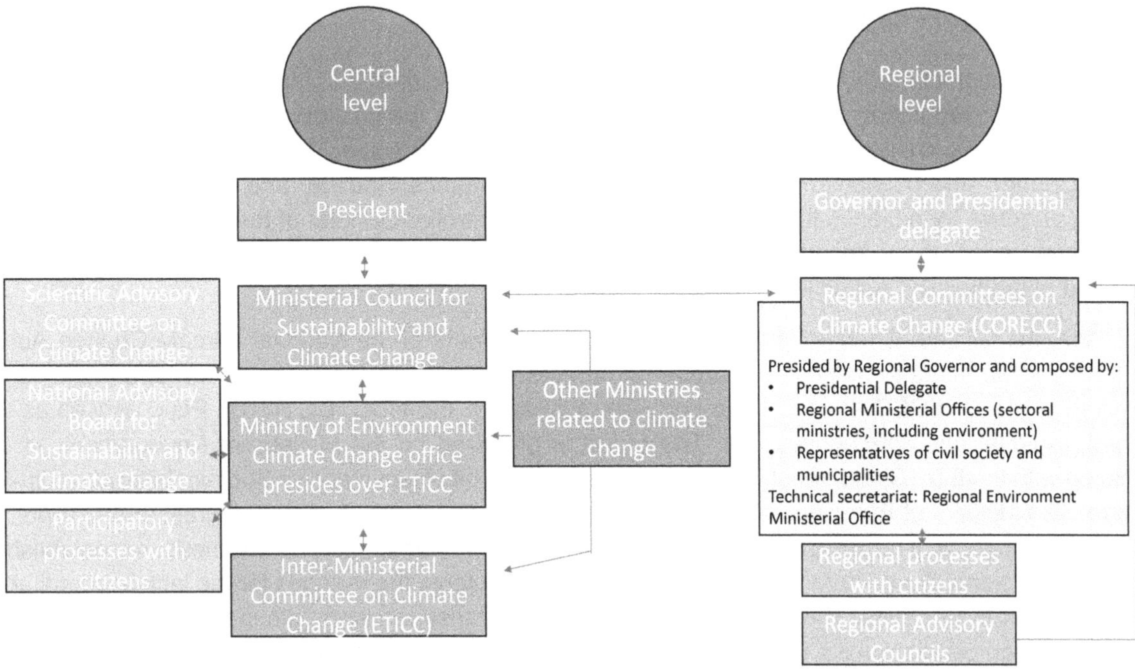

The Climate Change Law defines the following sub-national co-ordination bodies and their functions:

- Regional Committees: These are composed of the Regional Governor, who chairs the committee; the Regional Presidential Delegate and the sectoral Regional Secretaries; and representatives of the civil society-municipalities. Members of the Regional Council and the Environmental Advisory Councils may participate, with the right to speak. The Regional Committee is responsible for preparing the regional plans, thus participating directly in monitoring, reporting and verification, and evaluation. They must also define the objectives and instruments for climate change at the regional and local level, in line with the Long-Term Strategy, the sectoral mitigation and adaptation plans, communal mitigation and adaptation plans, and strategic plans for water resources. The Regional Committee also identifies financing sources and other means of implementation.
- Regional Governor and Regional Presidential Delegates: these are political authorities in every administrative region. The regional plans are approved by resolution of the Regional Presidential Delegate with the prior favourable agreement of the Regional Government. The Regional Ministerial Secretaries are co-ordinated by the Regional Presidential Delegate, while the Regional Government responds to the Regional Governor.
- Ministerial Regional Offices: these represent the sectoral ministries at the sub-national level. They carry out the sectoral management of climate change in co-ordination with the regional committee and in line with the regional plans.
- Municipalities: According to the Climate Change Law, local governments shall prepare Communal Plans, in line with the regional plans, and can participate in the Regional Committee individually, or collectively through municipal associations. The municipalities can establish local climate action roundtables, with representatives of civil society and with a focus on vulnerable groups, to propose, prioritise, and implement climate change management actions, in co-ordination with the Regional Committee.
- Regional Advisory Councils: these multi-sectoral bodies issue opinion and make proposals on climate management instruments, their progress, and the effects of their implementation.

3.3. Measuring progress in implementing adaptation policies

3.3.1. Legal and policy frameworks

The implementation of the NAP, CC Action Plans and sectoral adaptation plans is monitored annually by the Ministry of Environment, based on information collected from the institutions responsible. The results of this process are compiled in a report that is presented to the Council of Ministers for Sustainability and Climate Change and published on the Ministry of Environment's website, and thereby contributes to informing priorities for action in the next policy cycle. The Controller General of the Republic of Chile also audits compliance with the mandates of the different plans. An additional external review was developed at the end of the first CC Action Plan cycle.

In addition, the Climate Change Law mandates the development of the National Climate Change Action Report every two years to monitor and report on progress, in line with the Biennial Transparency Report submitted to the UNFCCC. It covers the Long-Term Strategy, the NDC, CC Action Plan, as well as the sectoral, regional and communal plans. The report is prepared by the Ministry of Environment, in co-ordination with the ETICC, and must be approved by the Council of Ministers for Sustainability and Climate Change. The Ministry of Environment must also provide a public account of the progress of the report to the Chilean Congress. If the action report reveals delays in the implementation of the measures established in the sectoral plans, the sectoral ministers responsible must clarify the reasons for the lack of compliance to the Chamber of Deputies. The Chamber of Deputies plays a supervisory role in the governance of the action report and can determine the political responsibilities of the sectoral authorities.

The Long-Term Strategy aims to implement a measurement system as part of the forthcoming NAP. Covering national and sectoral adaptation measures, it will aim to standardise processes and indicators to make information comparable and reliable, to enhance synergies among the reports of different policies, and avoid duplication of work. The measurement system, which will be publicly accessible, will also aim to facilitate reporting on national and territorial adaptation progress to the UNFCCC, as well as provide access to information on climate change to facilitate citizens' participation. In practice, however, the operationalisation of the adaptation measurement system requires the allocation of substantial financial and human resources to meet the deadlines established in the law. The Ministry of Environment, in collaboration with the responsible sectors, is working to define how the monitoring of the Long-Term Strategy goals and objectives, which includes a section on indicators, will be conducted.

3.3.2. Approaches for measuring progress on adaptation

Assessing the effectiveness of reducing climate risks is complex: it requires political commitment, conceptual and empirical agreement (e.g. on the variables to measure that help assess the result), and assigning responsibility in multi-sectoral contexts. In Chile, the institutions responsible for implementing adaptation measures carry out an assessment of progress that covers implementation (e.g. whether a measure been rolled out), the financial resources invested and their sources, and an overall "percentage progress" (e.g. what share of the total planned activities have been implemented, based on progress towards achieving goals or completing actions). Currently, this "percentage progress" is a value based on judgement by experts from the relevant institutions.

The external evaluation of the 2014 NAP concluded that the level of implementation of all cross-cutting measures (excluding measures in sectoral adaptation plans) had reached, on average, 72% of completion[3] since its launch (Ministry of Environment of Chile, 2021[6]). The evaluation also attempted to understand the level of effectiveness using a combination of quantitative and qualitative methods.[4] The evaluation was based on qualitative data obtained through interviews and workshops with the ETICC, where 24 questions were asked to assess the cross-cutting measures of the NAP and rationale for each response was sought. Examples of questions asked include:

- How do the actions relate to the desired objective? Has the NAP been consistent with other national policies and plans? Does the measure include the necessary elements for proper monitoring and follow-up in its design? etc.

Additional analysis was based on binary responses (Yes/No responses), which helped identify factors with the highest correlation with the level of progress of the measures, i.e., those factors whose presence (Yes response) correlates with greater progress on the measures, and their absence (No response) with less progress.

3.3.3. Monitoring and Evaluation Roadmap (2022-2024)

Findings of a study completed in 2022 showed that the evaluation system could be strengthened to better understand the effectiveness of adaptation actions (CCG UC, 2022[7]). The study presented a roadmap for improving the measurement framework (Box 3.1).

One of the key limitations addressed by the roadmap was the lack of a theory of change approach to justify the choice of measures. This approach determines how implemented actions lead to short-term outcomes, and in turn to long-term impacts. The need to generate a theory of change with the various sectoral actors is one of the challenges for the next update of the NAP, and is one of the pillars of the roadmap. Furthermore, the roadmap sets out to develop qualitative indicators; integrated risk assessments,[5] the development of 20 new climate risk indices, and the improvement of existing ones.

Box 3.1. A roadmap to strengthen Chile's adaptation measurement framework

In 2022, Chile developed the Monitoring and Evaluation Roadmap (2022-2024), which is yet to be implemented, to strengthen the country's adaptation measurement framework. It recommended strengthening and rolling out:

- The conceptual framework for monitoring and evaluating policies: the roadmap presented actions such as agreeing on definitions, standards and criteria for adaptation indicators; and considering international and national frameworks to facilitate the establishment of a comprehensive vision for adaptation.
- The strategic work plan for adaptation indicators: the roadmap presented actions to support sectoral needs for developing indicators and address conceptual challenges in attributing policies to outcomes. It also covered the need for a theory of change; cross-sectoral indicators; ways to illustrate the interconnectedness of climate risks; qualitative indicators; improved adaptive capacity indicators; gender indicators; mechanisms for continuous improvement; new impact chains; and mechanisms for collecting relevant data and information.
- Institutional arrangements and governance: The roadmap listed actions to improve the design of the system and the involvement of various stakeholders, including to strengthen their engagement and validation.
- Operationalising the monitoring and evaluation system: the roadmap identified technological and capacity-building requirements to improve transparency and facilitate feedback from information platform users.

Source: (CCG UC, 2022[7]), Informe Final "Desarrollo de indicadores para el monitoreo y evaluación del progreso de la adaptación al cambio climático a nivel nacional" [Final Report "Development of indicators for monitoring and evaluating the progress of adaptation to climate change at the national level"].

3.4. Information systems

Several articles of the Climate Change Law refer to the establishment of information systems for both mitigation and adaptation, in particular the need to generate information for developing indicators to characterise and assess vulnerability and the risks and effectiveness of the measures in sectoral adaptation plans. The Climate Change Law mandates the creation of several information-sharing platforms.

A climate adaptation platform is being developed to serve as a national information system for adaptation, including vulnerability and climate risk maps, and current and future climate projections. The platform aims to support the design of public policies, the implementation of measures and their evaluation, and improve public knowledge on climate risks. This platform will be managed by the Ministry of Environment with the support of the Ministry of Science, Technology, Knowledge, and Innovation. Publicly available, the platform provides data that can be used, among other applications, to meet the current obligation to incorporate the evaluation of climate risks in the projects presented to the Environmental Impact Assessment and the Strategic Environmental Assessment.

The climate adaptation platform will be based on the existing Climate Risk Atlas platform (ARClim) (Box 3.2), which presents indicators and methodologies to define climate risk indices. Most of these indices were calculated considering the climate risk for all 346 communes (Figure 3.2). It is being refined to improve indicators and methodologies to assess climate risks and will be continuously updated to also include information on the regional and communal plans.[6]

Figure 3.2. Snapshot from ARClim's climate risk maps in Chile

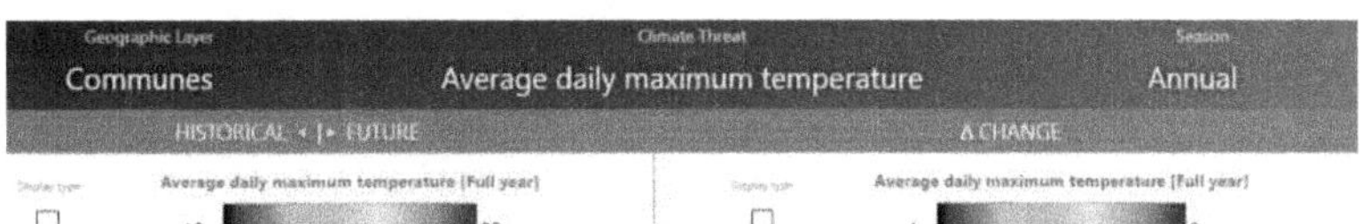

Note: ARCLim is a web-based platform with dynamic visualization of the main risks in Chile.
Source: (Ministry of Environment of Chile, 2024[8]), *Climate Risk Atlas*, https://arclim.mma.gob.cl/.

In addition, a climate change scientific repository will be set up to collect scientific research related to climate change, managed by the Ministry of Science, Technology, Knowledge, and Innovation. A national system of access to information on climate change and citizen participation is also planned to promote and facilitate citizen participation in the preparation, updating and monitoring of climate change management instruments. This system will include the information platform and repository mentioned above and other information systems related to mitigation.

To make better use of the existing information, such as the indicators included in ARClim, it is essential to increase their dissemination and the technical and human capacities to deal with climate risk information at different scales, especially at the local level. The integration of the various existing information sources is also a growing challenge. This requires, among other things, increasingly co-ordinated work on the multiple platforms with existing socio-environmental information and institutional co-ordination.

Box 3.2. Chile's Climate Risk Atlas (ARClim)

The Climate Risk Atlas (ARClim) is a national climate risk assessment platform that contains climate projections with a spatial resolution of 5km and information on hazard, exposure, vulnerability and risk from climate change at the communal level. The climate hazard explorer provides downloadable gridded data for all of continental Chile. Climate hazard indices were developed from General Circulation Models and downscaled with meteorological stations data to replicate the climate system and project future climate. Climate simulations were initially based on the CMIP5 initiative of the Fifth Assessment Report (AR5) of the Working Group II of the Intergovernmental Panel on Climate Change (WGII-IPCC) and were recently updated based on the Sixth Assessment Report (AR6). Hazards consider climate change between the historical (1980-2010) and future (2035-2065) periods, under a pessimistic greenhouse gas emissions scenario or *Shared Socioeconomic Pathway* based on fossil fuel development (SSP5-8.5). ARClim identifies 62 distinct climate hazards across thematic areas encompassing heat, cold, precipitation (separated into rain and snow), wind, humidity, and insolation.

ARClim's climate risk indices were developed following the guidelines of the AR5 by sectoral actors and the scientific community. Climate risk assessments are conducted individually for different impact chains across key social, environmental and productive sectors or systems, by considering hazard, exposure and vulnerability factors. Such assessments result in risk indices that can be interpreted as the potential magnitude of damage in the face of changing climatic conditions. ARClim estimates risk for 80 impact chains and 12 sectors at the local scale. These assessments helped prioritise adaptation actions to reduce exposure and vulnerability. Following the development of ARClim, the Global Change Centre project built new impact indicators and improved existing ones to close gaps related to adaptive capacity indices. Other climate risk assessments have focused on gender in mining, fisheries, and agriculture.

Sectoral impact assessments have been used as a basis for developing climate policies. In turn, the development of climate change adaptation instruments has allowed the creation of new risk assessments that have provided ARClim with updated impact chains, both at the sectoral and regional levels. While this dynamic and close relationship between science-based knowledge and decision-making in sectoral and regional adaptation is one of ARClim's main strengths, it also entails certain challenges. Ensuring a regular update of studies and continuous generation of useful and timely indicators is crucial to maintain a close alignment between risk assessments and policy priorities and objectives. Moreover, the ongoing process exchanging information between science and policy-making requires the establishment of a robust management system for updating and continually ensuring the quality of the platform's information.

Note: The Climate Risk Atlas (ARClim) project was funded by the Deutsche Gesellschaft für Internationale Zusammenarbeit (GIZ); co-ordinated by the Ministry of Environment and built through multidisciplinary work between the Centre for Climate and Resilience Research (CR2), the Catholic University's Global Change Centre (CCG), and Meteodata.
Sourc (Ministry of Environment of Chile, 2024[8]) e: (CR2, 2015[9]) (CCG UC, 2022[7]).

3.5. The development and use of adaptation indicators

3.5.1. Chile's indicator framework

Adaptation-related indicators have been included to varying extents in Chile's adaptation policy documents (Table 3.2). The first NAP lacked indicators, a shortfall that the forthcoming NAP aims to address. Several of the approved sectoral plans also lack indicators. At the regional level, the plans include varying numbers of indicators depending on their scope. The indicators that will be part of the national indicator framework for adaptation are yet to be defined.

The aforementioned study of indicators (CCG UC, 2022[7]) identified a potential framework involving three groups of indicators, based on quantitative and qualitative information:

- Implementation indicators: to measure progress in executing the instruments and their measures, including compliance with implementation goals and budget, deadlines, time management, and the entities that implement them, among others. Chile has advanced in recent years in the development of implementation indicators.
- Progress indicators: the effect of adaptation measures on reducing vulnerability and exposure to climate change or increasing adaptation capacity and resilience. Although considerable work has been done to generate climate risk assessments through ARClim, the effective integration of these into public policies is still in its early stages. The NAP external evaluation flagged gaps in progress indicators (Ministry of Environment of Chile, 2021[6]).
- Results indicators: these do not necessarily refer to a specific adaptation measure, but instead indicate how climate risk changes as a result of the adaptation process as a whole.

Table 3.2. Adaptation indicators in Chile's policy documents

	Policy	Number	Examples
National	CC Action Plan II	19	*Implementation*: • Percentage of territorial zones with flood, overflow, and landslide maps out of the total defined territorial zones. • Set of georeferenced vulnerability maps *Progress*: not available *Results*: not available
	NAP 2014	0	
	Sectoral plan: Energy	41	*Implementation*: • Number of studies by Ministry of Social Development aimed at integrating adaptation into the social assessment methodology. • Number of programmes generated to protect land from heavy rainfall, at the regional or national level. *Progress*: not available *Results*: not available
	Sectoral plan: Infrastructure	25	
	Sectoral plan: Forestry and agriculture	4	
	Sectoral plan: Tourism	37	
	Long-Term Strategy	0	
	National Strategy for Vegetation Resources and Climate Change	30	
Regional	Regional plan – Atacama	75	*Implementation*: • Number of monitoring stations (meteorological, hydrological, groundwater, snow, for floods, quality). • Amount of investment in climate change adaptation measures as a percentage of total state investment in the region. *Progress*: • Annual volume/flow of water by productive sector. • Annual tons of recycled waste. *Results*: • Conditions/state of algae meadows. • Conditions/state of marine ecosystems
	Regional plan – O'Higgins	56	
	Regional plan – Los Ríos	6	
	Regional plan – Los Lagos	6	

Source: Authors, based on (CCG UC, 2022[7]).

3.5.2. Impact evaluation

ARClim's methodology is based on the development of so-called "impact chains", which help understand the factors that contribute to climate impact in a specific system (e.g. natural, human, or productive). This builds on the concept of impact chains proposed by the German development co-operation agency (GIZ) and the International Institute of Sustainable Development (GIZ & IISD, 2014[10]). The development of impact chains in Chile has benefited from valuable sector-specific experts who contributed to the identification of climate impacts.

ARClim assesses impact chains through empirical and quantitative analyses in some cases, and also used expert interviews for qualitative assessment. A total of 62 climate risk indices formulated in through impact chains were developed in the Climate Risk Atlas when it was initially constructed. Table 3.3 shows selected impact chain indicators used in ARClim – those for which data are available.

Table 3.3. Impact chains in Climate Risk Atlas (ARClim)

Sector	Indicators
Water resources	Floods due to River Overflows; Flooding in urban areas; Risk in surface water use for irrigation purposes; Hydrological droughts; Risk to the availability of surface water for environmental purposes.
Energy	Impact of diminishing wind resource; Impact of temperature rise on transmission lines; Impact of the change in solar radiation; Impacts of water resource depletion.
Coastal Infrastructure	Increased downtime at state ports; Downtime of fuel discharge ports; Increase in Downtime for Fishing Harbors.
Agriculture	Change in Almond Crop Productivity; Change in Beef Cattle Carrying Capacity; Change in Dairy Cattle Carrying Capacity; Change in Cherry Crop Productivity; Change in Bean Crop Productivity; Change in Corn Crop Productivity; Change in Red Apple Crop Productivity; Change in Walnut Crop Productivity; Change in Sheep Carrying Capacity; Change in Irrigated Potato Crop Productivity; Change in Rainfed Potato Crop Productivity; Change in Pasture Productivity; Change in Irrigated Wheat Crop Productivity; Change in Rainfed Wheat Crop Productivity; Loss of Pisco Grape due to Increased Frequency of Heat Waves; Loss of Pisco Grape due to Increased Frequency of Droughts; Change in Chardonnay Grape Crop Productivity.
Mining (under revision)	Impact of Drought on Mining Operations; Impact of High Rainfall on Mine Tailings
Aquaculture	Salmon Farming: Loss of Production due to Reduced Freshwater Supply; Loss of Salmon Biomass due to Harmful Algal Blooms; Loss of Salmon Biomass due to Increased Parasites; Loss of Mussel Biomass in Fattening Phase due to Increased Harmful Algal Blooms; Loss of Mussel Seed Biomass due to Increased Salinity
Artisanal Fishing	Loss of Artisanal Fish Landing; Loss of Artisanal Clam Fishery Landing due to Changes in Upwelling; Loss of Artisanal Clam Fishery Landing due to Changes in Temperature; Loss of Oyster Aquaculture Production due to Changes in Upwelling Regime; Loss of Oyster Aquaculture Production due to Changes in Sea Surface Temperature; Reduction of Seaweed Meadows
Tourism	Loss of Winter Tourist Attraction in High Mountain Resorts; Loss of Tourist Attraction due to Forest Fires; Increased Presence of Jellyfish due to Rising Sea Temperatures; Increased Presence of Portuguese Man-of-War due to Rising Sea Temperatures; Beach Erosion; Loss of Tourist Attraction in Sun and Beach Destinations; Loss of Tourism in Sun and Beach Destinations due to Increased Swells
Biodiversity	Loss of Fauna due to Changes in Precipitation; Loss of Fauna due to Changes in Temperature; Loss of Flora due to Changes in Precipitation; Loss of Flora due to Changes in Temperature; Degradation of Coastal Wetlands; Changes in the Presence of Blue Whales due to Rising Temperatures; Changes in the Presence of Humpback Whales due to Rising Temperatures; Changes in the Presence of Sperm Whales due to Rising Sea Temperatures; Changes in the Presence of Bottlenose Dolphins due to Rising Sea Temperatures; Changes in Species Composition due to Rising Sea Surface Temperatures; Changes in Functional Diversity due to Rising Sea Surface Temperatures; Changes in Marine Species Richness due to Rising Sea Surface Temperatures; Changes in the Presence of Humboldt Penguins due to Rising Sea Surface Temperatures; Changes in the Presence of Peruvian Diving-petrels due to Rising Sea Surface Temperatures
Native Forests	Wildfires in Native Forests; Greenness in Native Forests
Forest Plantations	Forest Plantation Fires; Greenness in Forest Plantations
Health and Wellbeing	Rural domestic water security (human consumption); Urban domestic water security (human consumption); Drinking water loss in Rural Health Services due to lack of precipitation; Effects of Urban Heat Islands; Effects of Frost in Cities; Fires in urban settlements; Environmental Thermal Discomfort; Effect of heat waves on human health; Net premature mortality due to temperature change; Premature heat-related mortality; Increased morbidity due to higher temperatures and heat waves; Floodings; Coastal settlements flooding.

Note: The project developed 11 new impact chains, one for each sector, and completed 11 impact chains from ARClim with adaptive capacity indicators. The indicators reflect different components of climate risk and impacts.
Source: (CCG UC, 2022[7]) (Ministry of Environment of Chile, 2024[8]).

A gap remains in adaptive capacity indices for calculating the level of vulnerability. The Capacity-building Initiative for Transparency (CBIT) project aimed to reduce this gap by recalculating 11 of ARClim's climate risk indicators, including adaptive capacity, and developing 11 new impact chains to improve the understanding of adaptive capacity and explore adaptation possibilities (CCG UC, 2022[7]). The process involved a series of workshops with stakeholders from key sectors to discuss aspects of adaptive capacity related to specific risks, and the weight to be assigned to the indicators and availability of information. The project has helped to advance the development of adaptive capacity indicators and to shed light on the effectiveness of associated measures. Table 3.4 presents an example of indicators for the impact chain "Operational downtime of energy ports".

Table 3.4. Example of impact chain for energy ports

Component	Description	Data used
Hazard	Change in the wave (swell) regime, expressed in terms of probability.	
Exposure	Quantity of fuels unloaded at each port, measured by energy content.	Energy imports by port; Calorific value of energy.
Sensitivity	Number of port closure hours 2008-2017 by sea conditions.	Port closure days.
Adaptive capacity	Liquid fuels storage capacity, by macro-zone.	Fuel storage capacity; Annual fuel sales; Calorific value of energy.
Impact	Increased downtime of larger vessels, calculated at the port entrance. Port closures have an impact on the energy logistics chain.	
Geographic aggregation	9 ports: 2 public and 7 private.	

Source: authors, based on (CCG UC, 2022[7]), Informe Final "Desarrollo de indicadores para el monitoreo y evaluación del progreso de la adaptación al cambio climático a nivel nacional" [Final Report "Development of indicators for monitoring and evaluating the progress of adaptation to climate change at the national level"]

For each ARClim impact chain a detailed analysis of risk factors was developed (CCG UC, 2022[7]). The different impact chains incorporated the components of hazard, exposure, and vulnerability in different ways, while maintaining the characteristic that increasing the value of each component also increases the value of risk. ARClim identified 36 different climate hazard variables (e.g. "Increased precipitation intensity with respect to the current scenario" or "Variation in the combined occurrence of droughts and heat waves between historical [1980-2010] and future climate [2035-2065 under RCP 8.5 scenario]"). It also assessed exposure (e.g. number of individuals, species or activities present in a risk zone; metrics related to the performance level of a productive activity subject to risk; densities, areas and/or a combination of different aspects of a system that are summarised in an exposure index). It proved challenging to develop vulnerability indices because of the differences revealed in the working groups in defining the concept of vulnerability and its relationship with notions such as "sensitivity", "susceptibility", "dependence" or "resilience", as well as its cross-cutting nature.

Nonetheless, of the 62 impact chains, 47 combine different factors of vulnerability and summarise them in vulnerability indices, generating specific indicators or using existing indices to determine the impact chain. Some working groups selected factors that influence specific sector vulnerability. For example, for the coastal areas sector, the vulnerability index for the impact chain "Beach erosion" is determined by a sensitivity index composed of the factor "structural sensitivity" and "normalised erosion rate". Other working groups included broader and cross-cutting aspects (such as education and access to safety nets). Still other working groups relied on historical observations that identify which valuable elements have been more vulnerable.

Although vulnerability is approached through a combination of different factors that contribute to the resulting vulnerability, it could be linked to other factors that were not included in the index, or even the specific weight of each factor could vary, aspects that are not captured with this approach. The estimated vulnerability depends on the variables considered for the index construction, as well as the scales for each of the metrics included within the index. The methodological design of the vulnerability approach largely depends on the criteria of the working groups responsible for its development, compared to those chains that rely on historical statistics.

3.5.3. Capturing adaptation progress across different localities and sectors

Local indicators

While ARClim provides a baseline assessment of climate risks and impacts at different geographical scales, further work is required to assess risks at settlement level, as well as interactions between different risks and aggregate risks at sector level. Regional and local indicator frameworks are not yet implemented in Chile. The Climate Change Law sets ambitious deadlines for closing this gap, notably by setting out to define the mechanisms and resources needed to establish adaptation measurement at sub-national scale.

ARClim can be used as a reference to build indicators for sub-national policies, and reciprocally the results from the sectoral and regional plans can be incorporated in ARClim. Climate risk assessments have been developed for the first four regional plans for the regions of Atacama, O'Higgins, Los Ríos and Los Lagos, including adaptation indicators. More recently, 18 new impact chains were developed to prepare the regional plan for the Coquimbo Region (Ramajo et al., 2022[11]). In the sectoral and regional plans of Los Ríos and Los Lagos, the scale for generating risk-related results is regional, which provides a broader estimation without considering local-scale specificities, unlike ARClim, which provides data at the municipal level.

Cross-sectoral indicators

The ARClim indicators were reviewed as part of the CCG study to identify those that could be grouped by sector (e.g. biodiversity, health, etc.). There are indicators that are also closely related to those from other frameworks such as water management and disaster risk reduction. Cross-sector indicators, such as protected land area, are relevant not just for biodiversity, but also for several sectors such as the agricultural, forestry, water, infrastructure and tourism sector and cross-cutting issues such as gender (Box 3.3). The study defined 21 relevant cross-sector indicators for climate adaptation in a participatory manner (CCG UC, 2022[7]). In addition, it identified 12 indices related to "provision sectors" (e.g. water resources, energy, infrastructure, and coastal zones), which affect the results in other sectors as well as the vulnerability indices. For example, the indicator on annual hours of closed ports (result indicator) is relevant for several sectors (e.g. agriculture, mining, infrastructure, fisheries).

However, as those indicators were not developed with an inter-sectoral approach they present several limitations for monitoring cross-sector adaptation. While the different indicators have relevance across policy areas and across different jurisdictions, cross-sector climate risk indicators and assessments are still a gap in monitoring and evaluation of adaptation to climate change in Chile. In particular, within the development and selection of indicators, the maladaptive potential must be analysed. In the Chilean case, maladaptive practices are mostly identified through a sectoral approach in relation to the impacts on other sectors, especially when considering systems interconnected by shared resources like water.

Box 3.3. Developing gender-related adaptation indicators

Efforts were carried out to identify indicators that have disaggregated statistical data by gender at the regional and municipal levels across a series of sectors to shed light on the exposure, sensitivity, and adaptive capacity of women and to inform policy making. Some examples based on the ARClim impact chains are shown in Table 3.5. While it was observed that women have a higher sensitivity to climate change in general, the risk can be more unfavourable for either men or women depending on the impact chain. The adaptation measures proposed to address gender concerns include, for example, conducting workshops and training at the community level on the protection of water resources in households led by women; and creating mechanisms to achieve equitable participation between men and women in agricultural credit programmes, agro-climatic insurance and agricultural training initiatives.

Table 3.5. Gender-related indicators

Sector	Impact chain	Risk factor/ dimension	Indicator
Biodiversity	Population affected by the loss of ecosystem services caused by coastal wetland degradation due to flooding.	Sensitivity / Economic-productive	Dependency of local employment on women/men in the tourism industry.
		Adaptive capacity / Financial capital	Credit to tourism-related businesses and microenterprises offered to women/men.
Cities	Urban domestic water insecurity.	Sensitivity / Economic-productive	Rate of participation in unpaid household chores and caregiving, by type of unpaid work (laundry and shoe cleaning, meal preparation, pet and plant care, and house cleaning) (men/women).
		Adaptive capacity / Social capital	Percentage of women/men who have participated in any social organisation.
Agriculture	Productivity change in dryland wheat cultivation.	Sensitivity / Sociodemographic.	Percentage of indigenous female/male agricultural producers.
		Adaptive capacity / Political & institutional	Participation of women in the Rural Women Programme.
Fisheries & Aquaculture	Effect of salmon biomass loss on aquaculturists.	Sensitivity / Economic-productive	Proportion of temporary male/female workers in salmon farming centres.
	Effect of loss of fish landings on artisanal fishermen.	Adaptive capacity / Physical and natural capital.	Index of ownership of fishing vessels (male/female).

Source: (UNDP, 2023[12]); (Ministry of Environment of Chile, 2024[8]).

References

CCG UC (2022), *Informe Final “Desarrollo de indicadores para el monitoreo y evaluación del progreso de la adaptación al cambio climático a nivel nacional” [Final report Development of indicators for monitoring and evaluating the progress of adaptation to climate change]*, Proyecto ejecutado para para el Ministerio de Medio Ambiente de Chile (MMA) a través GEF (Global Environment Facility) y PNUMA (Programa de las Naciones Unidas para el Medio Ambiente). [7]

CR2 (2015), *Informe a la Nación La megasequía 2010-2015: Una lección para el futuro [Report to the Nation The 2010-2015 megadrought: A lesson for the future]*, Center for Climate and Resilience Research (CR2). [9]

GIZ & IISD (2014), *Developing National Monitoring Systems and Adaptation Assessment: A Guidebook*, https://www.iisd.org/publications/guide/developing-national-adaptation-monitoring-and-evaluation-systems-guidebook. [10]

Government of Chile (2021), *Long-Term Strategy*, https://cambioclimatico.mma.gob.cl/wp-content/uploads/2021/11/ECLP-LIVIANO.pdf. [1]

Government of Chile (2020), *Chile’s Nationally Determined Contribution*, https://unfccc.int/sites/default/files/NDC/2022-06/Chile%27s_NDC_2020_english.pdf. [2]

Ministry of Environment of Chile (2024), *Atlas de Riesgos Climáticos [Climate Risk Atlas]*, https://arclim.mma.gob.cl/. [8]

Ministry of Environment of Chile (2021), *Final External Evaluation of the National Adaptation Plan and the Sectoral Adaptation Plan for Biodiversity*, http://catalogador.mma.gob.cl:8080/geonetwork/srv/spa/resources.get?uuid=ffb44b07-2b3f-4de0-837a-1a899a5be8a4&fname=Evaluacion%20PNACC-PACCBD.pdf&access=public. [6]

Ministry of Environment of Chile (2020), *Informe de seguimiento 2019 del Plan de Acción Nacional de Cambio Climático 2017 - 2022 [2019 monitoring report of the National Climate Change Action Plan 2017 - 2022]*. [4]

Ministry of Environment of Chile (2014), *National Adaptation Plan*, https://cambioclimatico.mma.gob.cl/wp-content/uploads/2020/07/Plan-Nacional-Adaptacion-Cambio-Climatico-version-final.pdf. [3]

Ministry of Environment of Chile (2008), *Plan de acción nacional de cambio climático 2008-2012 (PANCC) [National Climate Change Action Plan 2008-2012]*, https://mma.gob.cl/cambio-climatico/plan-de-accion-nacional-de-cambio-climatico-2008-2012-pancc/. [5]

Pica-Téllez, A. et al. (2020), *Informe Proyecto ARClim: Atlas de Riesgos Climáticos para Chile [ARClim Project Report: Climate Risk Atlas for Chile]*, Centro de Ciencia del Clima y la Resiliencia, Centro de Cambio Global UC y Meteodata para el Ministerio del Medio Ambiente a través de La Deutsche Gesellschaft für Internationale Zusammenarbeit (GIZ). [13]

Ramajo, L. et al. (2022), *AdaptaClim: Indicadores Climáticos para la Adaptación en la Región de Coquimbo [AdaptaClim: Climate Indicators for Adaptation in the Coquimbo Region]*, Proyecto ejecutado por el Centro de Estudios Avanzados en Zonas Áridas (CEAZA) para el Ministerio de Medio Ambiente de Chile (MMA) a través GEF (Global Environment Facility) y PNUMA (Programa de las Naciones Unidas para el Medio Ambiente). [11]

UNDP (2023), *Report on Mapping the Gender Component in Data and Legislation in the area of Climate Change, Environment and Biodiversity*, https://www.undp.org/sites/g/files/zskgke326/files/2023-04/ReportGenderClimate26042023.pdf. [12]

Notes

[1] The Minister Council of Sustainability was established by law in 2010, with the focus on climate change added by the 2022 Climate Change Law.

[2] Ministers of Transport and Telecommunications; Agriculture; Finance; Health; Economy, Development and Tourism; Energy; Public Works; Housing and Urban Planning; Transport and Telecommunications; Mining; Family and Social Development; Education; and Sciences, Technology, Knowledge, and Innovation.

[3] This corresponds to the implementation of the cross-cutting measures of the NAP (excluding sectoral plans). It is generated based on the review of the annual NAP reports, considering the information on the degree of implementation of each measure, as declared by institutions responsible for their implementation, and generating a simple average of all the cross-cutting measures in the NAP.

[4] Further details on the method are explained on pp 47-52 of (Ministry of Environment of Chile, 2021[6]).

[5] The final report of ARClim describes this gap by establishing: "an integration of the results of different impact chains to evaluate the interactions of different climatic hazards jointly and the added risk for specific systems and/or territories" (Pica-Téllez et al., 2020[13]).

[6] https://arclim.mma.gob.cl/

4. Measuring progress in adapting to a changing climate: the case of Korea

This chapter presents the results of the country case study carried out in Korea. It reviews Korea's adaptation measurement framework, providing an overview of the policy and institutional framework and the methods used to measure progress in implementing national and local adaptation policies. It also highlights indicators that have been developed in the country to shed light on adaptation progress.

4.1. Summary and key findings

Korea has established a whole-of-government approach to adaptation policy and planning. Korea is currently developing its third National Adaptation Strategy (NAS). The national strategies are implemented through short-term national adaptation plans (NAPs), with the third plan released in 2023. The NAPs are accompanied by detailed sectoral implementation plans developed by 17 ministries. In addition, 17 metropolitan cities and provincial governments and 226 local governments have established five-year Local Adaptation Plans. Other public institutions are also mandated to develop adaptation actions and to report on them.

Adaptation measurement is a core part of Korea's well-established adaptation policy framework. Korea was among the first OECD countries to make adaptation measurement a legal requirement, in its Framework Act on Low Carbon and Green Growth, which it enacted more than a decade ago and updated in 2021. The act requires the government to monitor progress on the implementation of the adaptation plan annually, and to provide a progress report to the Ministry of Environment and subsequently to the 2050 Carbon Neutrality Committee. The act emphasises accountability and learning by requiring areas that need improvement to be reflected in future adaptation policies.

Korea's climate change risk assessments are an important basis for policy making. The 2020 Korea Climate Change Assessment Report identified 84 climate risks across 6 key policy areas (e.g. ecosystems, agriculture and fisheries, health, industry and energy, water management and national land and coastal areas). The risks were analysed according to their urgency and Korea's adaptation capacity. At the local level, an indicator-based risk assessment tool was developed to facilitate local risk understanding of hazard, exposure, and vulnerability.

Korea relies on well-structured and complementary methods for its adaptation progress reviews. Since its second NAP, the plan is reviewed frequently, through annual, interim (year 3) and final evaluations (year 5). This regularity helps ministries build capacity to identify implementation gaps, take corrective action and use resources efficiently. All adaptation projects (341 in the last round) are reviewed annually for budget execution and implementation progress, and a selection of 100 critical projects are put under greater scrutiny:

- Every year, implementing ministries carry-out self-evaluations for all projects using a standardised template, which are then reported to the 2050 Carbon Neutrality Committee. Ministries score the project based on several qualitative criteria (e.g. level of collaboration, compliance with the budget, target achievement...) and measured on a four-point scale (very good, good, normal, insufficient).
- The annual self-evaluations are further assessed as excellent, fair or poor by an expert review group, which also identifies best practices to be replicated.
- Additional information on adaptation engagements is collected at the local level and collated at the national level.
- In addition, for a selected shortlist of critical projects (49 projects in the third NAP), Korea has introduced a public evaluation group/citizen review that assess project implementation based on qualitative criteria. Allowing citizens to directly participate in the review of the implementation progress is a valuable practice that can help raise awareness of the need to adapt, increase acceptance for projects and provide insights on the prevailing level of awareness of the need for adaptation.

Korea's set of adaptation indicators has evolved over the years. There is currently a shortlist of key indicators as well as a longer list, respectively reflecting the national NAP and the sectoral plans. The indicators, which are both quantitative and qualitative, vary according to the sectoral plans and the nature of projects. A combination of key performance indicators for each sector and indicators to assess sectoral progress is used. For the third NAP, Korea established two lists of indicators: (i) one referring to "policy indicators" (20 indicators) that relate to the level of implementation towards quantified targets for 2025, such as the expansion of flood forecasting points; and (ii) one referring to so-called "public perception indicators" (16 indicators), which measure the usefulness and relevance of policy progress, such as "number of national drought information portal users".

Measurement gaps remain. The measurement of adaptation investments remains the focus of implementation progress, including budget execution rates, and lacks an appreciation of results and effectiveness of actions. Also the adaptation indicators reflect progress in the inputs and outputs of each action, rather than their outcomes. The expert judgements used for evaluating policy effectiveness criteria are a step in the right direction, though an expansion of methods and indicators beyond them would be useful to develop in the future.

4.2. Introduction

The Republic of Korea is home to about 51.8 million people, 90% of whom live in densely populated cities. Its geography is characterised by mountains, covering 70% of its land area, surrounded by the sea. The average annual temperature for the past 30 years (1991-2020) has been about 13.7℃, the annual accumulated precipitation is about 1315.5 mm, and the four seasons are distinct. In summer, it is warm and humid, including the rainy season, and in winter, the climate is cold and dry due to the influence of the northwest monsoon. However, climate change is already causing continuous adverse effects through slow-onset processes (e.g. change in season length, sea temperature rise, etc.) and extreme climate events (e.g. heatwaves, floods, droughts, cold waves, etc.).

Korea has been developing and implementing climate change adaptation policies for more than a decade, building on the 2010 Framework Act on Low Carbon, Green Growth and the revised 2021 Framework Act on Carbon Neutrality and Green Growth for Coping with Climate Crisis (FACNGG). The Framework Act also provides the legal basis for measuring progress in implementing adaptation policies. This process contributes to sharing the experiences of various implementing actors and informing decision making to improve adaptation planning and its effectiveness, as well as the efficiency of resources engaged.

4.3. Korea's adaptation institutional and policy context

4.3.1. Roles and responsibilities

The Framework Act on Low Carbon, Green Growth institutionalised the roles and responsibilities of a large number of ministries and agencies for the design, implementation and monitoring and evaluation (M&E) of adaptation policies in Korea (Figure 4.1). The Ministry of Environment (MoE) is the competent ministry responsible for decision making and public affairs. It is supported by analysis from the Korea Adaptation Centre for Climate Change (KACCC) at the Korea Environmental Institute (KEI), and the National Institute of Environmental Research (NIER) for monitoring climate impacts. The MoE is in charge of developing the National Adaptation Strategy (NAS) for a 20-year planning period and National Adaptation Plans (NAPs) for a 5-year planning period, in consultation with the agencies responsible for adaptation implementation. In addition, to respond to the latest scientific findings on climate change, it has also developed an enhanced strategy for climate adaptation covering 2023 to 2025 (Ministry of Environment Korea, 2023). Most central government agencies develop sectoral adaptation plans (SAPs) while 15 develop so-called detailed implementation plans (DIP) that lay out how the SAPs will be specifically implemented.

The 2050 Carbon Neutrality Committee[1] (CNC), an inter-ministerial body set up by the Framework Act, also plays a deliberating and decision-making role, in consultation with the MoE, for establishing some adaptation policies (e.g. approving the NAP) and assessing their implementation status, as part of their wider mandate for climate policy planning. The Korea Adaptation Centre for Climate Change (KACCC), comprising approximately 30 experts, has supported adaptation policy development and implementation since 2009, notably at state and local government level, but also for public institutions and the private sector.[2] In addition, it develops climate change risk assessment tools (e.g. MOTIVE, VESTAP, CRAS; see Section 4.3.3); supports domestic and international co-operation on adaptation, education and awareness raising for mainstreaming adaptation; and participates in international research activities.

All central ministries need to prepare annual self-evaluation reports to assess progress in implementing the NAP. Based on these reports, the MoE and KACCC conduct an evaluation, which is then reported to and annually reviewed by the CNC. As necessary, the CNC then requests implementing agencies to supplement and improve projects that have made insufficient progress according to the NAP. The requests need to be reflected in the respective agencies' projects.

Figure 4.1. Main bodies in charge of adaptation policy design and implementation in Korea

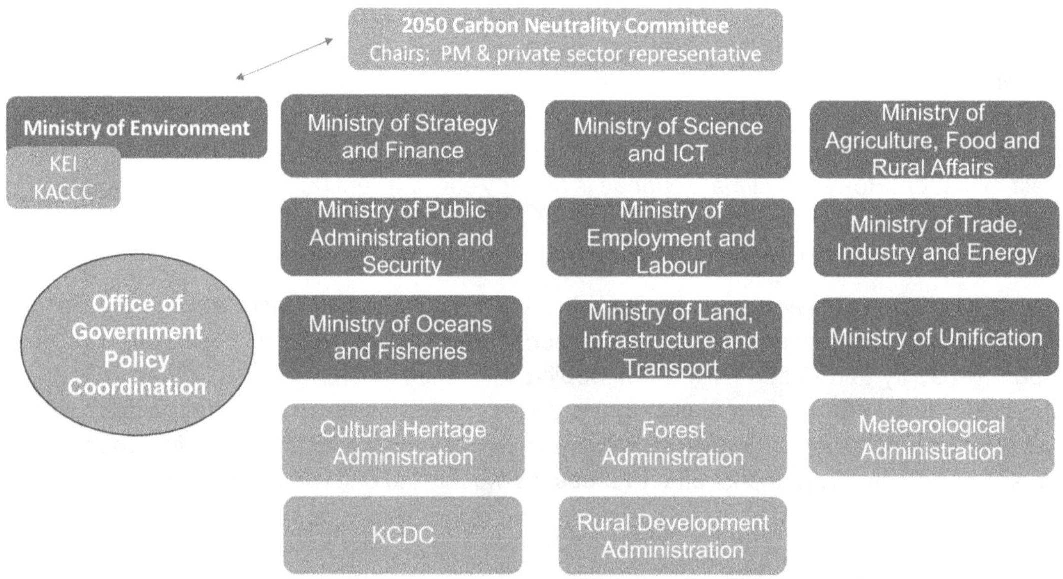

Note: Green: co-ordinating and decision-making bodies; dark blue: ministries; light blue: government agencies. KACCC=Korea Adaptation Centre for Climate Change; KCDC = Korea Disease Control and Prevention Agency; KEI= Korea Environmental Institute.

Local adaptation policies (LAPs) are also developed and reviewed. Notably, 17 metropolitan city and province governments as well as 226 basic local governments (cities, counties and districts) have established five-year LAPs and respective action plans. Regional research institutes review and provide advice on the LAPs. Since 2022, public organisations that operate major social infrastructure must also establish and implement adaptation plans every five years and review implementation results annually. They do so with capacity-building support from central government (e.g. guidelines for adaptation measures, development of climate risk assessment tools, integration and provision of adaptation information).

Although there are no legal requirements for establishing adaptation plans in the private sector, interest is increasing (e.g. through Task Force on Climate-Related Financial Disclosures) and mandatory disclosure of environmental, social and corporate governance (ESG) data that include climate risk is envisaged from 2030. In industry, the Industry Adaptation Partnership has been launched with associations representing key industries (e.g. materials, transportation, consumer goods) to prepare adaptation manuals for each industry and assess climate change impacts.

4.3.2. Adaptation policies in Korea

The Framework Act on Low Carbon, Green Growth provides the legal basis for climate adaptation policies in Korea, mandating the establishment and implementation of the NAP, NAS and LAPs. It also provides the legal basis for implementing local climate change adaptation projects and establishing adaptation plans for public organisations. These include, as of 2022, 62 of the 250 institutions that manage major infrastructure such as water, highways and electricity. With regard to adaptation measurement, the act mandates the government to develop measures to monitor and forecast climate change and its impacts, to assess climate impacts in all relevant sectors, and to assess progress in the implementation of NAP measures and detailed implementation plans (Korea Legislation Research Institute, 2021). The act was updated in 2021, keeping the mandate to monitor and evaluate adaptation implementation progress. The revised act covers both mitigation and adaptation, laying out mid-term goals and policy measures.

Korea's adaptation policy cycle is structured by the long-term (20-year) national adaptation strategy (NAS) and the five-year NAPs. The NAS is informed by regular climate change assessment reports (Figure 4.2). Korea is currently developing its latest long-term National Adaptation Strategy (NAS),[3] which builds on both the first (2016) and second (2019) NAS.[4] The second NAS sets out the goal "to prepare for 2°C warming by mainstreaming climate change adaptation" and outlines a set of actions to enhance adaptation in five key sectors, strengthen climate change monitoring and forecasting, as well as adaptation evaluation, and mainstream climate change adaptation across all sectors and actors.

In addition to the NAS, Korea has developed a series of National Adaptation Plans, starting with the *National Climate Change Adaptation Comprehensive Plan (2009-30)*, adopted in 2008, followed by the first (2011-15), second (2016-20) and third (2021-25) National Climate Change Action Plans, adopted in 2010, 2015 and 2020 respectively. Throughout the NAPs' evolution, there has been an increasing focus on participatory processes and a strong grounding in climate risk assessments. The third NAP benefits from a multi-stakeholder process, including youth and civil society, and builds on the national climate change risk list (84 risk items in 6 sectors) and the *2020 Korea Climate Change Assessment Report* (Lee, et al., 2022; Republic of Korea, 2021).

To improve the implementation rate and expected impact of the NAP, a so-called detailed implementation plan (DIP) has been established as a complement to the NAP. It lists individual projects to be implemented to achieve the NAP's goals, acting as an action plan. As with the NAP, the DIP is developed by relevant ministries every five years. The third DIP consists of a total of 286 projects and involves 12 major tasks in 36 key areas. Of these, 49 projects have been selected as critical to achieve the main directions of NAP3.

Figure 4.2. Timeline of key policy documents for adaptation

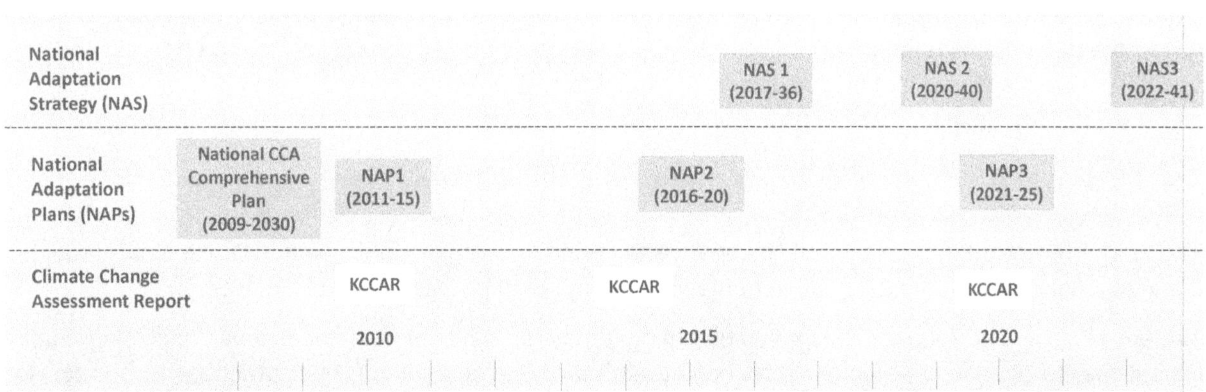

Note: NAS=National Adaptation Strategy; NAP=National Adaptation Plan; KCCAR= Korea Climate Change Assessment Report.

In accordance with the Framework Act, all local governments across Korea are establishing and implementing five-year LAPs. The regional governments and local governments have established their third LAPs based on the NAS and the third NAP, in line with the MoE's LAP establishment guidelines. They also benefit from the support of the risk assessment tool developed and continuously improved by the MoE. Once the plans are developed, they are reviewed and approved by the MoE and KACCC. The detailed projects included in the LAPs are centrally managed through a web-based LAP implementation check system developed in 2020 (Korea Environment Institute, 2022). The MoE also supports public institutions in developing adaptation plans through guidelines and training for those in charge of setting up the plans.

4.3.3. Climate risk assessment

The *Korea Climate Change Assessment Report* (KCCAR), prepared by the MoE and the Korea Meteorological Administration (KMA), and published in 2010, 2014, and 2020, provides the scientific basis for establishing adaptation plans. For the KCCAR, 120 experts analyse scientific evidence of observed trends and projections of climate change and impacts as well as adaptation measures. Based on expert judgement, the reliability of findings is categorised into three levels (firm, intermediate or limited agreement). The findings inform a national climate risk list, which, in turn, informs adaptation plans. In 2019, the list was updated to a total of 93 risks in 7 key sectors based on an analysis of causality relationship maps to understand how different risks might affect different sectors (Song & Lee, 2022).

As a basis for the KCCAR, the KMA develops detailed climate change scenarios in Korea looking to 2100 with 1km horizontal resolution. The scenarios are provided for both Representative Concentration Pathways (RCP) and Shared Socio-economic Pathways (SSPs), and the data are publicly available through the KMA's climate information portal (Korea Meteorological Administration, 2017). In addition, the MoE has developed the Model Of inTegrated Impact and Vulnerability Evaluation of Climate Change (MOTIVE) system, which quantitatively predicts future climate change impacts across seven sectors (Korea Environment Institute, n.a.). It also includes models to assess inter-sectoral linkage scenarios, projected economic impacts, and spatial planning. The system provides a web GIS-based display system to allow relevant decision makers and stakeholders to easily view and use model results.

The MoE has also developed VESTAP, an indicator-based climate risk assessment tool to support adaptation planning at the local level. The tool showcases indices related to hazard, exposure and vulnerability.[5] For example, in the health sector 15 evaluation items are assessed, such as vulnerability to heatwaves. This item is evaluated based on data on exposure areas such as perceived temperature, relative humidity and highest temperature; vulnerability data, which cover vulnerable populations and the number of heat-related fatalities; and adaptive capacity, based on the number of medical facilities and personnel. By allocating weights to risk items based on expert judgement, the tool allows for local governments to prioritise actions. MoE and KACCC are continuously conducting research to expand and update the risks and improve the indicators and weights.

4.4. Measuring progress in implementing national adaptation policies

The 2021 Framework Act on Carbon Neutrality and Green Growth for Coping with Climate Crisis provides the legal basis for evaluating the implementation of adaptation policies (Republic of Korea, 2021)(

Table 4.1). The act requires each implementing entity at national and local level, including public institutions, to provide an annual report on the status of implementation, best practices and areas for improvement. This must be submitted to the Minister of Environment, who is required to synthesise the information and report it to the 2050 Carbon Neutrality and Green Growth Committee. Public institutions also need to submit their annual reports to the heads of their respective central administrative agencies and local governments. The process is laid out in Table 4.1, and is described in detail in the following sections.

Table 4.1. Overview of adaptation measurement process

As prescribed in the Framework Act on Carbon Neutrality and Green Growth for Coping with Climate Crisis

		National government	Local government
NAP/LAP	Reporting period	3rd year of implementation, 5th year of implementation	5th year of implementation
	Reporting entity	Ministry of Environment, KACCC, specialist review committees for each field	Specialist review committees for each field
	Approach	Expert evaluation for each field	Expert evaluation for each field
	Data	Annual evaluation results and self-assessment reports based on plans	Annual evaluation results and self-assessment reports based on plans
	Results	Achievements and limitations of the implementation of NAP	Achievements and limitations of the implementation of LAP
All DIPs	Period	Annually	Annually
	Entity	Departments responsible for developing DIPs, Ministry of Environment, KACCC, specialist review committees for each field	Agencies responsible for formulating local DIPs, specialist review committees for each field
	Approach	1. Self-evaluation reports on planned evaluation items	1. Self-evaluation reports on planned evaluation items
		2. Review of evaluation results through expert review committees by field	2. Review of evaluation results through expert review committees by field
	Data	Self-evaluation reports	Self-evaluation reports
	Results	Performance and achievements in implementing DIPs	Performance and achievements in implementing DIPs

Note: DIP=Detailed Implementation Plan; LAP=Local Adaptation Plan; NAP=National Adaptation Plan
Source: authors, based on (Republic of Korea, 2021), Framework Act on Carbon Neutrality and Green Growth for Coping with Climate Crisis

4.4.1. Measuring progress at the national level

The national framework for measuring adaptation progress has been gradually established since the second NAP, with the focus on DIPs. Figure 4.3 outlines the key steps in the NAP3 implementation evaluation procedure. The evaluation of performance of the third NAP, based on policy indicators and public perception indicators, will be brought together in the following processes (see also Table 4.2):

- An annual review of the NAP's DIP and a joint performance evaluation of the relevant ministries including the expert committee, informing an action plan for the following year.
- A mid-term evaluation (in 2023) jointly carried out by the MoE, KACCC and the expert committees of each ministry.
- A comprehensive (end-of term) evaluation, led by the MoE, to be carried out in 2025 to inform the fourth NAP (2026-30). It will be complemented by an updated KCCAR 2025.

Figure 4.3. Timing of the NAP3 implementation evaluation procedure

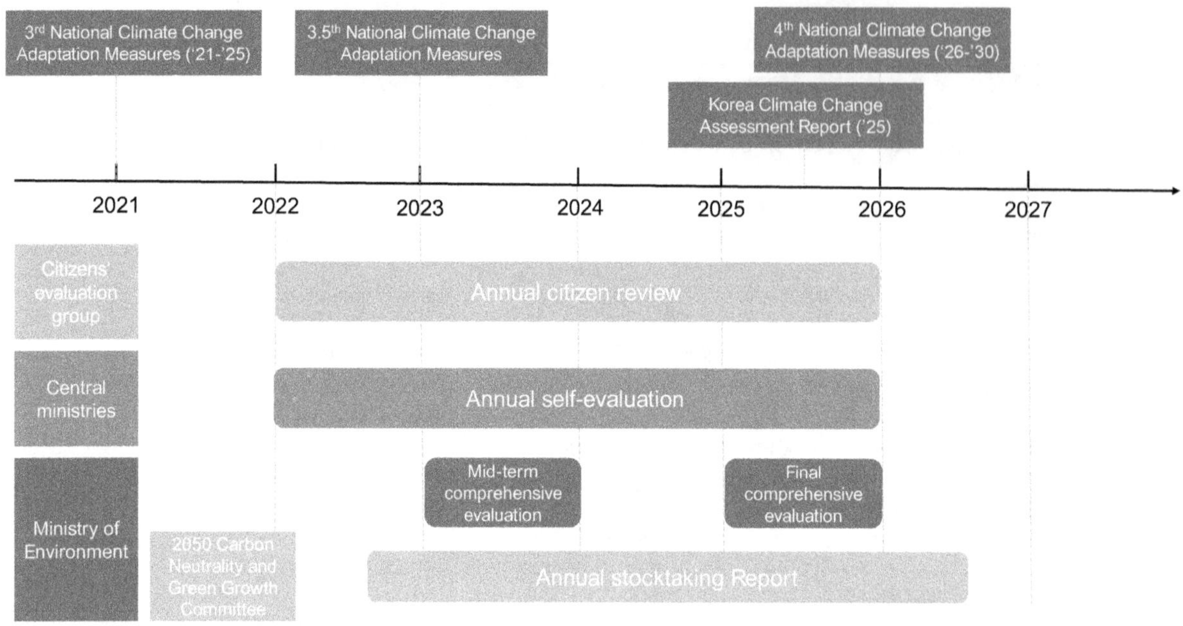

Table 4.2. Overview of implementation evaluation system for NAP3

Cornerstones/plans	Overall NAP	All DIPs	Critical projects
		Annual evaluation	
What is evaluated?		All projects in DIPs	Projects for public evaluation group/citizen review
Evaluation interval	• 2023 (Mid-term evaluation) • 2025 (Comprehensive (end-of-term evaluation)	Annually since 2021	Annually since 2021
How is progress evaluated?	• Qualitative self-evaluation (Expert committee of each ministry) • Quantitative evaluation (based on indicators)	Qualitative (Expert) + Quantitative	• Qualitative self-evaluation (Expert committee of each ministry, citizens' evaluation group) • Quantitative evaluation based on indicators

The annual review is divided into an evaluation of all the projects in the NAP's DIP and a more in-depth evaluation of the critical projects in the DIP. The DIP evaluation (first conducted in 2022 for NAP3) is a two-step process:

1. Each ministry that has a sectoral adaptation plan conducts a self-evaluation, based on a standardised template, of its respective DIP.
2. Each departments' expert review committee, as well as the national evaluation group, review the DIPs simultaneously to foster credibility. This sectoral self-evaluation of the DIP assesses the preparation, implementation and results using a number of indicators (Table 4.3, see section 4.5.1). An overall progress rating is assigned based on the points achieved for each indicator, namely very good, good, average or insufficient.

Table 4.3. DIP evaluation criteria and indicators used in NAP3

Progress area	Indicator (max. score out of 100)	Sub-indicator (max. score possible)
Preparation	Readiness of project implementation (max. 20 points)	Comparison to results of previous year & degree of adaptation to internal and external conditions
Implementation	Adequacy of implementation process (max. 40 points)	Project site monitoring, inter-ministerial collaboration, policy communication (max. 20 points)
		Compliance with schedule and budget execution (max. 20 points)
Performance	Performance goal & policy effect (max. 40 points)	Ratio of actual goal achievement to the target value in DIP (max. 20 points)
		Adaptive capacity & policy effectiveness (max. 20 points)

Total points (out of 100)	Rating score
90 and above	Very good
80 and above	Good
70 and above	Average
Less than 70	Insufficient

Note: If there have been additional achievements in adaptation mainstreaming such as establishing a horizontal co-operative organisational system, up to 5 additional points can be given.

For a selected shortlist of projects (49 projects in NAP3) considered critical during the consultation with responsible ministries in the development of the NAP, Korea introduced a public evaluation group/citizen review in NAP3, which, together with the expert review group, selects and reviews these so-called "critical projects" and identifies best practices among them (Table 4.2). The establishment of a public evaluation group a novel feature of NAP3 (2021-25) involving all implementing actors (i.e. government, metropolitan and local governments, experts, civil society, youth, and industry representatives) to monitor and evaluate implementation status. The group selects outstanding projects with the aim of increasing public policy acceptance. The evaluation of critical projects is conducted according to the results of the self-evaluation and qualitative/quantitative evaluation using a group of experts in each field. The objective of the assessment is to select best practice projects among the critical projects. The evaluation assesses project-site efforts and collaboration and communication efforts, how well the project is mainstreamed across relevant ministries and stakeholders, to what extent the project achieved its overall goal and its effectiveness (Table 4.7).

The mid-term and comprehensive (end-of-term) evaluations are carried out in the third and fifth year respectively of the NAP's five-year planning period. The last mid-term evaluation of NAP2 was conducted in 2018. It is carried out by an expert evaluation team for each field, who evaluate qualitative and quantitative indicators. The mid-term evaluation aims to improve the efficiency in achieving the overall performance goal with appropriate measures and by monitoring the execution and performance of individual projects by sector in adapting to changing circumstances. The last end-of-term evaluation of NAP2 was conducted in 2020, in which qualitative indicators were added to the indicators used in the mid-term evaluation, helping to understand performance and limitations for the NAP overall. The next end-of-term evaluation will be in 2025, with the aim to better assess the effectiveness of the implementation of NAP3 and inform NAP4 based on updated scientific evidence established in the KCCAR.

4.4.2. Measuring progress at the local level

Local governments are now in the third iteration of their LAPs. Each LAP also has a DIP, which also includes a selection of critical projects. Due to the similar structure of the NAP and LAPs, adaptation measurement at the local level reflects the measurement approach at the national level. Each LAP's DIP is reviewed annually through self-evaluation by the local department responsible for the development of the LAP. The evaluation compares the performance of LAP implementation with the plan's goals and budget execution. The evaluation results are brought together and shared with decision makers so as to inform future DIPs. MoE and KACCC have developed a web-based LAP implementation evaluation system[6] where each local government can upload information on the individual DIP projects and report on their evaluation results. The system allows dedicated LAP support staff in the MoE and KACCC to monitor and analyse progress in each local government. Similar to the NAP, the LAP evaluation comprises:

- An overall evaluation, conducted every five years at the end of the LAP period, assessing achievements and limitations of the current LAP.
- An annual review of all projects in each LAP's DIP.
- An annual review of selected critical projects in the LAPs' DIPs.

The annual review of all projects is carried out in line with the MoE's guidelines for implementation evaluation for local governments, which attempt to account for the different characteristics of each local government. They suggest that the heads of local governments collect opinions on implementation progress, for instance through public hearings or surveys, from stakeholders such as local residents, councils, NGOs, experts in the field and related organisations. The opinions collected are compiled to derive implications for the final evaluation results and used to inform future plans.

4.5. The development and use of adaptation indicators

4.5.1. Adaptation indicators to assess progress at the national level

Since the establishment of NAP2, Korea has used qualitative and quantitative indicators to assess progress in its implementation (NAP1 only included qualitative targets, and no indicators). Indicators have been developed to assess the DIPs, the selected critical projects and to evaluate the overall NAP at both the mid-point and the end of the implementation period. The indicator set is constantly evolving to improve the quality of evaluation as necessary. NAP3 saw the indicators evolve to include additional indicators on public (i.e. citizen) perception. These assess critical projects from the general public's point of view and help make citizens aware of climate adaption.

NAP3 is assessed using 20 policy indicators for 12 different sectors/domains, and 16 public perception indicators for 8 climate impacts/domains that are monitored annually (Table 4.4). Each indicator is associated with a target to be achieved by the end of the NAP implementation period (2025). The majority of policy indicators are linked to those of other relevant plans (e.g. water management, biodiversity, etc.).

Table 4.4. Policy and public perception indicators for NAP3

Area	Indicator	Current situation (2020)	Target (2025)
Policy indicators			
Water management	Number of flood forecasting points	65 locations	218 locations
	Establishment of national drought information system (INDIS)	Not yet established	Tool has been built
Ecology	National ecosystem climate change information management integration platform	Not yet established	Tool has been built
	Restoration of core ecological area of the Korean Peninsula	456ha	1,000ha
Inland & coastal area	Number of public rental housing units that undertook green remodelling	-	225,000 units
	Expansion of the number of coastal erosion survey points	250 points	300 points
Agriculture & fisheries	Number of disaster-resilient facility standards	68 standards	75 standards

	Number of types of crops in cultivation areas	17 types of crops	25 types of crops
Health	Establishment of Climate Health Impact Assessment	Established legal basis	1st evaluation conducted
	Participation in infectious disease information-sharing platform	1	4
Industry & energy	Number of manuals for adaptation for industries vulnerable to climate change	-	10
	Number of households with smart power grid	150,000	5 million
Observation	Number of variables of climate change satellite monitoring	29 variables of weather and ocean	96 variables of weather, ocean, and environment
Prediction	Up-to-date scenario production for Korea	AR5 based	AR6 based
Assessment	Publication of Korea climate change assessment report	AR5 based	AR6 based
Policy promotion	Climate change adaptation assessment system	-	Enforcement
	Establishment of adaptation plan for public institutions	-	Obligatory since Framework Act on Carbon Neutrality and Green Growth for Coping with Climate Crisis
	Operation of monitoring group for implementation of local government's adaptation plan	-	100% of cities
Climate resilience	Number of adaptive infrastructure standard pilots	-	5
Co-operation network	Operation of an adaptation research institute consultative body (KACCC as operator of a number adaptation-related institutes)	Body has been composed	Consultation twice a year
Public perception indicators			
Flood	Flash flood forecasting system	-	Built
	Priority management area for sewerage maintenance	114 locations	180 locations
Drought	Annual number of national drought information portal users	110,000	400,000
	Number of smart water supply management system locations	-	209 locations
Biogenesis	Establishment of database of genus occurrence and possible species	-	Established
	Development of eco-friendly control guidelines	-	Developed
Forest disaster	Advancement of the landslide prediction system	Forecast with 1-hour lead time	Short-term forecast
	Development of climate change forest fire risk map	-	Developed
Food security	Number of climate-adapted species	288 species	363 species
	Number of municipalities with farm-tailored early warning system	29	110
Health protection	Development of mobile app with health management platform to cope with climate change	-	In operation
	Number of facilities for people vulnerable to climate impacts seeking protective shelter such as from heat or cold	-	1,000
Protection of the vulnerable	Development of plan to select a climate risk hot spot	-	Developed
	Annual development of adaptive infrastructure (local government)	-	10 places per year
Public participation	Citizen's life lab (Living Lab) project units	-	20 units
	Development of disaster information citizen participation platform	-	Developed

Source: (Republic of Korea, 2020).

Indicators for annual reviews of the detailed implementation plan

Korea has improved the indicator framework for the third DIP, going beyond the second DIP's simple assessment of whether the budget was executed and the target performance achieved. The DIP is now assessed using two different sets of indicators – general project indicators and public perception indicators – which measure progress in each of the projects (Table 4.5). A total of 396 indicators have been created to assess the implementation of the 286 projects in the third DIP, and each project can be assessed by multiple indicators. The indicators are set by the implementing body, taking into account the overall goals of the NAP, the type/nature of the project and the characteristics of the respective ministries. Thus, the characteristics and levels of indicators differ between projects.

Table 4.5. Examples of indicators to assess the third DIP

General project indicators	Public perception indicators
Number of regional stations for climate adaptation measures	Development of climate change adaptation impact assessment system
Number of implemented pilot projects	Number of established adaptive infrastructure (by local government)
Extent to which climate adaptation has been mainstreamed	Number of standard models for urban climate change vulnerability reduction project
Number of consultations conducted to support the establishment of adaptation strategies for industries vulnerable to climate change	Number of civic life lab (Living Lab) projects (cumulative)

Source: (Republic of Korea, 2020)

In addition, the ministries responsible for establishing the DIP prepare a self-evaluation report for each of their assigned projects using evaluation indicators. These indicators assess the level of performance of individual projects in a standardised format, reporting on six sub-indicators to assess project preparation, implementation and results as well as degree of mainstreaming efforts (Table 4.6). To improve the interpretation of the results, the final evaluation result is presented by assigning 4 grades according to the overall score (out of 100): very good, good, normal and insufficient (Table 4.6). Evaluation results for the first annual DIP of NAP3 showed that 91.9% of projects were evaluated as good or above (79.9% very good, 12% excellent).

Table 4.6. Evaluation indicators for all projects of DIP3 and scoring grid

Evaluation indicators (points)		Sub-indicators (points)	Detailed review criteria
Preparation	Readiness for implementation of the plan (20)	Comparison to evaluation results from previous year & changes in internal and external conditions (20)	Compare to evaluation results from previous year Consider changes in internal and external social conditions
Implementation	Adequacy of the implementation process (40)	Project monitoring, inter-ministerial collaboration and policy communication (20)	On-site inspection by project (on/offline) and collaboration/policy communication (private/private)
		Compliance with implementation schedule and budget execution (20)	Degree of project implementation and budget execution according to implementation plan for each project
Result	Performance goals and policy effects (40)	Achievement of performance goals (20)	Ratio of actual goal achievement to goal of the project plan
		Policy effectiveness (20)	Enhancement of capacity to adapt to climate change and awareness of stakeholders and the general public according to project implementation
Extra points	Establishment of mainstreaming foundation (5)	Establishment of the basis for mainstreaming related to the implementation of DIP (5)	Achievement of mainstreaming by establishing a horizontal co-operative organisational system including relevant ministries and stakeholders

Note: Each indicator is rated on a 4-point scale: very good (90 points and above), good (80 points and above), normal (65 points and above) and insufficient (less than 65 points)
Source: Authors

Indicators for annual reviews of critical projects

The implementation of the DIP's selected critical projects is assessed separately by the expert review committee and the public evaluation group. The public evaluation group uses three overall evaluation indicators – implementation, mainstreaming efforts and achievement of goals – and four sub-indicators (Table 4.7). Best practice is identified based on the overall score (out of 100 points). In 2022, seven projects were selected for their best practice examples.

Table 4.7. Evaluation indicators for critical projects in the third DIP

Area	Evaluation indicator (points)	Sub-indicator	Detailed evaluation criteria
Communication & Co-operation	Project implementation (25 points)	Inspection of projects and communication and collaboration/policy (25 points)	Inspection of projects (on-site inspection and online response, etc.) and collaboration and policy communication efforts (publicity, etc.)
	Establishment of the basis for mainstreaming (25 points)	Building governance for DIP (25 points)	Achieving mainstreaming by establishing a foundation for horizontal collaboration including relevant ministries and stakeholders
Project performance	Achievement level (50 points)	Achievement of performance goals (25)	The ratio of actual goal achievement to the goal of project plan
		Policy effectiveness (25)	Improving the ability to adapt to climate change according to the project implementation and raising the awareness of stakeholders and the general public

Source: Authors.

Indicators for overall NAP evaluation

Finally, Korea also uses an indicator set for its mid-term and end-of-term evaluation of the NAP. The end-of-term evaluation of NAP2 in 2020 was conducted through four discussions amongst evaluation group of experts related to each sector[7] (Song, Young-Il, Hong, Je-woo, Jung, Huicheul, & Park, S, 2023). It used four evaluation areas and eight indicators to assess overall progress:

1. **The adequacy of the selection of implementation projects**: this first evaluation area is measured by the following three indicators rated on a five-point scale:
   - The correlation between a specific climate risk, based on the national climate change risk list for NAP2, and the project for each sector. For instance, the risk of increased mortality from heat waves is assessed using the indicator of health damage caused by heatwaves and cold periods and then rated based on the five-point scale.
   - Suitability of the project, considering the degree of risk association identified. This assesses whether the establishment of a DIP was appropriate. The appropriateness was assessed qualitatively by the expert evaluation committee members – including experts responsible for the different sectors in the NAP – based on whether individual projects could contribute to reducing climate change risks. The committee prepares an evaluation report synthesising the results of each department's self-evaluation of the DIP and develops policy recommendations for each sector.
   - The performance and limitations of each sector's projects based on the results of the performance evaluation of all DIP projects (qualitative).
2. **The degree of projects' contribution to reducing climate risks** (87 risks identified in NAP2), based on the results of the first evaluation area. The level of contribution was decided by consensus of the evaluation group on a five-point scale, and where necessary, the objectivity of the evaluation was secured by laying out project details.

3. **Proposal for establishing a NAP3 measure.** A qualitative evaluation looked at all the projects in NAP2 to decide which needed to be retained in NAP3 and to identify new projects to be added in consideration of current issues and the environment.
4. **Overall performance and limitations for each sector of NAP2.** The overall evaluation result was derived through an integrated discussion for all divisions with a representative of each division's evaluation group. The evaluation results for each division were derived using the results of the completed evaluation area and the results of the past performance evaluation.

4.5.2. Adaptation indicators to assess progress at the local level

Quantitative and qualitative indicators are also used to evaluate the implementation of local governments DIPs. The final result is divided into four levels: very good (more than 90%), good (more than 80%), average (more than 65%), and insufficient (less than 65%) measured for two axes, achievement of the goal and the budget execution rate.

References

Korea Adaptation Centre for Climate Change . (2017). *Korea adaptation centre for climate change.* doi:https://kaccc.kei.re.kr/

Korea Environment Institute. (2022). *LAP Implementation check system.* Retrieved from http://lap.kei.re.kr

Korea Environment Institute. (n.a.). *Model of integrated impact and vulnerability evaluation of climate change.* Retrieved from http://motive.kei.re.kr/

Korea Environment Institute. (n.a.). *VESTAP 기후변화취약성 평가도구 시스템.* doi:http://vestap.kei.re.kr

Korea Legislation Research Institute. (2021). *Framework Act on Low Carbon and Green Growth.* Retrieved from https://elaw.klri.re.kr/eng_service/lawView.do?hseq=53039&lang=ENG,%20date%20of%20search

Korea Meteorological Administration. (2017). *Korea Climate information portal dashboard.* Retrieved from http://www.climate.go.kr/home/

Lee, D., Shin, J., Song, Y., Chang, H., Cho, H., Park, J., & Hong, J. (2022). The development process and significance of the 3rd national climate change adaptation plan (2021–2025) of the Republic of Korea. *Science of the Total Environment, 818*(151728). doi:10.1016/j.scitotenv.2021.151728

Ministry of Environment Korea. (2023). *제3차 국가 기후위기 적응 강화대책 수립 [Establishment of the 3rd National Climate Crisis Adaptation Enhancement Measures].* Retrieved from http://www.me.go.kr/home/web/board/read.do?boardMasterId=1&boardId=1608350&menuId=10525

Presidential Commission on Carbon Neutrality and Green Growth. (2023). *First National Carbon Neutrality and Green Growth Basic Plan (2023-2042).* Retrieved from https://www.2050cnc.go.kr/base/board/read?boardManagementNo=2&boardNo=1469&searchCategory=&page=3&searchType=&searchWord=&menuLevel=2&menuNo=16

Republic of Korea. (2020). *An introduction to the Third Round of Korea's National Climate Change Adaptation Plan (2021-2025).*

Republic of Korea. (2021). *Framework Act on Carbon Neutrality and Green Growth for Coping with Climate Crisis.* Retrieved from https://elaw.klri.re.kr/eng_service/main.do

Republic of Korea. (2021). *The Republic of Korea's Enhanced Update of its First Nationally Determined Contribution.* Retrieved from https://unfccc.int/sites/default/files/NDC/2022-06/211223_The%20Republic%20of%20Korea%27s%20Enhanced%20Update%20of%20its%20First%20Nationally%20Determined%20Contribution_211227_editorial%20change.pdf

Song, Y.-I., & Lee, S. (2022). Climate change risk assessment for the Republic of Korea: developing a systematic assessment methodology. *Landscape and Ecological Engineering, 18*, 191-202. doi:10.1007/s11355-021-00491-6

Song, Young-Il, Hong, Je-woo, Jung, Huicheul, & Park, S. (2023). *Research on Monitoring and Evaluation System for Climate Change Adaption Policy in Korea.* Korea Environment Institute.

Notes

[1] The committee comprises between 50 to 100 members and is chaired by the Prime Minister and private experts appointed by the President.

[2] See their website, https://kaccc.kei.re.kr/ (in Korean).

[3] An adaptation chapter is included in the *First National Carbon Neutrality and Green Growth Basic Plan (2023-2042)* published in 2023 (Presidential Commission on Carbon Neutrality and Green Growth, 2023).

[4] The *First Basic Plan for Climate Change Response* (2017-2036) and the *Second Basic Plan for Climate Change Response* (2020-2040).

[5] VESTAP, see http://vestap.kei.re.kr.

[6] http://lap.kei.re.kr

[7] Further details are provided in the preliminary version of this case study available on the KEI's website ((Song, Young-Il, Hong, Je-woo, Jung, Huicheul, & Park, S, 2023): https://library.kei.re.kr/pyxis-api/1/digital-files/51fa3cb7-3cca-4e76-b9ba-af6acd0279d4

5. Measuring progress in adapting to a changing climate: the case of the Slovak Republic

This chapter presents the findings of the case study carried out in the Slovak Republic. The full case study was released as an OECD Environment Policy Paper, which provides an extensive overview of the country's adaptation measurement framework and practices. It puts a specific focus on the methodology developed for measuring climate change risks at the municipal level to inform adaptation priorities and budget allocation decisions.

5.1. Summary and key findings

Slovakia has recently established a robust, national policy framework for climate adaptation. Slovakia established a formal adaptation policy framework with the adoption of its National Adaptation Strategy (NAS) in 2018 and its subsequent National Adaptation Plan (NAP) in 2021. This has been an important step to mark a move away from a reactive approach to dealing with the impacts of extreme events and towards a proactive approach that strengthens adaptation investments. The NAS and the NAP identify strategic priorities and objectives, specify their implementation actions and define actors responsible for their execution. 16 local adaptation plans reinforce the national policy instruments. Slovakia's Ministry of Environment plays a driving role in promoting and mainstreaming adaptation across ministries and levels of government.

While adaptation measurement is part of the implementation reporting planned to be carried out as part of the NAS and the NAP, there is limited progress to date. Adaptation measurement is mentioned as a key objective in Slovakia's NAP, aiming to inform future adaptation policy adjustments. Specifically, the NAP recommends the adoption of an evaluation system and to monitor the relationship between adaptation costs and benefits. Thus far, information is available on progress achieved in implementing the short-term (as opposed to the medium-term) measures proposed in the NAP, but a framework and methodology to systematically measure adaptation progress is not yet operational.

As a first and important step of adaptation measurement, Slovakia conducted a nation-wide, downscaled climate risk assessment. The assessment aims to inform and improve the objective setting process for adaptation actions and to better align future funding allocation with adaptation priorities. The CRA analyses three climate hazards, considered to be the most prevalent in Slovakia, namely extreme heat and precipitation as well as drought. By identifying a set of indicators, which link socio-economic and land cover data with observed and projected climate hazard information, the methodology determines each municipality's level of climate risk and geospatially maps them. With this methodology Slovakia develops vulnerability indicators for the whole country, at the local level and in a quantified manner, building on information such as the age of inhabitants, their employment status, their income as well as their access to drinking water.

The climate risk assessment shows that different climate risks prevail in different parts of Slovakia and that this may in turn change under climate change. For example, more than 16% of the Slovak population live in areas at high risk of extreme temperatures, notably in the south of Slovakia. Districts with low access to healthcare and a high proportion of young children are particularly exposed. Droughts pose notable risks to districts in the southwest, including critical agricultural land and areas with large drinking water reservoirs, though this risk might become more prevalent still in the countries western parts in the future. Access to public water supply has been identified as key vulnerability to droughts. In contrast, extreme precipitation presents a risk to districts in the north as well as the east. Municipalities with a high share of Roma populations exhibit the highest level of risk to extreme precipitation.

The full paper is available at:

OECD (2023), "Adaptation measurement: Assessing municipal climate risks to inform adaptation policy in the Slovak Republic", *OECD Environment Policy Papers*, No. 35, OECD Publishing, Paris, https://doi.org/10.1787/dad34bb3-en.

Annex A. OECD cross-country survey

Overview

The cross-country survey on adaptation measurement gathered information on existing practices, achievements and persisting challenges faced in measuring adaptation progress at the national level. The survey consisted of 26 open-ended and multiple-choice questions on adaptation policy context, measurement processes and approaches and key challenges as well as emerging good practices. The survey was sent to 48 countries and targeted national government officials working on climate adaptation. The countries included 38 OECD Members, 6 OECD accession countries (Argentina, Brazil, Bulgaria, Croatia, Peru, Romania) and 4 OECD key partner countries (China, India, Indonesia, South Africa) and the European Union (EU). The OECD received 30 countries responses, which corresponds to a 62.5% response rate.

Survey

Adaptation policy context

1. If available*, please indicate if your country has developed the following documents and provide the respective links (or indicate planned publication date if they are currently being developed or revised).

[please check all that apply]

☐ National or sectoral climate risk assessment

Please insert links:

☐ National adaptation strategy (NAS)

Please insert links:

☐ National adaptation plan (NAPs)

Please insert links:

☐ Additional sectoral (SAPs) or sub-national adaptation plans

Please insert links:

* Note for federal countries: additional information about sub-national policy documents can be provided.

** Note for EU countries: This question can be skipped if the information is already available on the EU Climate-Adapt website (https://climate-adapt.eea.europa.eu/countries-regions/countries).*

2. **If a climate risk assessment has been developed, what does it assess?**
   [please check all that apply]

☐ Past and/or projected climate hazards

☐ Past and/or projected vulnerability

☐ Past and/or projected exposure

☐ Past and/or projected socio-economic and environmental impacts

☐ Other: [*please specify*]

Note: The definitions of the terms hazards, vulnerability, exposure and impacts can be found in IPCC, 2022.

3. If a climate risk assessment has been developed, to what extent does it inform the development of adaptation policies in terms of priority and objectives setting?

[please check on a scale from 1 (not at all) to 5 (fully aligned)]

1 (not at all)	2	3	4	5 (fully aligned)
☐	☐	☐	☐	☐

Measuring progress in implementing national adaptation policies

4. Does your country define the following elements in its NAS/NAP/SAP?
   [please check all that apply]

☐ A vision for adaptation (e.g. people and ecosystems are resilient to climate change)

☐ Objectives or goals (e.g. reduce vulnerability and/or exposure, enhance capacity, strengthen the knowledge base for adaptation)

☐ Targets (e.g. "keep the share of climate-related economic losses per year within 0.08% of the national GDP")

☐ Adaptation actions (e.g. "develop a Coastal Zone Management Programme, restore damaged wetlands")

☐ Financing or investment options for implementing adaptation actions

☐ Monitoring and evaluation (e.g. a framework, which may include indicators, to monitor and evaluate progress on the implementation of the NAS/NAP/SAP)

☐ Other: [*please specify*]

Please share a link where more information related to the above can be found:

5. If applicable, at what level are adaptation objectives or targets formulated?
   [please check all that apply]

☐ At the national level

☐ At the subnational level

☐ At the sectoral level (e.g. transport, energy, water…)

☐ None of the above

☐ Other: [please specify]

6. If applicable, what is the process followed for developing the objectives and targets?

[please check all that apply and if available, provide additional details in the box]

☐ Stakeholder engagement

☐ Expert consultation

☐ Inter-ministerial consultation

☐ Subnational consultation

☐ Other: [please specify]

If available, please share additional details (e.g. number and types of consultations):

7. If applicable, please characterise the objectives and/or targets:

a.In general, are the objectives and/or targets defined qualitatively or quantitatively?

	None	Some	Most	All
Qualitative (e.g. strengthen disaster risk management against the impacts of climate change)	☐	☐	☐	☐
Quantitative (e.g. restore 75% of terrestrial and freshwater sites to favourable condition; 100% of residents living in flood risk areas with flood protection equipment by 2030)	☐	☐	☐	☐

b.In general, are the objectives and/or targets time-bound?
(i.e. the intended year of achievement of the objective is indicated)

☐ No

☐ Yes, some objectives and/or targets

☐ Yes, all objectives and/or targets

c.Have indicators been developed to measure progress towards the objectives?
(e.g. number of people and properties at risk of surface water flooding)

☐ No

☐ Yes, for some objectives

☐ Yes, for all objectives

d.In general, are the objectives and/or targets associated with a baseline (e.g. a reference year or period against which progress towards the objectives or targets can be compared)? (e.g. excess deaths due to extreme cold temperatures *compared to first records* in 1950)

☐ Yes, some objectives and/or targets

☐ Yes, all objectives and/or targets

☐ No

If not, please explain why:

e.Have entities responsible for reaching the objectives and targets been defined? (e.g. Ministry of Environment, Environment Agency, Department for Transport)

☐ No

☐ Yes, for some objectives and targets

☐ Yes, for all objectives and targets

☐ Other: [*please specify*]

Please share any links where more information related to Question 7 can be found:

8. Does your country measure inputs, outputs, outcomes or impacts (see examples in brackets below) in measuring the implementation of national adaptation policies?
   [please check all that apply]

☐ **Inputs** – Specific actions implemented as part of a policy (e.g. amount of spending on flood defences; environment agency staff trained to respond to flood incidents)

Please provide an example and indicate any challenges in measuring progress in terms of inputs:

☐ **Outputs** – The deliverables resulting from a policy action (e.g. number of dykes installed; building codes integrating adaptation to flood risk)

Please provide an example and indicate any challenges in measuring progress in terms of outputs:

☐ **Outcomes** - The likely or achieved short- or medium-term change generated by adaptation output(s) (e.g. changes in the share of buildings located in hazard prone areas (exposure); changes in the level of building damages due to floods recorded annually (climate impact); condition of flood defence assets (vulnerability))

Please provide an example and indicate any challenges in measuring progress in terms of outcomes:

☐ **Policy impacts** - The contribution of policy outcomes to the achievement of overarching goals aimed at reducing climate risk (i.e. reducing vulnerability, exposure, hazard and/or increasing resilience and adaptive capacity) that can be attributed to a particular intervention

Please provide an example and indicate any challenges in measuring progress in terms of policy impacts:

☐ **Other**: [please specify]

Please provide an example and indicate any challenges in measuring progress in other terms:

9. Have there been any activities undertaken or studies conducted in your country to measure the effectiveness of adaptation actions in achieving corresponding adaptation outcomes (i.e. the extent to which an adaptation action, in terms of inputs and outputs, has reduced climate risk)?

If yes, please share links or describe:

10. What are the roles and responsibilities of the following institutions or stakeholders in the process of measuring progress on adaptation?

Please check all that apply and provide a short description of roles and responsibilities (e.g. providing or collecting information relevant for adaptation measurement; carrying out or participating in the measurement process; communicating results).

☐ **Ministries** (e.g. Ministry of Environment, Inter-ministerial working group…)

☐ Other **government agencies** (e.g. Environment Agency; National Office for Statistics; Scientific agencies (e.g. meteorological institute) or Audit Office, or similar)

☐ **Independent body focused on climate change** (e.g. Climate Change Council, Committee, or Centre, or similar)

☐ **Sub-national level institutions** (e.g. at the provincial/state, regional or municipal/city levels)

☐ **Non-governmental organisations**

☐ **Academia**

☐ **Civil society**

☐ **Other**: [please specify]

11. How is relevant data and information to measure progress on adaptation collected or generated?

[Please check all that apply]

☐ Existing data (e.g. data on species abundance can be used as proxy indicator for vulnerability of a habitat to climate change)

☐ Requested data (e.g. information templates filled out by different entities, or questionnaires)

☐ Expert or stakeholder interviews

☐ Other: [please specify]

12. Is local level information on adaptation measurement aggregated at the national level? If so how?

Please describe:

13. Is progress on the implementation of adaptation policies documented in a report?

☐ Yes. *Please specify (e.g. progress, update, monitoring and evaluation or assessment reports)*:

☐ No

☐ Other: [*please specify*]

14. If yes, at what frequency are they published?

☐ Regularly (e.g. every 1, 2, 3, 4 or 5 years): [*please specify*]

☐ In the middle of the implementation period

☐ At the end of the implementation period

☐ On an *ad hoc* basis

15. If yes, how can results be accessed?

Please describe (e.g. publicly, upon request, available across government, only for selected officials) and share a link if applicable:

16. If yes, how do the results inform policy-making?
[Please check all that apply]

☐ The results are disseminated and discussed among policy-makers

☐ The results inform priorities for action in next NAS/NAP/SAP

☐ The results inform the budget cycle, notably for future adaptation finance/investments

☐ Results do not inform policy-making

17. Have you developed indicators to help measure progress on policies that support adaptation?

[Indicators may measure input, output, outcome, impact and/or progress towards objectives or targets set in the NAS/NAP]

☐ Yes, and they are used to measure progress

☐ Yes, but they have not been used yet to measure progress

☐ No

☐ The development is underway [*please indicate the publication date*_________])

Please provide an example and, if available, a link to a document containing a more comprehensive list of indicators:

18. If yes to question 17, what criteria drive indicator selection?

	Yes	No
Data availability and quality (e.g. temporal and geographic coverage)	☐	☐

Usefulness and policy relevance	☐	☐
Links with other topics/sectors (e.g. biodiversity, disaster risk management)	☐	☐
Other: [*please specify*]	☐	☐

19. If yes to question 17, please describe if and how indicators facilitate the understanding of progress on the implementation of adaptation.

[For example, the indicators can show percentage of target achieved, display an upward trend direction to indicate success, a rate of change, or enable the assignment of traffic light scores]

Please describe:

20. If yes to question 17, at what scale do indicators apply?

[Please check all that apply]

☐ Sub-national

☐ National

☐ Sectoral

☐ International

21. What challenges have you encountered in *defining* and *using* adaptation indicators?

Please describe:

Key challenges and emerging good practices

22. In your view, to what extent are the challenges in measuring progress listed below experienced by your country?

[Please indicate on a scale from "Not challenging at all" to "very challenging"]

	Not challenging at all	Slightly challengin g	Moderately challenging	Q uite challengin g	Very challengin g
(i) Measuring effectiveness	☐	☐	☐	☐	☐
(ii) Aggregating information across	☐	☐	☐	☐	☐

geographic and jurisdictional scales					
(iii) Comparability over time and across jurisdictions/ sectors	☐	☐	☐	☐	☐
(iv) Lack of data and information relevant to adaptation measurement	☐	☐	☐	☐	☐
(v) Complexity of adaptation (e.g. measuring adaptation to climate risk; interdependent and cascading climate risks)	☐	☐	☐	☐	☐
(vi) Inadequate technical, legal and financial resources to undertake measurement	☐	☐	☐	☐	☐
Other: [please specify]	☐	☐	☐	☐	☐

Note: Discussions held at two recent OECD events distilled key challenges in measuring progress, notably (i) measuring the effectiveness of adaptation actions and policies due to the difficulty of attributing outcomes to specific actions, (ii) aggregating, often individually collected, information across scales, (iii) comparing the information overtime and across jurisdictions/sectors, (iv) lack of data due to resource constraints, and (v) the difficulty of measuring progress due to adaptation's inherent complexity, notably due to future uncertainty of how climate impacts unfold in a particular location and cross-sector interactions and (vi) inadequate technical, legal and financial resources to undertake measurement efforts.

23. What, if anything, have you done to try to overcome some of the challenges?

Please describe and provide examples of good practices/solutions to overcome the challenges.

Key challenges	Examples of good practices/solutions
(i) Measuring the effectiveness	
(ii) Aggregating information across geographic and jurisdictional scales	
(iii) Comparability over time and across jurisdictions/sectors	

(iv) Lack of data and information relevant to adaptation measurement	
(v) Complexity of adaptation (e.g. measuring adaptation to climate risk; interdependent and cascading climate risks)	
(vi) Inadequate technical, legal and financial resources to undertake measurement	
Other: [*please specify*]	

24. Please describe (or share a link to) any initiatives that measure progress on adaptation at the provincial / regional / local level that you wish to highlight.

Please describe (or share a link to):

25. Please share any additional insight or information that is relevant, but not covered in the questions above.

Please share information:

26. In your view, how can the OECD help support your country in measuring progress on adaptation?

Please describe:

Annex B. Guidance for case study structure

Adaptation policy context

- Overview of adaptation as a policy priority (providing short historical context) and main national adaptation policies (key strategies and documents such as NAS, NAP, NDC and sectoral);
- Brief characterisation of responsibility for designing, implementing and reporting on adaptation policies at national level, across sectors, and at sub-national levels of government
- Brief characterisation of whether and how policy objectives are formulated (quantitatively, qualitatively, on a sectoral level, disaggregated to local level, etc.)
- What informs national priority setting process and how? (hazard, risk assessments, or similar)
    - Hazard assessment: definition; types of climate hazards are assessed; level of downscaling and coverage; frequency of updates;
    - Vulnerability, exposure, risk assessments: definition, types of risks assessed; level of downscaling and coverage; frequency of updates;
    - Other: description of other key characteristics of the risk assessment process (including on how it has evolved, if several iterations have been conducted)
- Discussion of strengths and challenges, such as: how well has the actual hazard/risk assessment informed priority setting process? Can this be improved, and how? How clearly have objectives been formulated in the main policy documents? Can this be improved, and how?

Measuring progress in implementing adaptation policies

- Overview of main approaches/efforts to measure progress in implementing adaptation policies/adaptation measures,
    - Description of main approaches/efforts
- Characterise what gets measured and how (i.e. indicators[1] or other)?
- Institutional arrangements
    - What is the role of the lead ministry in steering the measurement process?
    - What is the role of other actors at national and subnational levels? How do national and subnational actors interact?
    - What is the role of non-government actors, if any?
- Characterise the process to determine indicator (or other measurement type) selection, including:

[1] *The bullets below are examples of categories for indicators, which can be different in different country practices.*

- Adaptive capacity (e.g. capacity of exposed individuals, systems or institutions to adjust or cope with potential impacts from climate change) (e.g. percentage of communities with local building code regulations integrating adaptation requirements
- Adaptation process (Implementation of strategies and plans through policy action or allocation of financial and human resources (inputs) (e.g. percentage of transport infrastructure revised to account for climate change)
- "*Intermediate*" outcomes (results of adaptation policies and plans on climate risks (e.g. increase in the water supply coverage of previously water deprived communities)).
- Others.

- Who decides and how and on the basis of what objectives?
- Do they apply to specific sectors?
- Is data availability the key criterion for selecting an indicator or is the criterion itself the objective and on that basis the data collection is strengthened?

- Characterise the data collection method underlying the indicators or other:
    - Responsibility for information collection, reporting process, reporting frequency and method, etc
- Information sharing
    - Are there central repositories sharing information that gets collected?
    - If so, how frequently are there updated? How easily accessible are they?
- Opportunities and challenges: Discussion of country experience in establishing indicators and data collection processes; description of current strengths and weaknesses; discussion of specific measurement challenges such as uncertainty.

Use of adaptation data & indicators for measuring implementation progress and effectiveness

- Do collected data & indicators inform policy decisions at different levels of government and across sectors? If so how?
- What role do collected data & indicators play in informing project appraisals of specific adaptation measures (including in CBA's, CEA's, MCA's or similar)? Are different data sets generated for such appraisals?
    - Characterise the use of methods, data and indicators to appraise different types of adaptation measures?
    - What types of adaptation measures get evaluated based on project appraisal methods (e.g. physical measures or organisational measures (e.g. changes in planning prescriptions, or similar))?
    - What are the challenges posed in the appraisal process?
- Do collected indicators inform (causal) impact evaluations, i.e. the effect of implementation of adaptation policies on the reduction of certain climate related risks? If so, could you characterise when and how and by whom such studies are carried out and what relevance they have in policy making?
- Use of nationally collected data to report on internationally agreed objectives/commitments
    - How does collected information feed into SDG, Sendai Framework reporting, if at all?
- Discussion of opportunities and challenges

www.ingramcontent.com/pod-product-compliance
Lightning Source LLC
Chambersburg PA
CBHW061218240926
51846CB00006B/1270